Living Latin

Other Latin books from Evertype

Aliciae per Speculum Trānsitus (Quaeque Ibi Invēnit)
(Lewis Carroll, tr. Clive Harcourt Carruthers, forthcoming)

In Perendinum Aevum: Carmina Latina
(Stephen Coombs 2015)

Alicia in Terrā Mīrābilī
(Lewis Carroll, tr. Clive Harcourt Carruthers, 2011)

Living Latin

*The Heritage of Latin Phrases
and Quotations in English*

John Parker

evertype
2016

Published by Evertype, 73 Woodgrove, Portlaoise, R32 ENP6, Ireland. www.evertype.com.

First published by Cressar Publications, Penzance, ISBN 978-0-9535399-5-6.

A catalogue record for this book is available from the British Library.

ISBN-10 1-78201-193-5
ISBN-13 978-1-78201-193-4

Typeset in Baskerville by Michael Everson.

Cover design by Michael Everson, based on *La Primavera* by Botticelli.

Printed and bound by LightningSource.

In Memoriam
Ronald E. Taylor

TABLE OF CONTENTS

TABLE OF CONTENTS

TABLE OF CONTENTS

TABLE OF CONTENTS

TABLE OF CONTENTS

LIVING LATIN

INTRODUCTION

Latin is commonly regarded as a dead language, but bits of it still live on in phrases and quotations. This book lists a sizeable number of them and comments and reflects on many of them.

A book of this nature can never be "finished". Any author, if his reading continues to be sufficiently wide, will always be coming across new Latin phrases which deserve inclusion, or fresh examples of the use of existing phrases by past or by present-day authors, or even by speakers. There will always be a small treasure store waiting to be added to the "next edition".

There may be no more than one edition of the present book but I hope it contains enough information to enlighten and satisfy most of those who happen to open its pages. It has three main purposes.

Imprimis, it celebrates Latin as a beautiful language, displaying for the pleasure of the present reader some of its multitude of treasures.

Item, it tries to help readers divine the meaning of at least some of the Latin phrases they may encounter in their own reading. A few modern writers use Latin phrases in their work, and writers in the past have certainly done so. As an example, Lawrence Durrell published *Mountolive* in 1958, and in the book we come across "the *caput mortuum* of a love scene", "*taedium vitae*", "*alter ego*", "*loquitur*", and "*ex voto*" as well as a reference to the delivery of "a small mouse" by Mahomet if not by the Mountain. This book provides explanations of all these references.

Item, it seeks to encourage readers to continue to use such Latin phrases as already figure in their own speech or writing, and perhaps to risk adding new ones to their vocabulary. This last purpose is as important as the other two. There are those who advocate using only English words and phrases in English speech and writing, but I believe these people have little soul and no ear for the music of language. English owes much of its colour to the occasional appearance of a foreign word or phrase, such as "tête-à-tête" or "Schadenfreude" or "in situ", et cetera. Lately the use of Latin has been discouraged in English courts of law: but what harm is there in using terms such as "in camera" or "sine die" or "pro bono", phrases easily understood as they stand and with no succinct English equivalent? Without the power to draw on foreign languages to express what are often foreign ideas and concepts, English becomes clumsy and loses its music. It also loses force. In the opinion of Doctor Samuel Johnson, "a scripture expression may be used like a highly classical phrase to produce an instantaneous strong impression." (James Boswell, *The Life of Samuel Johnson, LL.D.*)

I have given examples of the use of many phrases together with their sources, hoping that the curious reader may be drawn to look more closely at the books in which the quotations have been used. Many of these books are among my favourites and I can recommend them to other readers.

Some of the single words and short phrases which appear in this book have been passed down orally from one generation to the next and have been absorbed as part of the mother tongue. One hears in childhood such phrases as "et cetera", "pro tem.", "infra dig.", "in toto", "per se", and later on reads them in books and newspapers with the addition of less familiar terms such as "in flagrante", "non sequitur", "quid pro quo", "sine qua non". They can be counted as being quasi-English by virtue of their frequent and long-standing use.

The longer phrases and quotations may not be on everybody's lips, but writers over the centuries have seen fit to use them when the occasion calls for them. Short phrases such as "pari passu", "ceteris paribus", "in extenso", cropped up frequently in everyday speech in an era when scholars conversed in Latin, as they often did up to the end of the nineteenth century. Longer quotations were committed to memory by the schoolboy in his formative years, and formed part of the adult writer's immediate vocabulary. A fruitful source of these was Horace's Odes, which provided "integer vitæ scelerisque purus", "O matre pulchra filia pulchrior", "carpe diem", "non omnis moriar", among many others. When Dr Johnson was being tossed about in an open boat between Scalpa and Raasay in the Hebrides, we are told he recited an apposite ode of Horace, and he could not have been the only scholar of his time who knew many of these odes by heart. In addition to Horace, writers such as Virgil, Caesar, Catullus, Ovid and Cicero appear frequently as sources in this book, giving "ave atque vale", "tempus edax rerum", "varium et mutabile semper femina", "Gallia est omnis divisa in partes tres", et cetera.

Even though dead, Latin still seems to have a certain cachet in some quarters. The names chosen by pop groups such as Status Quo and Procul Harum exemplify this. The Austrian symphonic black metal band Hollenthon have entitled their first album Domus Mundi—"Home of the World", and have given Latin names to all eight tracks, among them Hinc Illae Lacrimae, Non Omnis Moriar, Pallida Mors, Ultima Ratio Regum, and Lex Talionis (*qq.v.*). More sober institutions use Latin in the same way:

a magazine described as "the thinker's garden quarterly" is called "Hortus", which is "garden" in Latin.

It has frequently been pointed out that a great part of the English language is anyway no more than thinly-disguised Latin. To a Roman of 100 B.C. the words "intricate" and "influence" would have seemed curiously familiar, reminding him of *in-tricæ* and *in-fluere*. He might study the word "ubiquitous" and wonder perhaps if it had any connection with *ubique*. He might see in "circumvent" a curtailment of *circumventus*, and so *ad infinitum* (or very nearly so). A further point which has been made is this. Many words of Latin origin were brought into Middle English to dignify the vocabulary of philosophy or of the natural sciences, to fill gaps where there was no suitable English word available, or to supply single words in place of English phrases—"dignify" in place of "make worthy", "vocabulary" in place of "word list". But when we use a word like "intervene" as a more elegant alternative to "come between", we should realize that to our Ancient Roman the word "*intervenire*" meant literally nothing less that "come between", and that to *intervenire* in a quarrel meant putting oneself bodily between the two who were fighting it out. When the Romans wanted words to supply gaps in their own philosophical lexicon, they borrowed from Greek.

I hope this book, incomplete though it may be, will encourage the reader to continue to use Latin phrases whenever they are appropriate and to add a few new ones to his arsenal. Only in this way can these bits of left-over Latin survive, by constant warming-up.

John Parker
Cressar, Ludgvan 2016

PRONUNCIATION

Until around 1920, Latin was pronounced in Britain as though it was English. The old pronunciation still persists in such phrases as *et cetera*, *prima facie*, *sub judice*, and *vice versa*. Then scholars decided that if the language was to be taught at all in schools and colleges, it should be spoken as the Romans spoke it (according to the scholars' conjecture about Roman pronunciation, there being little if any record of how the average Roman actually spoke); and from that time forth uncertainty reigned, and spoken Latin in Britain entered on a decline.

The Romans used the letter V for writing both V and U: what they pronounced as "unus" they wrote "vnvs", and the letter V in Latin was pronounced either as U [u] or as W [w], but never as V [v]. Likewise where the Romans used I at the start of a word, followed by another vowel, as in "ianitor", we tend to use J (janitor); however they pronounced the initial I not as J [dʒ] but as Y [j]. They pronounced C as K [k] and not as S [s] or CH [tʃ], and G was a hard [g] as in "girl" and never a soft [dʒ] as in "gentle". Their vowel sounds were much the same as they still are in Rome nowadays, so if we use present-day Italian values for the vowel sounds, we shall not go far wrong. So the word "vice" should strictly speaking be pronounced as "wee-kay" ['wike] and "judice" as "you-dee-kay" ['judike], and it is clear why Latin scholars became torn between tradition and their own conscience, and grew shy of using Latin in everyday speech, other than those words and phrases such as "verbatim", "ex officio", "versus", "Julius Caesar" *et alia*, which had become anglicized beyond redemption. (The Latin version of "Wikipaedia" on the Internet is "Vicipaedia": both words are pronounced in exactly the same way.)

Sellar and Yeatman, in *1066 and All That* used the confusion to some effect in their opening chapter, suggesting that when the Ancient Britons heard Julius Caesar's dictum "Veni, Vidi, Vici", pronounced correctly in the Roman manner, they thought he was referring to them as being "Weeny, Weedy and Weaky", so that they "lost heart and gave up the struggle, thinking that he had already divided them All into Three Parts". (*Vide:* "**Gallia est omnis...**" below.)

PRONUNCIATION

To confuse matters further, two words when heard in Christmas carols or church music attract the Italian pronunciation of C as CH [tʃ]: they are *Coeli* as in "Regina Coeli", "re-jigh-na chaily" [re'dʒaɪna 'tʃeli], "Queen of Heaven"; and *excelsis*, "ex-chelsis" [eks'tʃelsis], as in "Gloria in excelsis Deo", "Glory to God in the highest". Here the (benign) influence of the Roman Catholic Church can be seen at work, the pronunciation of Ecclesiastical Latin recommended by Pope Pius X being made clear in the *Liber Usalis*, a former chant book for Mass (readily accessible through the Internet).

How should we pronounce Latin words when they occur in English? Most word and phrases present no problem. There is a limit to the number of different ways in which we can say *ipsissima verba* or *in articulo mortis*, and there is everything to be said for sticking to the traditional English pronunciation of most phrases. The letter "v" can present a problem—should "*vis*" in *vis inertiae* be pronounced "vees" [vis] or "wees" [wis]? And many people, perhaps through having learned a little Latin at school, tend to pronounce *Te Deum* as "tay day-um" [te 'deum] rather than as "tee dee-um" [ti 'dium] which was the old English way. (This tendency can be seen at work in English—"deity" was for centuries pronounced "dee-ity" ['diːʲɪti], but is now often pronounced as "day-ity" ['dejɪti].)

It is a matter of personal preference—there is no compulsion to use any particular one of the alternatives on offer. Those who want to use the Received Latin pronunciation are free to do so, and can find it explained in any grammar book. Others might prefer to adopt the ecclesiastical pronunciation in the *Liber Usalis* referred to above. One's chosen pronunciation can be tempered by listening to Latin as spoken by the presenters of radio music programmes, who are frequently called on to announce the Latin titles of pieces of sacred music. Radio Finland (YLE Radio 1) broadcasts the news in Latin (*Nuntii Latini*) on national radio and on its Overseas Service. The pronunciation used there might be taken as a norm. The important thing is to use Latin, to learn a number of words and phrases, to use them in writing and then to use them in speech, pronouncing them as you think fit, and scorning those who mock you, but taking note of how other users pronounce them. Once these phrases become common currency again, their pronunciation will become fixed by use and by common agreement, as has happened in the past, and English will be the richer through the retention of some of its Latin jewels which at present are in danger of disappearing down the plug-hole.

Notes

A few Latin words, sometimes abbreviated, are used as instructions in this book. Each is explained as a separate entry in the book, but here is a list for easy reference.

cf. (*confer*)	compare
infra	below
passim	throughout
q.v. (*quod vide*)	which see
supra	above
s.v. (*sub verbo*)	under the word
vide	see

If a passage quoted is taken from a book or from a newspaper or magazine, the name of the book, etc., is set in italics, as in *The Newcombes* by W. M. Thackeray. If a passage quoted is taken from a short story, the name of the story is set in normal type within quotation marks, as in: Rudyard Kipling, "The Puzzler". Any passages not so attributed, and those credited to P. J. Dorricot or to Q. Q. Enwright, are from the unpublished writings of the present author.

I am greatly indebted to Mr Andrew Lownie for his erstwhile support and encouragement in the writing of this book, and to Mr James Cochrane, who has offered invaluable help and advice in correcting and improving the text.

LIVING LATIN

This book contains single words or short phrases in Latin which in the past have enriched or which in the present still enrich the vocabulary of English. It also contains quotations mostly from the classical Latin writers, together with a number of extracts from the Vulgate Bible, with corresponding English verses from the Authorized Version; and a number of extracts from the Ordinary of the Mass in the Roman Catholic Church, with their new English replacements. These last will be referred to simply as being extracts from "The Mass". The Vulgate translation of the Bible was made in the 4th Century by St. Jerome, was subsequently twice revised, and was the version of the Bible used in the Roman Catholic Church.

A

Abeunt studia in mores
—Ovid, *Heroides*, Epistle xv. 83
Studies (or habits) pass into (or create) character
This is the motto of the (teacher training) College of St. Mark and St. John in Plymouth, bearing touching witness to the belief of teachers that, despite the well-attested existence of academic rogues, education is a good thing. But perhaps Ovid wasn't thinking of middle-class morality. Francis Bacon in his essay "Of Studies" analysed the dictum:

> "Histories make men wise; poets witty; the mathematics subtile; natural philosophy deep; moral grave; logic and rhetoric able to contend. *Abeunt studia in mores.*"

The book *Abeunt Studia in Mores: A Festschrift for Helga Doblin* is written by Sarah A. Merrill.

(It is worth remembering that a Latin word ending in "a" could be a singular feminine noun, e.g., *stella, alea, angina*; or a plural neuter noun, e.g., *studia, acta, verba*. The singular of these neuter nouns, where it exists, usually ends in "-um".)

Abiit ad plures
—Petronius, *Satyricon* 42.
He has gone to join the majority, i.e., the dead
A stock reply to the Roman child's query: "Haven't seen Grandpa around lately—is he all right?" A classical euphemism, much on a par with "kicked the bucket" or "popped his clogs".

> "Roger [Needham's] career and his life's work are an inspiration for all in computer science and related fields.... *Abiit ad plures* now. His achievements will be remembered."
> *The Computer Journal*, 2003.

Not so applicable now, since it has been calculated that those alive today outnumber the dead and that we ourselves are the new "majority". In his *Religio Medici* ("The medico's religion"), Sir Thomas Brown quoted *abiit ad plures* as having been inappropriate also just after the Creation, until such time as Adam and Eve and their immediate family had begun to die off in sufficient numbers.

Abiit, excessit, evasit, erupit
—Cicero, *In Catilinam*, II, i. 1
He has gone, he is fled, he has eluded our watch, he has broken through our guards
The resourceful escaper was Catiline who had plotted to overthrow the government of Rome and who, being accused of treason, had deemed it a prudent move to flee Rome and join his army of rebels. (N.B. There appears to be no word in Latin, or in any other known language, for "escapee".) Cicero clearly wanted to leave his hearers in little doubt that Catiline had in fact gone away, and in doing so offered us a choice of four ways in which to say in Latin "he has slung his hook".

> "He [*sc.* the pig] bolts! He's off!—*Evasit! Erupit!*"
> Leigh Hunt, "On the Graces and Anxieties of Pig-driving".

> "Then *abiit*—what's the Ciceronian phrase? –
> *Excessit, evasit, erupit*—off slogs boy,
> Off like a bird, *avi similis*—(You observed
> The dative? Pretty i' the Mantuan!)—*Anglice*
> Off in three flea skips…"
> C. S. Calverley, "The Cock and the Bull".

Ab imo pectore
From the bottom of the heart, from the pit of the stomach
Literally "from the bottom of the breast", and a phrase said to be used first by Julius Caesar. Despite the efforts of Galen to educate the ancients into the geography of the human anatomy, it seems the Romans were not much clearer than we are from exactly which part of one's entrails a gut feeling should come.

I have a letter from a friend, now sadly long deceased, containing the apology "*Mea culpa (q.v.) ab imo.*"

> "[Henry] described (in words which were no doubt pathetic, for they came *imo pectore*, and caused honest Dick to weep plentifully)

his youth, his constancy, his fond devotion to that household that
had reared him;…"

W. M. Thackeray, *Henry Esmond*.

(Many Latin prepositions "govern" the ablative case of the noun, which
in the singular ends with a vowel. Here *imo* is the ablative singular of *imus*;
other examples are *ab origine, in absentia*, and *in situ*. The plural ablative
usually ends in "*-is*" or "*-ibus*", as in *in excelsis* or *de gustibus*.)

Ab incunabulo
From the cradle

Much the same as *ab initio* and *ab ovo, qq.v.* "Incunabula" were originally
"swaddling clothes", with the meaning later transferred to one's birth-place
or one's origins. Later still "incunabula" was the term used to designate the
earliest books printed in the West, (before 1501).

Sadly the "swaddling clothes" mentioned in the Gospel story of the birth
of Jesus are rendered in the Vulgate simply and unromantically not as
incunabula but as *panni* or "cloths". The baby Jesus was swaddled *in pannis*.

Ab initio
From the beginning, at the outset

"I tell you, Gillett, if the Romans had dealt faithfully with the Celt,
ab initio, this—this would never have happened."

Rudyard Kipling, "The Propagation of Knowledge".

"to 'tell it as it really is'—as if the poverty of that phrase did not *ab
initio* castrate the wish it implied!"

John Fowles, "Poor Koko".

A tale told *ab initio* gladdens the heart of such as the King of Hearts in
Alice in Wonderland, who commands the White Rabbit to: "Begin at the
beginning and go on until you come to the end: then stop." For a tale begun
in the middle, *vide "**in medias res**" infra.*

In science *ab initio* is used to mean "from first principles". For example, a
particular system may be advertised to those in the know as consisting of
"*ab initio* programs for molecular electronic structure calculations".

Ab initio software have produced a unique administration package
specifically for the Double Glazing Industry.

Ab initio also refers to the initial stages of flying training and is the motto
of No. 1 Elementary Flying School of the R.A.F.

Ab origine

From the beginning, from the source

Aboriginal inhabitants of a country, or *aborigines*, ("abos" to some) have evolved there, or at least have been minding their own business there for a long time, in contrast to later immigrants.

The St. John's first annual Children's Art Show on Environmental Concerns for young artists between the ages of 5 and 17 years of age, had the theme *Ab Origine.*

> "These ladies sat side by side with young females destined to be *demoiselles de magazins*, and with some Flamandes, genuine aborigines of the country."
>
> Charlotte Brontë, *The Professor.*

> "This man [*sc.* Goldsmith's schoolmaster] must have been of the Protestant religion; but he was of the aboriginal race, and not only spoke the Irish language, but could pour forth unpremeditated Irish verses."
>
> Lord Macaulay, "Essay on Oliver Goldsmith".

In a book review in *The Guardian*, Mary Hoffman notes that the early Venetians, from about the eighth century B.C., traded salt from the marshes: "Venetians were merchants *ab origine.*"

Ab ovo

From the egg, from the start

Perhaps as of a bird hatching, but also used of a feast which begins with an egg and finishes off with an apple. (*Ab ovo usque ad mala*—Horace, *Satires* I, iii. 6.) (Horace's longer phrase might also refer to your friend and mine who monopolises the conversation at a meal from start to finish.)

> "Do you suppose that [dinner-time] is a pleasant period, and that we are to criticize you between the *ovum* and the *malum*, between the soup and the dessert?"
>
> W. M. Thackeray, *Roundabout Papers.*

Ab Ovo is a fast growing, innovative and independent ICT services and products provider; a French electronic duet; and a Latvian rhythm, beat and ethnic project headed by Nils Ile.

Ab ovo may be used synonymously with *ab initio (q.v.)*

Absit omen

May no portent be present

"May no portent of evil be attached to the words I speak." The phrase sounds more elegant than "Touch wood!"

> "Months of calm before you—I touch upon wood: *absit omen*—
> months of mental calm,..."
>
> Patrick O'Brian, *The Fortune of War.*

> "They were sailing their little boats upon the Serpentine,... and
> as I looked on, Master Hastings Huckaback's boat went down!
> *Absit omen*, Pendennis! F. B. hopes that the child's father's argosy
> may not meet with shipwreck!"
>
> W. M. Thackeray, *The Newcomes.*

In Joseph Conrad's *Lord Jim*, Marlow recalls leaving Jim on the brigantine which was to take him, *D. V.*, to Batu Kring. Jim raised his cap on high in farewell. Marlow could see the face of the brigantine's captain, "the shape and colour of a ripe pumpkin, poked out somewhere under Jim's elbow. He too raised his arm as if for a downward thrust. *Absit omen!*"

For no clear reason Sellar and Yeatman dedicate their book *1066 and All That* to "Absit Oman (*sic*)".

Ab urbe condita (AUC)

From the founding of the city (Rome)

Every civilization uses a calendar in which years are numbered from some landmark event in the past. For the Jews it is the Creation, for the Muslims it is the Hegira, for the Western nations it is the birth of Christ. For the Romans it was the year in which Rome was founded. All happenings in Roman history were dated from this point, which we know as 753 B.C. but which to the Romans was their year dot (or rather year 1). Lord Macaulay prefaces his poem "Horatius", one of the "Lays of Ancient Rome", with the words: "A Lay Made about the Year of the City CCCLX", which is about (754—360) = 394 B.C. (Note that if A.U.C. 1 is 753 B.C., then A.U.C. 2 is 752 B.C., and the two corresponding numbers will always add up to 754.) An alternative form is "*Anno urbis conditae*"—"In the year of the founding of the city".

Frank Morley, in *The Great North Road*, transfers the phrase from Rome to London. "Concealed for the many centuries, the north front of the Wall [of London] was now disclosed,... as it was *ab urbe condita*."

In *Angels and Insects*, A. S. Byatt has Natty Crompton agree that the name of the Blood-Red Ants' nest should be "Red Fort", and that he would embark on its geography and history "if not *ab urbe condita* then from our discovery of it."

If the Romans ever needed to pin dates on events which happened before 1 A.U.C., they used the formula *ante urbem conditam*, "before the founding of the city".

Acta non verba
Deeds not words

This is precisely the sort of motto which, being pithy and easy to spell, was likely to appeal to aristocratic families who valued the busy life of the court and the hunting field over the less congenial and often more strenuous pursuits of reading and writing. It could almost be translated as "War, war, not jaw, jaw". It is the motto of the Jameson family, whose best-known member is Sir Leander Starr Jameson. Sir Leander put the motto into practice in December 1895 by leading the "Jameson Raid" into the Transvaal in the hope of stirring up rebellion against the president, "Oom" Paul Kruger. He failed, but his attempt apparently inspired Rudyard Kipling to write his poem "If—".

*Vide "**facta non verba**" infra.*

Ad astra per alas porci
To the stars on a pig's wings

The young John Steinbeck was told by his tutor that pigs would fly before he became a successful writer. He subsequently and gleefully made sure that the words *Ad astra per alas porci* appeared in the title page of each of his books.

Ad captandum vulgus
To catch the rabble

This phrase is by no means flattering, since it implies that someone, usually a demagogue or lesser (or even greater) politician, is no more than a rabble-rouser, employing specious arguments to his own ends, and exuding insincerity and duplicity with every word he utters to a credulous audience.

> It was curious how vulgar Nature could be at times,—meretricious,
> *ad captandum vulgus* effects –…
>
> Patrick O'Brian, *H.M.S. Surprise.*

"Why did Mr Disraeli take the duties of the Exchequer with so much relish? Because people said he was a novelist; an *ad captandum* man… that could not add up."

W. Bagehot, *Literary Studies*, "Shakespeare".

"The pretext given, 'tis clear, was *ad captandum vulgum*, powder to blind other eyes…."

John Fowles, *A Maggot*.

(Here Mr Fowles treats "vulgus" as a masculine noun, whereas it is normally treated as neuter. *Cf. "mobile vulgus", "odi profanum vulgus", infra.*)

(Some Latin prepositions govern the accusative case of the noun, which in the singular usually ends in "-m", as in *ad infinitum, ad hominem* and *ad nauseam*. The plural accusative usually ends in "-s" as in *ad auras* and *inter alios*, the exceptions to these rules being some neuter nouns such as *vulgus* and *funus*, plural *"funera"*.)

Addenda
Things which are to be added
The endings "-anda" and "-enda" denote the "gerundive" of the verb, indicating that something has to be done. *Cf.* agenda, corrigenda, propaganda, pudenda, videnda, etc. "Addenda" is plural: if a single item only has to be added, this is an "addendum".

Adeste fideles
Come, ye faithful
The first line of the Latin version of the hymn "O come, all ye faithful", with music composed by John Reading (*ob.* 1692), organist at Winchester and author of *Dulce Domum (q.v.)*. The first verse runs:

Adeste fideles,	Come, ye faithful,
Laeti, triumphantes,	Joyful, triumphant,
Venite, venite in Bethlehem.	Come, come to Bethlehem.
Natum videte,	Behold him born
Regum angelorum.	King of angels.
Venite adoremus, Dominum.	Come let us adore him, the Lord.

Adeste is the second person plural imperative of *adire*—"to approach". The more usual verb for "come" is *venire* whose corresponding imperative is *venite*, as in line three. Most similar imperatives end either in *-ite* or in *-ete*, hence *videte* in line four. Further into the book we find *benedicite, credite, currite*

8

and *favete*. The first conjugation imperatives end in *-ate* as in *cantate Domine*—"O sing unto the Lord", but are comparatively rare. Note that in English the imperative is often reinforced by "O", as in "O come all ye faithful".

Ad hoc
For this (special purpose)

An "ad hoc" committee, as opposed to a "standing" committee, is set up to consider a specific issue or problem. When the issue has been resolved or the problem solved, the ad hoc committee is disbanded.

> "A paramedic is employed on an ad-hoc basis, whenever he is needed."
>
> Report in *The Cornishman.*

The Ad Hoc Theatre Company of South Wales was formed expressly to enact plays at the Minack Theatre, Cornwall.

The phrase should be used with circumspection. A statement that "the matter will be investigated by an ad-hoc public enquiry" sounds sensible enough until one asks how an "ad-hoc" enquiry differs from an ordinary enquiry, since both must sooner or later present their report and then be disbanded.

Ad infinitum
To infinity

> "Lord Chesterton himself was not easier on matters of morality. [Sir Timothy Shelley] used to tell his son [Percy Bysshe Shelley] that he would provide for natural children *ad infinitum*, but would never forgive his making a *mésalliance*."
>
> W. Bagehot, *Literary Studies,* "Percy Bysshe Shelley".

Was Sir T. ever called on to fulfil his promise, (or indeed did young Percy fulfil his own early limitless promise in the matter)? When the latter was nineteen he married, in defiance of his father's wishes, sixteen-year-old Harriet Westbrook, who we imagine funnelled Percy's philoprogenitive energies into acceptable channels, to coin a phrase.

The invention of the microscope gave mankind a new insight into the dimensions of comparative size, and provided a glimpse into hitherto unseen vistas of life ("animalcules") on earth. As a result several microscopists claimed that:

"Great fleas have little fleas
Upon their backs to bite 'em,
And little fleas have lesser fleas,
And so *ad infinitum*."

Augustus de Morgan: "A Budget of Paradoxes", (1865).
Also Swift: "On Poetry", (1737).

This phrase, like many another, is susceptible to *tmesis*:

"calls… from one police department to another; one State to other States; calls for one set of records that referred to another set of records that led… *ad* apparently *infinitum*."

Colin Dexter, *The Jewel that was Ours*.

Ad libitum (ad lib)
At pleasure

In a stage play, an *ad lib* is a line or comment which does not appear in the script, but which the actor speaks notwithstanding, at his own pleasure if not at that of the director. Cynics may claim that most lines spoken by most actors are ad libs.

John Ayto, writing in *The Observer*, noted that television newsreaders used the phrase "explanation into" in three successive bulletins, "so it was presumably a faithful representation of the written autocue, not an *ad-lib* aberration".

If you are offered something *ad libitum*, you are free to accept or to reject the offer as you see fit. Written on a doctor's prescription, the abbreviation *ad lib* means "to be taken freely".

"The men get a little more sociable… and tell lies against each other sociably…. Lies *ad libitum*; and every true Australian bushman must try his best to tell a bigger out-back lie than the last bush-liar."

Henry Lawson, *While the Billy Boils*.
(*Vide* also *s.v.* "***seriatim***" *infra*.)

Ad majorem Dei gloriam (A.M.D.G.)
To the greater glory of God

This is the motto of the Society of Jesus (*alias* "The Jesuits"), and also of St. Ignatius College in Middlesex. It is a favourite dedication for war memorials, rolls of honour and stained glass windows up and down the land, as well as being the standard dedication for the compositions of Johann Sebastian Bach.

Ad nauseam
Until it makes you sick
The nausea is usually brought on by repetition.

"He undermined his best images by repeating them *ad nauseam*".
Art criticism in *The Observer.*

"[Marco Pierre] White rarely, if ever, mentions taste and flavour in his discussion of cooking. What he does bang on about, *ad nauseam*, is the look of a plate."
Book review in *The Guardian.*

Variety is the spice of life and hearing the same old spiel over and over again can prompt in the listener not only nausea but also murderous propensities.

"In his dotage, Uncle Walter was given to recounting *ad nauseam* his wartime exploits in the Navy, so that in the end we half wished he had been vouchsafed a heroic and watery grave alongside the less fortunate of his shipmates."
P. J. Dorricot, *Nursery Tales.*

Ad valorem
According to value
In 1953 I had some worn-out clothing sent from England to Kenya to be used as rags for dusting around the house. The Kenya Customs charged me fifteen shillings in import duty, at 22½ per cent *ad valorem*. In a letter replying to my strong objections, they agreed with me that the rags *per se* had no value, but since they were required to charge the duty, they simply placed an arbitrary value on the package and charged on that. No one should be surprised to learn that this incident somewhat coloured my attitude to Customs and Excise world-wide from that point on.

Aegri somnia (vanae)
—Horace, *Ars Poetica*, 7
The dreams of a sick man
There seems to be some confusion over the meaning and origin and correct form of this phrase. The full sentence in Horace runs: *velut aegri somnia, vanae fingentur species*—"like the dreams of a sick man, creating empty visions". Here *vanae* qualifies *species*, but the phrase *aegri somnia vana* is also

used, which can be translated as "the empty dreams of a sick man", with *vana* qualifying *somnia*. Ovid also talks of *somnia vana* in *Metamorphoses* ii. 614.

> "[Henry, wounded,] was passing the days in these crazy fancies and *vana somnia*, whilst the army was singing *Te Deum* for the victory."
>
> W. M. Thackeray, *Henry Esmond*.

Jules Verne uses *Aegri somnia* as the title of chapter 23 of volume I of *Twenty Thousand Leagues under the Sea*, while *Aegri Somnia Vana* is the title of a poem by Willowdown of the *Tír na nÓg* poetic community to be found on the ezboard website.

Aegrotat
He is ill

Anyone too nervous or too drunk (or even too ill) to sit the final examination for a university degree, but whose work has shown sufficient merit up to that point, may on that evidence be granted the degree: his (or her) name will appear on the pass list, accompanied by the word *ægrotat*.

On the title page of Sellar and Yeatman's *1066 and All That*, Walter Carruthers Yeatman's accreditation appears as "Aegrot: Oxon:" (Passed by virtue of illness at Oxford). (*Vide "***absit omen***" supra* and "***fatigatus et ægrotus***" *infra.*)

Aetatis suae
Of his (or her) age

Strictly speaking this should, and sometimes does, read *anno ætatis suæ*— "in the year of his age". It is frequently shortened to "ætat" or even to "æt". In any of these forms the phrase appears on many old tombstones and memorials.

> "He [Peroo] must needs make love to Baktawri,… , and she being betrothed to Akhmed Buksh's son, *ætat* nine, very properly threw a cow-dung cake at his head."
>
> Rudyard Kipling, *From Sea to Sea*.

It may even be shortened to "atat". It is recorded that John Gibbs of Clyst St. George, Devon, died in 1652 "At at plus minus 82", the *plus minus* or "more or less" reminding us how easy it was before birth certificates became obligatory to forget one's exact age, especially after eighty-odd years.

Sometimes the phrase offered more of a promise than a delivery. Elizabeth Marker's epitaph in Ottery St. Mary Church, Devon, finishes

with a defiant flourish: "ob. MDCCXI ætatis suæ"—"died 1711 aged".
Coyness about age not infrequently extended beyond the grave.

Affidavit

He has declared upon oath

Or "he has sworn on oath". A written affidavit, properly signed and
witnessed, is equivalent to a sworn testimony and is as good as (and infinitely
preferable to) a personal appearance in the witness box.

Afflavit Deus et dissipantur

God breathed and they are scattered

These words were inscribed on a medal struck by order of Queen
Elizabeth I to commemorate the defeat of the Spanish Armada, giving due
credit to God but not necessarily thereby devaluing the contributions of Sir
Francis Drake *et al.* Drake himself acknowledged God's part in his many
successes by having the motto *Auxilio Divino*—"By divine aid"—on his crest.

The words *Afflavit Deus et dissipantur* also appeared on a medal struck in
1797 to commemorate the dispersal by storms of a French invasion fleet
off Bantry Bay.

A fortiori

With stronger reason

> "These criticisms of the employees must apply *a fortiori* to the
> employers whose orders after all the employees were simply
> carrying out."
>
> > Report in *The Observer*.

> "Malebranche... was murdered.... Leibnitz, being every way
> superior to Malebranche, one might, *a fortiori*, have counted on *his*
> being murdered;..."
>
> > Thomas de Quincey: "On Murder considered
> > as one of the Fine Arts."

> "He means more than this: that she fears and despises the whole
> subject—and, *a fortiori*, its adherents."
>
> > Julian Barnes, *Arthur and George.*

(*A fortiori* as used here has a faint odour of the *non sequitur* about it—what
"stronger reason" is in evidence? Mr Barnes is on slightly firmer ground in
the following passage from *Something to Declare.*)

"How to explain what Sartre calls 'this scandalous occurrence: an idiot who becomes a genius'? And how, *a fortiori*, to explain it when the documentary evidence is thin… ?"

Agenda
Things to be acted upon

"Agenda" is the plural of "agendum". Being already plural, it has no plural of its own, but English ingenuity has supplied the deficiency with "agendas" (which is infinitely preferable to "agendae"). It does not suffer alone in its plurality; its woes are shared by "data", "strata", and "media" (*qq. v.*) which are also plural forms but which are often treated as though they were singular.

Agnosco veteris vestigia flammae
—Virgil, *Aeneid*, iv. 23
I feel the stirrings (literally "traces") of the former fires (of love)

Dido is confiding to her sister Anna that for Aeneas she is beginning to feel stirrings of that same love which she felt for her dead husband Sychaeus. (N.B. The "old flame" was internal and was not a former admirer.)

> "*Agnosco veteris vestigia flammae!* Something dim and far removed…
> —stirring beneath the surface—coming to life…"
> C. S. Lewis, "Psycho-analysis and Literary Criticism".

Agnus Dei, qui tollis peccata mundi, miserere nobis
—The Mass
Lamb of God, who takest away the sins of the world, have mercy on us

"Tollis" may not look much or sound much on its own, but in this context it seems to me to exert a certain power.

The origin of the passage is St. John's Gospel, i. 29: "The next day John [the Baptist] seeth Jesus coming unto him and saith, Behold the Lamb of God, which taketh away the sin of the world." In the Vulgate this is: *Ecce agnus Dei, ecce qui tollit peccatum mundi*—"Behold the Lamb of God, [behold him] which taketh away the sin of the world."

The *Agnus Dei* is frequently said or sung as part of the Communion Service of the Church of England, although it does not in fact appear in the Communion section of the *Book of Common Prayer*.

Agnus Dei is also the name given to a cake of wax or dough stamped with the figure of a lamb carrying the banner of the Cross, and distributed by the Pope on the Sunday after Easter. Such a symbol also appeared stamped on ingots of tin produced in the past in Cornwall.

Ecce agnus Dei qui tollit peccata mundi is the motto of the Tallow Chandlers Company.

Alea iacta est
The die is cast

At this point there is no going back. Julius Caesar is said by Plautus to have quoted this proverbial saying (in its original Greek form, ἀνερρίφθω κύβος, "*anerrhíphtho kúbos*", derived from Menander) after crossing the Rubicon with his legions on 10th January, 49 B.C. (A.U.C. 705). He should by rights have told his soldiers to fall out and go home, and then have gone on to Rome *solus*, but in view of what happened to him eventually, he could hardly be blamed for neglecting to disband his bodyguard. But by so crossing the Rubicon, the "point of no return", he rejected the authority of the Senate and precipitated the civil war between himself and Pompey.

For some reason *Alea Iacta Est* is the name of a research training programme network in tissue engineering.

The fact that he said *Alea iacta est*—"the die (two or more of which make dice) is cast", suggests that Caesar was a gambling man at heart, and had he lived in our day and age and been a musician, he might have taken pleasure in aleatory music, tunes composed by such chance methods as throwing dice. In reply to those (and there were some) who could have sworn that he said not "Alea iacta est" but "Iacta alea est", he would have doubtless replied to the effect that the order of words in Latin is immaterial—he could have said "Est iacta alea" or any other of the six different arrangements possible of three different words, and still have made his meaning clear. On the other hand, since it was claimed that Caesar spoke in Greek, the above conjectures seem somewhat pointless.

Alias (dictus)
At another time (under a different name)

We seem to be in danger of losing the useful word *alias* to the unattractive Americanism "aka"—"also known as". The only thing to be said for "aka" is that it might be used for contemporaneous aliases, when someone uses different names according to circumstances. If Yusuf Islam was formerly known as "Cat Stevens" but no longer chooses to use this name, then he would then be "*alias* Cat Stevens": if he is Yusuf Islam in private but Cat Stevens when performing, then, fair enough, he is "aka Cat Stevens". Fortunately "aka" has as yet no plural, so we are forced instead to use *alias* in such statements as "Jones travelled under a variety of aliases" (and as in the second sentence above) even though *alias* has no plural in Latin.

> "'Twisdon's the name, isn't it?' 'No,' I said. 'I mean to say. Yes.' I had forgotten all about my *alias*. 'It's a wise conspirator that knows his own name,' he observed, grinning broadly...."
>
> John Buchan, *The Thirty-Nine Steps*.

Alibi
Elsewhere

To have an alibi is to be able to prove you were elsewhere when the crime was committed and must therefore be innocent of it. Robin Goodfellow could put a girdle round about the earth in forty minutes but even at that speed he couldn't be in two places at once.

An alibi is not, never has been, and, *Deo volente,* never will be, the same as a mere excuse, although a section of the English-speaking media is doing its best to hide the proper meaning of this noble word.

> "Vell," said Mr Weller, "now I s'pose he'll want to call some witnesses to speak to his character, or p'raps to prove a alleybi.... I've got some friends as'll do either for him, but my adwice wud be this here—never mind the character, and stick to the alleybi. Nothing like a alleybi, Sammy, nothing."
>
> Charles Dickens, *Pickwick Papers*.

Aliquando bonus dormitat Homerus
Even good Homer nods at times

Good Homer nodded off permanently a few centuries ago but the phrase is still pertinent today: for "Homer" simply substitute the name of any cricket umpire. It is often used to excuse anyone's lapse of memory or inattention to detail, but it is in fact a variant on a critical remark of Horace, who, in *Ars Poetica* 359, says: *Indignor quandoque bonus dormitat Homerus*—"I deem it unworthy of him if Homer, usually good, nods for a moment." Horace will happily accept human frailty in any artist, but Homer?—of him he expects only the best.

> "for if *aliquando bonus dormitat Homerus*, they should remember how long he stayed awake...."
>
> Miguel De Cervantes, *Don Quixote*.

LIVING LATIN

Gideon Haigh in *Silent Revolutions* tells of how Errol Hunte, a West Indian test cricketer, was usually referred to in *Wisden's Cricketers' Almanack* as R. L. Hunte. Haigh comments on this error: "*Quandoque bonus dormitat Homerus* of course."

Alma mater
Nourishing mother, foster mother

Young people removed from the bosom of their families at a tender age to be boarded out at a public school have no choice but to accept this school as an *alma mater*. My own minor grammar school had a School Song (which I remember with affection—it was a great song to sing on special occasions) which referred to the school as *nostra mater altera*—"our second mother". This did no great harm, since ours was a day school and each day after school we went rejoicing back to our first mothers.

> "An interview with Steven Pinker referred to his 'almer mater'; we meant alma mater."
>
> Correction in *The Guardian*.

Alter ego
Second self, other self

Francis Lenton in *Characterismi* wrote: "A true friend is a man's second self", better than a brother, as good as a twin. Other phrases suggesting a similar relationship are *alter ipse amicus* or *amicus est tamquam alter idem*—"a friend is a second self".

> "[Leicester] appeared daily to advance in the Queen's favour. He was perpetually by her side in council—willingly listened to in the moments of courtly recreation... the *alter ego*, as it seemed of the stately Elizabeth..."
>
> Sir Walter Scott, *Kenilworth*.

An *alter ego* could also be one who has full powers to act for another. However the phrase is frequently used nowadays to indicate that someone from time to time takes on a different *persona* (*q.v.*): "Once behind the wheel of his car, he reveals his *alter ego*." For another phrase containing *alter*(a), *vide* **"alma mater"** *supra*.

Alumnus

A foster son, a former student

This is the next generation down in the family of the *alma mater*, both *alumnus* and *alma* being derived from the same root. It is normally, though not exclusively, used of an Old Boy (or Girl, *alumna*) of a school, or of a graduate of a university.

> "In his youth Uncle Waldemar had been a cat-burglar of some note. Later he decided to settle down to a more virtuous life as a time-share salesman, but remained quietly proud of being an alumnus both of Brixton and of Wormwood Scrubs."
>
> P. J. Dorricot, *Tales out of the Nursery.*

Amantium irae amoris integratio est

—Terence, *Andria*, 555

Lovers' quarrels are the renewal of love

This is perhaps one of the most controversial statements to have come down to us from the Latin writers, and probably more loving couples have fallen out arguing about it than for any other reason. Nevertheless a Latin T-shirt website offers a shirt with this inscription as "a gift for your lover after an argument".

W. M. Thackeray heads chapter 66 of *Vanity Fair* and Anthony Trollope heads chapter 73 of *Phineas Finn* with *Amantium Iræ*.

In *The Oxford Book of English Verse* Richard Edwardes' poem "In going to my naked bed" is given the heading *Amantium Irae*. The last line of each stanza reads: "The falling out of faithful friends renewing is of love."

Ambo

Both (together)

"Ambo" is used to indicate in a duologue or duet that both persons are to talk or sing together.

From Peele's *Arraignment of Paris*:

PARIS:	… Thy love is fair for thee alone, and for no other lady.
OENONE:	My love is fair, my love is gay, As fresh as bin the flowers in May…
AMBO:	Fair and fair and twice so fair, As fair as any may be: The fairest shepherd on the green, A love for any lady…

Ambo is also used in parish names to indicate that two settlements comprise the parish. Thus the parish of Fulfords Ambo in the East Riding of Yorkshire embraces the villages of Gate Fulford and of Water Fulford.

The game of "Ames-ace" requires the player to throw aces on both dice at once.

*Vide "**arcades ambo**" infra.*

Amo, amas
I love, thou lovest

When John O'Keefe wrote his more or less nonsensical poem starting "*Amo, amas, /* I love a lass, / As cedar tall and slender;..." he was touching a chord in the heart of anyone who had ever learned Latin from a standard text-book. The verb *amo* is used as a paradigm for verbs of the first conjugation (out of four or five) in the language. In the present tense it runs as follows:

amo	I love	amamus	we love
amas	thou lovest	amatis	you (plural) love
amat	he, she or it loves	amant	they love

The sequence, *amo, amas, amat, amamus, amatis, amant,* when chanted aloud, has a rhythm of its own which helps fix it in the memory. The perfect tense—"I have loved, thou hast loved, etc."—is likewise fixed in the memory, although the rhythm of this passage is a little wayward: *amavi, amavisti, amavit, amavimus, amavistis, amaverunt.*

Angina pectoris
A pain in the chest

"Angina" was the Latin for "quinsy", which is suppurative tonsillitis. Through association with "anguish" (French, *angoisse*) "angina" has come to mean "pain", a pain in the muscles of the heart caused by a lack of oxygen.

It may not be good Latin but by analogy *angina collis* sounds appropriate enough for "a pain in the neck". For the full translation into English of *angina natium*, "a pain in the *nates*", the reader is referred to any good dictionary.

Anglice
In English

The termination *-ice* (pronounced "icy") usually gives warning that a phrase is about to be translated into a different language (*vide s.v.*

*"**confiteor**" infra*). However S. T. Coleridge in his "Notes on The Merry Wives of Windsor" uses the word *Cambrice* to mean "in a Welsh manner" rather than "in Welsh": "Shallow no sooner corrects one mistake of Sir Hugh's,... but the honest Welshman falls into another, namely,... *Cambrice* 'cot' for coat."

In "Notes on Titus Andronicus" Coleridge extends the use of the termination *-ice* to a person rather than to a language: "as Theobald most *Theobaldice* phrases it..." (Coleridge reminds us earlier that Theobald is pronounced "Tibbald", so the style is succinctly *Tibbaldice*.)

Anno

Anno Christi (A.C.) *In the year of Christ*
Anno Domini (A.D.) *In the year of our Lord*
Anno Graciae (A.G.) *In the year of Grace*
Anno Salutis (A.S.) *In the year of Salvation*

All four of the above inscriptions or their abbreviations can be found on old tombstones and memorials, although A.D. is by far the most common.

In the Western world (which was a Roman world) for some centuries after the birth of Christ, dates were still reckoned in the Roman style (*vide* "***ab urbe conditæ***" *supra*). It was Dionysius Exiguus in the early sixth century who fixed the date of the Nativity (at A.D. 1 or A.U.C. 754), but his computation was probably up to half a dozen years out, and Christ may actually have been born a bit before his time in about 5 B.C.

Anno Domini can still be heard used as an excuse for personal shortcomings wherever two or three middle-aged persons are gathered together. It also still appears in print: "His latest work shows lamentable signs of *Anno Domini*". Book review in *The Guardian*.

It can in fact get worse:

"Nothing really wrong with him—only *anno domini*, but that's the most fatal complaint of all, in the end."

James Hilton, *Goodbye, Mr Chips*.

For some time now there has been a move to replace A.D. and B.C. with alternative terms which do not have an implied connection with Christian tradition, and which can be used, if they so prefer, by followers of other faiths or of none. Thus A.D. 1066 can be written as 1066 CE (Common Era) and 55 B.C. can be written as 55 BCE (Before the Common Era). The author of the present book prefers to stay with A.D. and B.C.

Annus horribilis

A horrible year

This is the opposite of *annus mirabilis q.v. infra*, and the phrase appears to have been coined *ca.* 1985.

"Gardeners writing off 2006 as their 'annus horribilis'."
Headline in *The Cornishman*.

Annus mirabilis

The year of wonders

The original "Year of Wonders" was 1666, remarkable for the Great Fire of London and for British military successes over the Dutch. An interesting extension of the phrase is *dies mirabilis*, "wonderful day", used by Geoffrey Lean writing in *The Observer*: "It took weeks to learn… to walk again, first with physiotherapists,… then—*dies mirabilis*—with a Zimmer frame."

It was Dryden who, in his poem entitled *Annus Mirabilis*, celebrated the miracles of 1666, in which the Dutch were defeated and London escaped total destruction by fire. Philip Larkin also wrote a poem with this same title but with a slightly different subject: "Sexual intercourse began / in nineteen sixty-three…."

In a numerical sense also 1666 could be said to be an *annus mirabilis*. In Roman numerals 1666 is MDCLXVI: these seven numerals occur, from $M = 1000$ to $I = 1$, in decreasing order of size, with none missed out. Only 1666 B.C. also has this property.

The plural, *anni mirabiles*, forms part of the title of an essay on modernist poetry by R. P. Blackmur.

The reverse side of the coin, *annus horribilis* or "year of horrors" was quoted by H.M. Queen Elizabeth II, referring to A.D. 1992. An earlier year, 1349, the year the Black Death struck Europe, was the *annus terribilis*.

Ante

Before

In a game of poker, each player lays down a stake or "forced bet", the *ante*, before the cards are dealt. "Upping the ante" is to raise the amount to be laid down before the action begins. Mark Twain, in *Roughing It*, writes: "I reckon I can't call my hand. Ante and pass the buck".

"Ante" is also used in various compound phrases, e.g., "ante-natal", "ante-room", "ante-bellum" ("pre-war", especially the American Civil War). The paradoxically-sounding "ante-post" betting refers to bets placed prior to the overnight declaration stage of a race, usually 10 a.m. on the day before it takes place.

Ante meridiem (a.m.)

Before midday

This together with p.m. (*q.v.*) makes up the twenty-four-hour day.

One can but wonder what possessed the western civilizations to decide that the new day began in the middle of the previous night. The civilizations of the Near East took the reasonable view that the day began at sunrise, at around 6 a.m. western time. Thus in Acts ii. 15, Peter sets the time of the Pentecostal descent of the Holy Spirit on the disciples at "the third hour" or 9 a.m. Living for a few years in East Africa, I rapidly grew used to the local (Arabic and African) method of counting time from sunrise at 6 a.m. and from sunset at 6 p.m. so that 9 a.m. was then (in Swahili) "saa tatu ya siku"—"hour three of the day"; 11 p.m. was "saa tano ya usiku"—"hour five of the night", and so on.

Ante prandium (a.p.)

Before lunch

On a doctor's prescription "a.p." indicates that the pills are to be taken, perhaps with an anteprandial cocktail, before a meal; which itself may then be followed by a postprandial nap.

Anti

Against

Used in combination—"anti-gambling campaigners", "an anti-war protest", etc.—or as a free-standing adjective—"He was always very anti when he was at college".

During the Great Schism of the West (for the correct pronunciation of "schism" see any good dictionary), 1309-76, a succession of popes was elected in opposition to the pope in Rome. These popes resided in Avignon, and are known generally as the "anti-popes".

Apologia

A vindication

In 1864 Cardinal John Newman wrote an account of his life and opinions under the title *Apologia pro Vita Sua*—"A defence of the conduct of his life". Wilfred Owen wrote a poem—"Apologia Pro Poemate Meo [for my poem]"—beginning "I, too, saw God through mud." Over the years the term "apology" has acquired connotations of guilt, of *mea culpa*, but the original *apologia* was in no sense apologetic.

Sara Wheeler, reviewing in *The Guardian* a book on Iran, suggested that the book "is, above all else, an apologia for the unifying underlying meaning of Islamic art".

A posse ad esse
From potentiality to being

"Even before puberty Martin had felt that he possessed within him the makings of a great lover…. Samantha's initial response to his tentative but markedly amorous advances seemed to hold out hope of his proceeding shortly *a posse ad esse*."

P. J. Dorricot, *Beyond the Nursery Slopes*.

A posse ad esse is the motto (though referring strictly only to moral and intellectual potential) of Pierrepont School, Surrey.

*Vide "**posse**" infra.*

A posteriori
From events coming after

A posteriori reasoning identifies causes by studying the clear results of sensory experience.

"That it was Yorick's and no one's else:—It was proved to be so, *a posteriori*, the day after, when Yorick sent a servant to my Uncle Toby's house, to enquire after it."

Laurence Sterne, *Tristram Shandy*.

A Posteriori is the title of a studio album of New Age electronic music by a German Group "Enigma".

In the poem "The Riddle of the Dinosaur" by Bert Taylor, occur the lines:

"The creature had two sets of brains,
The one in his head, the usual place,
The other at his spinal base.
Thus he could reason *a priori*
As well as *a posteriori*."

*Cf. "**a priori**" infra.*

Apparatus
Things prepared

A word adopted *in toto* into English from Latin but curious in that being a fourth declension noun *apparatus* as written may be either singular or plural. (The Romans pronounced the word differently however in the singular and in the plural, with a "short u" and "long u" respectively.) Only rarely do we talk about "an apparatus", though there is no reason why we should not do so. It is equally correct to say, "The apparatus is broken", and "The apparatus are broken". The usual way of avoiding this perhaps subconsciously–felt ambiguity is to talk about a "piece of apparatus".

When I was in training for my spell of National Service, we were instructed how to fall flat on our faces preparatory to firing our rifles. Our corporal suggested that we "grasp the rifle firmly in the left hand and fall forward on to the right hand, being careful to avoid the wedding apparatus as you go down."

A priori
From preceding events

A priori reasoning involves arguing from basic premises or from abstract first principles, independent of sensory perception or experience, and seeing to what conclusion the arguments lead. However, it is possible that the basic premises may nevertheless themselves be inferred from preceding events, so that by reasoning *a priori* we may simply be divining from evidence gleaned from the past what is likely to happen in the future, a sound statistical procedure.

> "Does not the whole vast structure of modern naturalism depend not on positive evidence but simply on an *a priori* metaphysical prejudice?"
>
> C. S. Lewis, "Is Theology Poetry?"

> "Melissa, sweet chuck, your *pater* is a celebrated war profiteer of the highest renown. He is also of a generous nature, exuding philanthropy from every pore. It doesn't take an Albert Einstein to work out *a priori* that as a wedding gift we ought to be able to sting the old boy for at least six hundred a year."
>
> P. J. Dorricot, *Beyond the Nursery Slopes.*

Cf. "***a posteriori***" *supra.*

Aqua fortis
Strong water

This is not water at all but nitric acid, used by "aquafortists" engaged in engraving designs on copper.

Aqua mirabilis
Wonderful water

Again not water at all but slightly less toxic than *aqua fortis*, being a concoction made by alchemists of cloves, nutmeg, ginger and "spirit of wine", i.e. alcohol. *Aqua mirabilis* combined the new spices of the East in a palatable medicine, perhaps not so very different in its ingredients from the Medicinal Compound of Lily the Pink.

Aqua pura
Pure water

This is water from the spring (or often even from the tap), uncontaminated and fit to drink, and hence is also known (though not widely) as *aqua fontana*. The schoolboy howler analyses it: "Water is made up of two gins, oxygin and hydrogin. Oxygin is pure gin, but hydrogin is gin and water."

Nil Sine Aqua—"Nothing Without Water"—was the motto of the South Staffordshire Waterworks Company.

Aqua regia
Royal water

Like *aqua fortis*, this is not water at all, and again like *aqua fortis* is certainly best not taken by mouth, being a mixture of one part of nitric with two to four parts of hydrochloric acid, which has the power to dissolve the king of metals, gold, and which would certainly make short work of the human digestive tract. However, it is used to clean the glass tubes used in nuclear magnetic resonance spectography, so would presumably do a good job on kitchen sinks.

Aqua vitae
The water of life

Once more not water at all but unlike *aqua fortis* and *aqua regia* is best taken by mouth, being some form of alcohol, usually brandy ("eau-de-vie"). The Gaelic form of the phrase, "uisge-beatha", gives us the word "whisky", while the Scandinavians are said to drink a caraway-flavoured spirit called "akvavit". *Aqua vitæ* was a *sine qua non* in the ingredients of the *elixir vitæ* (*q.v.*).

And yet it is said to be all a mistake, being the mis-rendering back into mediaeval Latin of the Spanish *acqua di vite*, "juice of the vine". The correct translation would be *aqua vitis*, but who cares? *Aqua vitæ* is a very happy error.

Aquila non capit muscas
An eagle does not catch flies
   This is a declaration that certain trivial annoyances and inconveniences
are beneath the notice of the well-bred. It is the motto of many well-bred
and aquiline families, including those of Illidge, Keevil, Manningham-
Buller and Yarde-Buller.

Arbiter elegantiarum
A judge of matters of taste
   Tacitus in *Annals* xvi. sect. 18 cites/designates Petronius as *elegantiæ arbiter*
of which *arbiter elegantiarum* is a later variant.

> "In his inmost heart he desired to be something more than a mere
> *arbiter elegantiarum*, to be consulted on the wearing of a jewel, or the
> knotting of a necktie, or the conduct of a cane."
> Oscar Wilde, *The Picture of Dorian Gray*.

> "In the 1950's, Mrs Lillicrap, who made her own clothes copied
> from pictures in the fashion magazines, was the neighbourhood
> *arbiter elegantiarum.*"
> P. J. Dorricot, *Beyond the Nursery Slopes*.

   Henry Fielding in *Tom Jones* introduces an arbiter of another kind,
"Heydegger, the great *arbiter deliciarum*, the great high priest of pleasure."

Arcades ambo
   —Virgil, *Eclogues*, vii. 4
Arcadians both
   The full line is *Ambo florentes ætatibus, Arcades ambo*—"Both in the bloom of
youth, Arcadians both". To Virgil they were well-regarded musicians, but
Byron rather unkindly diminishes them in *Don Juan*, Canto iv: "Arcades
ambo, *id est*, blackguards both".
   The suggestion is sometimes that they are a well-matched pair. In Patrick
O'Brian's *The Fortune of War*, Stephen Maturin says: "*Arcades ambo*. They
are the same species of curculio and there is nothing to choose between
them", suggesting that it is difficult to distinguish one weevil from another.
   Baroness Orczy, taking her cue from Byron, used *Arcades Ambo* as a
heading for chapter 8 of her *Eldorado*, which dealt with an underhand plot
to foil the Scarlet Pimpernel.
   (*Vide "**ambo**" supra et "**et in Arcadia ego**" infra.*)

Argumentum ad hominem

An argument to the man

Not involving so much an appeal to a man's better nature, but appealing to his inner nature, calling up his own deeply-held views and principles in support of the argument: "… that soft and irresistible piano of voice, which the nature of the *argumentum ad hominem* absolutely requires…" Laurence Sterne, *Tristram Shandy*.

The phrase *ad hominem* can also be applied to an attack made on a person's character so as to avoid having to counter his arguments. Writing in *The Observer*, Anita Brookner suggested that the tutelary genius of all commentators on eighteenth-century French painting was Diderot, "whose hectic *ad hominem* attacks and enthusiasms would not pass muster in today's world of professionals."

John Locke, in *Human Understanding*, writes: "Argumentum ad hominem—to press a man with consequences drawn from his own principles or concessions."

Arma virumque cano

—Virgil, *Aeneid*, i. 1

Arms and the man I sing

The opening words of the *Aeneid*, from which George Bernard Shaw took the title, *anglice*, of his play "Arms and the Man".

Patrick O'Brian in *H.M.S. Surprise* reports a harsh voice saying: " '*Arma virumque cano*,'… as some recollection of Diana's mad cousin set Stephen's memory in motion."

"Arms and the Man" is the motto of Number 2 Air Armament School of the R.A.F.

Armiger

A bearer of arms

On memorials in Latin it is not uncommon to find the deceased designated as *armiger*. The English translation is "esquire", still used occasionally as a courtesy title on envelopes: "William Boyd, Esq.," followed by the address. Originally those classed as Armiger or Esquire were minor aristocracy with no more resonant title to their name, who nevertheless, through their connection to a noble family, were entitled to an appropriate and often imposing coat of arms. A slightly lower class of wealthy commoners, often successful tradesmen or professional men, might acquire by purchase the right to a coat of arms, but their designation was merely "Gentleman" or *Generosus* (*q.v. infra*) in Latin. The practice of addressing letters to "James Conway, Gent." died out in the course of the nineteenth century, and "Esq." became generally used. Below the rank of "gentleman" came "yeoman", and at the bottom of the rural ladder was "husbandman". So the inventory of the property of Isaac Elliott who died in 1722 begins: "A trew and perfect inmatarey of all and singulier the goods and shatells of Isack Elliott of Woodbery in the County of Devon Hosbantman." It was a requirement, *de facto* if not *de jure*, for every person mentioned in an official document of that time to be labelled with his rank in society.

Ars est celare artem
True art lies in concealing art

A Latin proverb. Ovid may have had it in mind when he said (*Artis Amatoriæ*, ii. 213): *Si latet ars, prodest*—"If the art is concealed, it succeeds", the art here being the sly and subtle art of seduction.

Ars est celare artem was the motto chosen by the Central Signals Establishment of the R.A.F., but presumably not for its seductive implications. On the other hand, and I speak as an ex-R.A.F. man, who knows?

Ars gratia artis
Art for art's sake

Théophile Gautier (1811-72) coined the slogan "L'art pour l'art", which was taken up by Walter Pater and others in the Aesthetic movement in Britain, and rendered *anglice* as "Art for art's sake". The Latin version has become familiar to millions as the legend around the roaring lion (Leo) of the Metro-Goldwyn-Mayer films.

Not to be outdone by the art world, Edgar Allan Poe felt much the same about poetry, suggesting that the poem *per se* was what mattered, the poem being written solely for the poem's sake.

Ars longa, vita brevis
—Hippocrates; quoted by Seneca, *De Brevitate Vitae* (*Of the Brevity of Life*)
Art is long, life is short, or *So long a time to learn the art, so short a time to live*

The art was the art of healing, as one might suppose of Hippocrates. The phrase does *not* mean, as suggested in the schoolboy howler, "a short skirt on a fat bottom", although *Punch* magazine once added its own comment on an obituary notice: "John Longbottom, aged 3 months, dies: *Ars longa vita brevis.*"

Sir John Millais took *Ars longa, vita brevis* as his family motto. Longfellow translated it as: "Art is long but time is fleeting". *Vita Brevis* is the title of a book by Jostein Gaarder.

In *Doctor in the House*, Richard Gordon states that over the entrance to St. Swithin's Hospital was engraved "Hippocrates' discouraging aphorism 'The Art is Long'."

Arte et labore
By skill and hard graft
This is the motto of the Blackburn Rovers Football Club.

Artium Magister (A.M.)
Master of Arts
A scholar's qualification which, especially when appearing in a Latin inscription, might be written as A.M. rather than as the English M.A.

> "Jimmy Dunn was an A.M. of crookdom. He was an artist in the confidence line."
>> O. Henry, "The Gold that Glittered".

Occasionally the phrase appears in reverse: "... let us add at last in the tail of the number, Edmund FitzHenry Talbot, MAGISTER ARTIUM!" William Golding, *Close Quarters*.

Aspice Finem
Look to the end
This phrase was adopted as its motto by West Penwith Rural District Council, under whose jurisdiction came Land's End.

Audere est facere
To dare is to win
Or "He who dares, wins". This is the motto of Tottenham Hotspur Football Club.

Audi alteram partem
—St.Augustine, *De Duabus Animabus*, XIV. 2
Hear the other side
> "So far he has not been heard in his own defence. *Audi alteram partem*—hear the other side—is a well-established and fundamental rule of law on both sides of the border."
>> T. Winsor, letter to *The Guardian*.

Traditionally the statues of Themis, the Greek goddess of justice, show her holding her sword and scales, and blindfold. The statue of Justice standing above the portals of the Old Bailey in London has the sword and scales but not the blindfold. But blindfold or not, it is to be understood that whatever else is shut up her ears are wide open.

Aurora australis
The Southern Lights
Auster was the south wind; *auster nocens* was the bad south wind, the sirocco. Australia is the "southern" continent, originally designated as *Terra Australis Incognita*. *Aurora Australis* is the name of an Antarctic ice-breaker.

Aurora borealis
"Dawn in the north", the Northern Lights
Aurora is the pink glow in the eastern sky heralding the dawn. *Boreas* was the North Wind. *Ad auroram*—"to the dawn", is the motto of 255 Squadron of the R.A.F.

Ave atque vale
Hail and farewell
Catullus, visiting his brother's tomb near Troy for the first time while on his way to Bithynia, and not expecting to pass that way again, says in *Carmina* ci. 10: *Atque in perpetuum, frater, ave atque vale*—"And so for ever, brother, hail and farewell". (Although it means "Hail and Farewell", *ave atque vale* was a traditional Roman farewell to the dead.)

Colin Dexter heads the final chapter of *The Jewel that was Ours* with the last two lines of the poem: *Accipe fraterno multum manantia fletu / Atque in perpetuum, frater, ave atque vale*. "Accept (these gifts) drenched with many a brotherly tear, And so, etc."

Tennyson, sympathizing with Catullus, wrote a poem entitled "Frater Ave atque Vale". A. C. Swinburne wrote a poem "Ave atque Vale", in memory of Baudelaire. Had the film "Brief Encounter" been made in ancient Rome, its title might well have been "Ave atque Vale". Up to the end of the 1920's the termly magazine of my grammar school used "Ave atque Vale" for the list of names of those pupils who either had recently entered the school or had just left it.

Ave atque Vale is the official website of the book on the history of the Vale-Special sports car.

The heading "Ave Atque Vale" appeared in the *Radio Times* some while ago for a programme of music by Shostakovich, Charles Ives and Haydn. I am not quite sure why the "Ave", but the programme finished with Haydn's "Farewell" Symphony. In any case it was good to be reassured that the phrase was still alive and in good shape.

Ave Caesar morituri te salutant

—Suetonius

Hail, Caesar, those who are about to die salute thee

Suetonius reported that this was the cry of condemned prisoners who were crewing galleys in a mock battle on Lake Fucinus in A.D. 52. However tradition has it that it was also the tribute paid to Caesar by the gladiators about to engage in a fight to the death in the arena of the Colosseum and other places. It would seem that whether on land or sea the stiff upper lip— *labrum superius rigidum*—was not the invention of the English Public School, but was alive and flourishing in ancient Rome, at least for as long as it took to fight to the death. An alternative form is *Ave Imperator morituri te salutamus*— "Hail, Emperor, we who are about to die salute thee."

Longfellow's poem "Morituri salutamus" begins: "'O Caesar, we who are about to die / Salute you!' was the gladiators' cry."

Derived from this is *Morituri nolumus mori*—"we who are about to die don't want to", the motto of the mission dispatched in Terry Pratchett's *The Last Hero* to foil the plan of the gods to destroy Discworld. *Morituri nolumus mori* is also the name of a wargames website.

Julius Caesar handed on his cognomen of *Caesar* to his heirs; and subsequent Emperors of Rome, not to turn down a good thing, assumed the name as a title. The Romans pronounced the word as "Kigh-zar" and from *Caesar* came the word "Kaiser", a title adopted by the emperors of Germany. The same name was whittled down to "Csar" or "Czar", a title adopted by the kings of Bulgaria. "Czar" also flourished in Russia from the fifteenth century onward, though respelt as "Tsar" to make it look more Russian and less Bulgarian. The title Tsar was snuffed out in Russia at Ekaterinburg on 17th July 1918, although the name "Czar" has since been resurrected, we are told, in such titles as "War Czar" and "Energy Czar".

Ave Maria

Hail Mary

In Luke i. 28 the archangel Gabriel addresses Mary in these words: "Hail, thou that art highly favoured, the Lord is with thee, blessed art thou among women". The Vulgate has *Ave gratia plena, Dominus tecum...*—"Hail, full of grace, the Lord is with thee". In neither of these versions does the angel mention Mary by name, and the habit arose only later of making it clear exactly who the highly-favoured lady was. The version to be found for example in the Visconti *Book of Hours* has the angel say explicitly: *Ave Maria gratia plena* ... "Hail Mary, full of grace..."

The passage was a prayer to be repeated a set number of times as penance after Confession. In the rosary, the small beads were known as

Ave Maria beads, distinct from the larger Paternoster (*q.v.*) beads. The *Ave Maria* bell was sounded at six o'clock and twelve o'clock to invite the faithful to repeat the prayer.

Two farm workers were debating a serious problem. Should Jake remain faithful to Maria, his childhood sweetheart, or transfer his affections to Emily, the seductive new parlourmaid at the Hall? Suddenly Reuben had a bright idea. Jake should pray for heavenly guidance. The local Catholic church was close at hand, and Reuben persuaded Jake to go in and pray. Two seconds later, Jake was out again. "You ain't 'ad time to pray, surely!" said Reuben. "'Tweren't no need!" said Jake, his face aglow. "I got in through the door, and there 'twere writ up for me all in gold letters—''Ave Maria'!"

B

Benedicite
Bless you

An old form of greeting or mark of approbation. The canticle from the Order of Morning Prayer in the Prayer Book entitled "Benedicite" starts with the words: "O all ye works of the Lord, bless ye the Lord", which in Latin are: *Benedicite omnia opera Dominum*. The words of the canticle are taken from the "Song of the Three Holy Children" found in the Apocrypha.

> "And when this Yeman hadde this tale ytold
> Unto oure Hoost, he seyde, '*Benedicitee!*'
> This thyng is wonder merveillous to me,…"
>
> Chaucer, *The Canon's Yeoman's Prologue*.

Benedictus benedicat
May the Blessed One give a blessing

A brief form of Latin grace used in colleges and places where they use Latin and eat.

> "'*Benedictus benedicat, per Jesum Christum Dominum nostrum,*' [Mr Thursley] said at last in his praying voice, which was deep, with the suspicion of a tremolo, and charged with transcendental significance."
>
> Aldous Huxley, *Eyeless in Gaza*.

Beneficium accipere libertatem est vendere
—Publilius Syrus, *Sententiae*, 49
To accept a favour is to sell one's liberty

Judging by reports of the incidence of official corruption world-wide, the value placed on liberty sometimes doesn't seem to amount to very much.

Sententiae were thoughts put into the form of maxims or aphorisms, and many in this present collection are taken from Publilius Syrus. The word "maxim" itself derives from the phrase *maxima sententia*, a "greatest thought", or as one might say, a "lofty thought".

Bis dat qui cito dat

—Publilius Syrus, *Sententiae*, 6

He gives twice as much who gives quickly

A simplified form of *Bis dat qui dat celeriter*, which says exactly the same thing, *viz*, that a swift though modest response to a call to alms can be a cheap way of acquiring a reputation for generosity. From the recipient's point of view, a bird in the hand is worth two in the bush—*avis in manu duas in frutice valet*.

In theatrical or musical circles, "Bis!"—"twice", is of course the French for "Encore!"

Both *cito* and *celeriter* mean "quickly": the former in its comparative form appears in the motto of the Olympic Games: *Citius, Altius, Fortius*—"Faster, Higher, Stronger".

Bis peccare in bello non licet

In war one may not blunder twice

> "He pressed upon me the importance of planting (trees) at the first in a very sufficient manner, quoting the saying, *In bello non licet bis errare*; and adding, 'this is equally true in planting.'"
>
> James Boswell. *The Life of Samuel Johnson, LL.D.*

(*Peccare* is "to sin", *errare* is "to err".)

Bona-fide

In good faith, legitimate

A *bona-fide* (with or without the hyphen) offer is one made in good faith, without intention to deceive. For some reason, King Louis XIV of France was known as "Old Bona Fide".

> "'It's a *bona fide* proposition. brass-bound, silver-plated, copper-bottomed.' 'Hey, that's a pretty good description of my Aunt Agatha,' said Gerald."
>
> P. J. Dorricot, *Tales out of the Nursery.*

> "'… what made you put [the stanza] into your essay like that, in a way that suggested as strongly as possible that it was a bona fide part of Gray's poem?'"
>
> Kingley Amis, "Boris and the Colonel".

At one time, pubs were allowed to serve drinks out of hours only to persons on a journey, who were therefore "bona-fide travellers".

> "I reminded them that all public-houses were closed till six o'clock. Stillwood said: 'That's all right—*bona-fide* travellers.'"
>
> G. and W. Grossmith, *The Diary of a Nobody*.

The other side of the coin is *mala fide*—"in bad faith".

Bona fides
Good faith

Once all I had to do to establish my *bona fides* was to show that I was to be trusted, that I was *integer vitæ* (*q.v.*), etc. Now it all boils down to proving that I am who I claim to be, and I have to establish my *bona fides* via passwords, PIN numbers and my mother's maiden name. Anyone imprudent enough not to have acquired a password, pin or mother is doomed *in perpetuum* to be regarded with the deepest suspicion.

> "He said Twisdon would prove his *bona fides* by passing the word 'Black Stone' and whistling 'Annie Laurie'."
>
> John Buchan, *The Thirty-Nine Steps*.

To question someone's *bona fides* is to be suspicious of his intentions, of his good faith. In one of A. P. Herbert's *Misleading Cases*, the "Reasonable Man" is defined as one who, *inter alia*, "investigates exhaustively the *bona fides* of every mendicant before distributing alms."

Britt. Omn. Rex (Britanniarum Omnium Rex)
King of all the Britains

These words, inscribed on British coins of the late nineteenth and early twentieth centuries, made it clear, at least to the monied classes, that the monarch was ruler of all the Britains, both here and overseas. Victoria was *Britt. Omn. Regina*, Queen of all the Britains. There was none too much room round the edge of any coin, however large, to accommodate all the sovereign's titles, hence the abbreviations. In fact, Victoria often had to make do with a bare *Britt. Regina*. (*Cf. "Ind. Imp." infra.*)

Had Victoria reigned a hundred years earlier, she could have rejoiced in being Queen of France as well. Edward III had laid claim to the throne of France as far back as 1337. A medallion struck in the reign of Charles I is inscribed *CAROLVS I D:G MAG[NAE] BRITTANN[IAE] FRAN[CIAE] ET HIBERN[IAE] REX*—"Charles I, by the Grace of God King of Great

Britain, France and Ireland"; while in one of the early deeds of a former house of mine, dated 1754, appears a reference to "our Sovereign Lord George the Second by the Grace of God of Great Britain France and Ireland King Defender of the Faith and so forth"; and I have come across a deed of 1792 which still mentions France in the king's titles. Not until the Peace of Amiens in 1802 did the British monarch formally relinquish the title of King of France, after more than two centuries had elapsed since the loss in 1558 of Calais, the last possession held in France by Britain. *Vide* also "***fid. def.***" *infra.*

C

Cacoethes scribendi

An itch for writing

"*Cacoethes*" is not Latin but Greek. However the word was adopted into Latin by the normal process of language borrowing and this phrase is used by Juvenal, who is scathing about it—*insanabile cacoethes scribendi*—"the incurable itch for writing". The Irish poet Samuel Lover expands on this and offers some hope of relief: "When once the itch of literature comes over a man, nothing can cure it but the scratching of a pen. (But if you have not a pen, I suppose you must scratch any way you can.)" There is a writers' group called "Cacoethes-Scribendi".

Other cognate phrases are *cacoethes loquendi*, an itch for talking, and *cacoethes emendi*, an itch for going shopping, both being endemic in half the population, one might almost say from scratch.

Caeca invidia est

—Livy, xxxviii. 49

Envy is blind

Unlike jealousy, which is reported as having green eyes.

Caelum non animum mutant qui trans mare currunt

—Horace, *Epistles*, I, xi. 27

They change their skies but not their souls who flee across the sea

Caelum is sometimes spelled as *coelum*, which is said to be an error perpetrated in the Middle Ages and perpetuated ever since, so that the standard dictionaries of Latin use *coelum* in preference to *caelum*. The preference extended to the Latin used in the Roman Catholic church, *cf.* "***regina coeli***" *infra.*

Caelum non Animum is the motto of several prominent families, including Harper of Lamberts and Rhodes of Bellair.

Milton had a similar thought to Horace's; but whereas Horace's smacks much of the despair of one who by travelling is unsuccessfully trying to escape from the trammels of his own thoughts, Milton's gives boundless hope of mental freedom:

> "The mind is its own place and in itself
> Can make a Heav'n of Hell, a Hell of Heav'n."
>
> *Paradise Lost*, Book I.

Camera obscura
A darkened room

Not the "dark room" in which film is developed, but a darkish room, sometimes a mere box, in which an image from the outside world is projected *via* a series of lenses on to a screen.

> "The landscape has not the hues of the real world; it is modified in the *camera obscura* of the self-enclosed intelligence."
>
> W. Bagehot, *Literary Studies*, "Percy Bysshe Shelley".

The phrase clearly suggested the title of an English translation from the French of a meditation on photographs and memories by Roland Barthes: *Camera Lucida*, "a lighted room".

Caput mortuum
A dead head

Not so much a dead head as a dead bottom. *Caput mortuum* is the inert residuum left by a process of chemical distillation or sublimation, being known also as "sludge".

> "There is no *caput mortuum* of worn-out threadbare experience to serve as ballast to [Shelley's] mind; it is all volatile, intellectual salt-of-tartar,…"
>
> W. Bagehot, *Literary Studies*, "Percy Bysshe Shelley".

> "This is the caput mortuum of pain:
> Perhaps your splinters have a power to prickle…
> They are not pain, for pain is spiritual…."
>
> Alan Porter, "The Signature of Pain".

Caput mortuum is the name given to the pigment Cardinal Purple, derived from iron rust. It was also the name given to "Mummy Brown", a pigment made from ground-up mummified bodies, used widely by artists until they found out where it came from.

Carpe diem

—Horace, *Odes*, I, xi (the last line)

Reap the harvest of the day

It is difficult to walk the streets of any large town nowadays and not come across these words emblazoned on a T-shirt, the wearer presumably hoping to come across a kindred spirit anxious to make the most of what was to be reaped before the day was out. The complete thought is *Carpe diem quam minimum credula postero*—"Reap the harvest of the day, trust as little as possible in the morrow".

Many poets have written poems in the spirit of "Gather ye rosebuds while ye may" and "Youth's a stuff will not endure". Lawrence Hope gave the title *Carpe Diem* to one of his poems, while Byron uses the phrase in the last stanza of "Don Juan":

> "But *carpe diem*, Juan, *carpe, carpe*!
> Tomorrow sees another race as gay
> And transient, and devour'd by the same harpy..."

Erskine Childers in *The Riddle of the Sands* adapts the phrase, casting it in the subjunctive mood for "let us make the most of the day": "We abandoned ourselves, three youthful, hungry mariners, to the enjoyment of this impromptu picnic. Such a chance might never occur again—*carpamus diem*."

In Palgrave's *Golden Treasury*, *Carpe Diem* is the heading for Shakespeare's "O Mistress mine". *Carpe Diem* is also the title of a novel by Saul Bellow.

Carpe diem is often translated as "Seize the day", which makes sense of Terry Pratchett's choice of title for his book *Carpe Jugulum*, "Seize the Jugular".

Evidence that *Carpe Diem* has caught the public imagination so as to become almost a mantra lies in the fact that at least two commercial firms have adopted the title. One "Carpe Diem" offers "Celebration Parchments" for weddings and similar landmark events in one's lifetime: another offers "botanic water", presumably for serving up instead of champagne at weddings and similar landmark events in one's lifetime. The cogent argument that champagne has botanic origins seems churlish in the face of the enthusiasm the producers have for their own product, foreshadowed by Hippocrates two and a half thousand years ago in a treatise on the incomparable benefits of herbal brews.

Casus belli

A reason for war, for dispute

The invasion of Belgium in 1914, that of Poland in 1939, and the threat of weapons of mass destruction in Iraq at a later date, are each an example of a *casus belli*.

The term can also be use in a less destructive sense. Adrian Hamilton, writing in *The Observer*, says: "Yesterday the *casus belli* was the Social Charter, today it is the budget."

Casus, like *apparatus* (*q.v.*), is a fourth declension noun and the plural of *casus belli* is also *casus belli*. In *A Maggot*, John Fowles refers to an inquiry dealing with "heriot and farleu, thraves and cripplegaps, plowbote and wainbote, hedge-scouring and whin-drawing (and a hundred other obscure *casus belli* between landlord and tenant)…"

(*Vide s.v. "**sui generis**" infra.*)

Cave

Beware

At my grammar school, we imitated the public schools in various ways. We cried "cave", pronounced as "K.V.", at the first sight of danger, usually a master or a prefect. It was some years before I discovered this was the Latin for "Look out!"

Lt. Benét is describing some of the precautions he took in a clandestine love affair, which included employing Marion as a look-out:

"She was accustomed to keep *cave* for us."

William Golding, *Close Quarters*.

"The gigantic Front-de-Bœuf… bore on a white shield a black bull's head… bearing the arrogant motto, *Cave, Adsum.*"

Sir Walter Scott, *Ivanhoe*.

Cave adsum (Beware, I am here) is the motto of the Jardine family. *Vide "**cave canem**" infra.*

Caveat

Let him beware

If I am empowered to issue a Caveat on a particular matter, then no one may act on that matter without letting me know first. On the other hand, the word now seems to be used as a synonym for "warning". Janet Watts, writing in *The Observer*, says: "So Somerville will stay on course to become mixed. Amid gallantries to the young women and caveats to the college, the Visitor advises this should happen...."

For a description of an actual Caveat and its progress, *vide* Ch. II of Robert Graves' *Goodbye To All That.*

Caveat emptor
Let the buyer beware
A maxim in Latin law, and of perennial and universal relevance.

> "eBay itself is plastered with 'caveat emptor' warnings."
> Letter in *The Guardian.*

But the buyer is not the only person at risk. The reader may also be vulnerable. In *The Guardian*, Sara Wheeler, reviewing a book on Iran, noted that before a long essay on the origins and history of Islamic art, the author "inserts a *caveat lector* [my italics] advising uninterested readers to skip to the next chapter".

Cave canem
Beware of the dog
This famous warning, quoted by Petronius but dating back to the Greeks (if not to the first cave-dwellers), was discovered written in mosaic on the portal of a house excavated in the ruins of Pompeii.

James Thurber in "The Dog That Bit People" recorded that they buried the dog along a lonely road and put up a smooth board above his grave. "On the board I wrote with an indelible pencil 'Cave Canem'. Mother was quite pleased with the simple classic dignity of the old Latin epitaph".

Reports of sightings of the variants *Cave felem*—"Beware of the cat", and *Cave uxorem*—"Beware of the wife", are apocryphal at the time of writing but *verb. sap. (q.v.)*...

Ceteris paribus
Other things being equal
> "'*Ceteris paribus*, I think we'd better be going,' said Penfentenyou."
> Rudyard Kipling, "The Puzzler".

Sometimes and previously *cæteris (caeteris) paribus*. "A very rich man, from low beginnings, may buy his election in a borough; but *cæteris paribus* a man of family will be preferred." Dr Samuel Johnson.

Cf. "mutatis mutandis" infra. (Ceteris paribus and *mutatis mutandis* are both examples of "ablative absolute" phrases. For an explanation of this term, see any good Latin grammar book.)

Circa (c. or ca.)

About

Usually with reference to a point in time, time being a fluid quantity difficult to pin down. "I remember the coloured map of Britain *circa* 900... So far as that map was concerned, the Great North Road did not exist, *circa* 900." Frank Morley, *The Great North Road.*

> "The Celtic drive southwards down the Italian Peninsula was paralleled by another one *ca.* 350 B.C. into the Balkans and Greece."
>
> D. B. Gregor, *Celtic.*

Citius, Altius, Fortius

Faster, higher, stronger

This is the motto of the Olympic Games, presented in Latin presumably because it is a safe neutral language, even if few people can understand it. (A book on setting up a website suggests that using Latin text in a mock-up page helps you concentrate on the design: you can download Latin text from www.lipsum.com.)

(The comparative of adverbs in Latin is supplied by the neuter singular of the comparative of the adjective; e.g., "strong" is *fortis*, "stronger" is *fortior*, and "more strongly" is *fortius*, the neuter of *fortior*.)

Civis Romanus sum

—Cicero, *In Verrem*, V, lvii. 147

I am a Roman citizen

To be a Roman citizen was a qualification of no little value when the Empire was at its height. Cicero's case against Verres included the charge that under Verres' administration Roman citizenship had ceased to be a protection against injustice.

St. Paul was a Roman citizen:

> "And as they bound him with thongs, Paul said unto the centurion that stood by, Is it lawful for you to scourge a man that is a Roman, and uncondemned?
>
> "When the centurion heard that, he went and told the chief captain, saying, Take heed what thou doest: for this man is a Roman."—(*... hic enim homo civis Romanus est.*)
>
> Acts xxii. 25, 26.

Cogito, ergo sum

—Rene Descartes, *Le Discours de la Méthode*

I think, therefore I am

In French this was "Je pense, donc je suis". Brigitte Bardot used to sing a song: "Je danse, donc je suis" (*Salto ergo sum?*).

Descartes almost immediately after writing the *Discours* dropped the *cogito* and changed the phrase to "I am, I exist" (*ego sum, ego existo*).

> "'I could have mentioned *cogito ergo sum*, only I detest that shallow but influential maxim, now I'm glad to say discarded.'"
>
> Iris Murdoch, *The Message to the Planet.*

Coitus interruptus

Interrupted intercourse

Specifically a method of birth control by withdrawing before ejaculation. Its effectiveness seems to compare well with that of the rhythm method..

The withdrawal need not be voluntary. "On the night of the murder she [*sc.* the dead woman, but before she was murdered] had a client in bed with her, and if ever there was a *locus classicus* [*q.v.*] for what they call *coitus interruptus* this was it, because someone interrupted the proceedings." Colin Dexter, *The Remorseful Day.*

Coitus plenus et optabilis

Perfect and desirable coitus

Perhaps one of the most sought-after gifts in the average man or woman's Christmas stocking.

> "She had taken deep pleasure in sex until it became a hobby with almost slogan proportions: *coitum plenum et optabilem.*"
>
> Richard Condon, *Arigato.*

It is not clear why Condon puts the phrase in the accusative case rather than in the nominative, unless it is in remote apposition to "deep pleasure".

Compendium

An abridgement, a short cut

Pears Cyclopædia includes a General Compendium, "A collection of useful tables and data on a variety of unrelated subjects...."

Compos mentis

Of sound mind

Literally, "in complete possession of (one's) reason", or in full possession of one's mental faculties. The phrase was used by Cicero.

> "Despite her choosing to appear habitually in public dressed as Brünnhilde, the doctors decided that on the whole Aunt Ariadne was fully *compos mentis*, and medically fit to ride a motorcycle."
>
> P. J. Dorricot, *Tales out of the Nursery*.

Compos Mentis is the name of an Australian Funk band, and also of a Melodic Death/Rock Metal band ("Symphonic Rock from Hell") in Denmark.

Cf. "**non compos mentis**" *infra*. Both are legal terms.

Confederatio Helvetica (CH)

The Helvetican Confederation, (Switzerland)

"CH" is the International Vehicle Registration allocated to Switzerland and can be seen on the rear of Swiss cars and on their number-plates. The abbreviation for Swiss Francs is "CHF" and the Internet domain for Switzerland is ".ch".

Helvetia is the Latin name for Switzerland, home of the *Helvitii*, a powerful Celtic people. Since in all the four languages used in the country the name for Switzerland begins with S, it is not *prima facie* clear why S could not be used instead of CH, until one realises that Sweden got there first, just beating Switzerland to it in alphabetical order. SW would not have done instead (Schweiz, Suisse, Svizzera, etc.,) so CH is a good compromise, and Latin is a nice neutral language.

Confer (*cf.*)

Compare

"Confer" is the imperative of "conferre". In the past the English word "confer" meant "compare", in the sense of bringing two things together. The Latin "comparare" was also used to mean "to compare" in the sense of pairing things off. It all seems rather confusing.

Confiteor

I confess

The Latin version of the Public Confession in the Mass begins: *Confiteor Deo omnipotenti…*, or *anglice*, "I confess to Almighty God…"

A slight variant—*Confitebor tibi, Domine*—"I will confess to thee, O Lord", is the motto of the Milsom family.

Consensus
Agreement, unanimity

This has nothing to do with "census" and everything to do with "consent", so there can really be no excuse for misspelling it.

Consilio et animis
By wisdom and courage

This is the motto of the Ramsay-Steel-Maitland family and of Sheffield Wednesday Football Club.

Consummatum est
It is finished

The last words of Christ on the cross (John xix. 30). In Greek they are the single word τετέλεσται, "*tetélestai*". It is possible that Christ spoke the words in Aramaic, but it seems difficult to find out what they would have been in this language. Marlowe puts the same words into the mouth of Dr Faustus as he signs the bill of sale of his soul to Lucifer (*q.v.*).

Consummatum est is the title of a sculpture by Jacob Epstein in the National Gallery of Scotland.

Contra (con)
Against

Contra is generally used in compound words such as contradict, contraflow and contraindication. *Contra naturam* is "against nature".

So Hugh O'Shaughnessy, writing in *The Observer*, points out that Argentina is still one of the world's greatest food producers and that "to poke fun [at the Buenos Aires peach melba] would be *contra naturam*."

Vide also **nem. con.**, pros and cons, **versus**, *etc. infra*.

Coram populo
Before people, in public

Horace used this phrase in his *Ars Poetica* (line 185) when he suggested that certain dramatic business should be conducted off-stage rather than enacted on-stage. The two relevant lines run:

> *Ne pueros coram populo Medea trucidet,*
> *Aut humana palam coquat exta nefarius Atreus.*
> Let not Medea slaughter her boys in full view of the audience,
> Nor wicked Atreus openly cook human entrails.

45

(Atreus had killed his brother's sons and served them up to his brother as a tasty dish.)

Horace did not exclude clean slaughter from the public view: he would have accepted that the killing of Julius Caesar on stage would not overly offend the most squeamish of us, but he would have approved of Shakespeare's decision to have Macbeth beheaded in the wings.

Other things may, indeed should, be enacted in full view of as many people as possible. In 1953 the then Dean of Westminster, describing the ritual of the forthcoming coronation, told how by partaking of Holy Communion during the service, the Queen would present herself to be "a reasonable, holy and lively sacrifice to God". He stated: "She does this *coram populo*,…" as it were, in the face of the congregation.

Cornucopia
The horn of plenty, a source of unlimited wealth

Originally *cornu copiæ*, referring to the horn of the goat by which Zeus was suckled. Some say the goat's name was Amalthea, others (and it did happen a long time ago) that Amalthea was the name of the animal's owner. Be it as it may, it would seem that a grateful Zeus rather unkindly wrenched a horn from the goat and gave it to the goat's owner, promising that the horn would thenceforth be empowered "to scatter plenty o'er a smiling land."

> "Such a fertile imagination your father had, such a cornucopia of original ideas, and such a tragic loss he was to the construction industry when he tripped over that fork-lift truck."
>
> P. J. Dorricot, *Beyond the Nursery Slopes*.

Corpus
Body

Literally a body in the phrase *Habeas corpus* (*q.v.*), but also used metaphorically, as when *corpus* refers to a body of work on a particular subject by different authors. Roy Jenkins, reviewing in *The Observer* a biography of Sir John Simon, mentions "the large corpus of anti-Simon invective".

Corpus Christi
The body of Christ

This nowadays is the Eucharist, the bread of the Communion Service. It is also the name of a festival of the Church, kept on the Thursday after Trinity Sunday, in honour of the Eucharist. The festival was instituted by

Pope Urban IV in 1264, and was the usual time for the performance of the religious dramas of the trade guilds.

Corpus Christi College, Cambridge, is the only Oxbridge college to be founded by the citizens of the place.

Corpus delicti
The body of the crime

The *corpus delicti* does not have to be a corpse. It could be, e.g., a snatched handbag found on the person of the snatcher, or a burnt-out building after an arson attack. Whatever it is, living or dead, it must present clear evidence that a crime has been committed.

> "Rico asked me: What are you doing with St. Mawr? When I said we were taking him with us, he said: *Oh, the Corpus delicti!* Whether that means anything I don't know."
>
> D. H. Lawrence, *St. Mawr.*

(St. Mawr was the horse which had fallen on Rico, who thereby suffered two broken ribs and a crushed ankle.)

Corpus Delicti is the title of a Czech film of 1991 by Irena Pavlásková.

Corrigenda
Things to be corrected

Usually twinned with *addenda*, *q.v.* The singular is *corrigendum*. In English publications "addenda and corrigenda" are the remedy for "errors and omissions" (although in the reverse order).

Cras amet qui nunquam amavit,
Quique amavit cras amet
Tomorrow let him love who never loved before,
and whoever loved before, let him love tomorrow

These lines are the start and the refrain of *Pervigilium Veneris*—"The Eve of St. Venus", an anonymous love poem written *circa* A.D. 350. Evelyn Waugh used *Pervigilium Veneris* for the title of a chapter in *Decline and Fall*, which partly concerns the lamentably fleeting courtship of Paul Pennyfeather and Margot Beste-Chetwynde. The same lines conclude John Fowles' novel, *The Magus.*

Credite posteri
—Horace, *Odes*, II, xix
Believe me, you who are to come
A general call to posterity to believe the speaker or writer, however unlikely his statements may appear to be.

> "Ah, I remember a different state of things! *Credite posteri.* To see those nymphs—gracious powers, how beautiful they were!"
> W. M. Thackeray, *Roundabout Papers.*

Credo
—The Mass
I believe
Credo gives us our English word "Creed", and is the first word of the Creed of the Latin Mass: *Credo in unum Deum…*—"I believe in one God…"
The word is also used for the totality of a person's beliefs, secular as well as religious. "Cressida bent down and tenderly picked up the worm from the road and deposited it safely on the grass verge, for kindness to animals was a central part of her Credo."
A Credo need not belong to a single person. The firm of Johnson & Johnson publish a comprehensive "Our Credo" in which they declare their responsibility to all who use their services, to their employees, and to the local and world community, as well as to the stockholders.
Credo is the motto of the Lords Sinclair of Cleeve.

Credo quia absurdum est
I believe it because it is so unlikely
The origin of this phrase might lie in statements of Tertullian about Christian belief being independent of probabilities. In Aldous Huxley's *Point Counter Point*, Walter Bidlake adopted and adapted the phrase, avowing that he loved because it was unseemly and unworthy. "Knowing all, he could listen to anything that might be said about [Lucy Tantamount]. And the more atrocious the words, the more desperately he loved her. *Credo quia absurdum. Amo quia turpe, quia indignum….*"
[Huxley's lines translate as: "I believe because (it is) so unlikely. I love because (it is) shameful, because (it is) unworthy".]

Cucullus non facit monachum
The cowl (hood) does not make the monk
Do not judge by outward appearances. (The hoodie is no modern phenomenon.)

ESCALUS: "Signor Lucio, did not you say you knew that Friar Lodowick to be a dishonest person?"
LUCIO: "'Cucullus non facit monachum:' honest in nothing but in his clothes;…"

Shakespeare, *Measure for Measure*, V, i.

CLOWN: "Lady, cucullus non facit monachum, that's as much to say as I wear not motley in my brain…"

Shakespeare, *Twelfth Night*, I, v.

Cui bono (fuerit)?

—Cicero, *Pro Milone*, xii. 32
To whom is the profit? or Who stands to gain?

Cicero quotes Lucius Cassius Longinus, a judge, who asked this question in the search for a motive behind whatever illegal action he was looking into. The phrase does *not* mean "What good does it do?" This latter meaning might be supplied by a phrase like *Quid prodest?* which is the motto of the family of Webb of Knocktoran.

"Now it was you, Sherlock, who rightly asked the key question: *cui bono*? And you concluded that the real beneficiary was Wyndham."
Colin Dexter, "A Case of Mis-identity".

Cum

With

Used as a linking word, as in "The Parish of Winkworth-cum-Hobberton Magna". A picture caption in *The Observer* read: "John Taverner: Old Testament prophet cum Seventies hippy", while in the same paper Andrew Motion, reviewing a book by Konrad Lorenz, referred to it as "an autobiography-cum-diary-cum-analysis".
*Vide "***pax vobiscum***" infra.*

Cum grano (salis)

With a pinch (of salt)

The motto of the sceptic down the ages. Pliny in his *Naturalis Historia* told of how a grain of salt was a key ingredient in an antidote to a poison; now it is in itself an antidote to undue credulity.

"The tradition of an early British chief or king being buried in a gold coffin seems to have been curiously persistent… Personally, I take it *cum grano*."
Ernest Bramah, "The Secret of Headland Height".

"A good deal of medical argument has revolved round this subject. 'Hooper's deal' is actually said to have a pulverising effect on the Balakieff layer of the cortex. Myself, I take this *cum grano salis*."

Stephen Potter, *Gamesmanship*.

Cum Grano Salis is the name of a website which is "a place to moan and grump".

Cum omnibus suis pertinenciis
With all its appurtenances

A legal phrase which occurs frequently in old documents (*vide* **"inquisitio post mortem"** *infra*) detailing the bequest of property to someone or listing the property owned by a dead person.

Cum privilegio
With licence

A phrase to be found on the title page of certain books, especially bibles and prayer books, published by leave of the appropriate authorities.

Cupido dominandi cunctis affectibus flagrantior
The desire to dominate is stronger than all other human feelings

Tacitus mentions this urge in his *Annals*, xv. 53.

A variant appeared in a book review of Nigel Hamilton's "JFK" in *The Observer*. F. P. Smoler wrote: "Joseph Kennedy was a… coward whose regular passions were restricted to greed and *libido dominandi*…" *Libido* is Latin merely for "desire", although now the word has acquired firm sexual connotations.

> "Every man is born *cupidus*—desirous of getting; but not *avarus*—desirous of keeping."
>
> James Boswell, *The Life of Samuel Johnson, LL.D.*

Currente calamo
With running pen, fluently

Anything written *currente calamo* is not subject to erasure or revision or second thoughts, but as the words stream from the mind, so they flow from the pen.

> "Accordingly his letter to Sir Nicholas was written *currente calamo*, with very little trouble."
>
> Anthony Trollope, *Barchester Towers*.

Curriculum Vitae (CV)

Course of life, life history

A *curriculum* was originally a chariot, and by extension came to mean the course along which chariot races were run. A school curriculum outlines the course of study which its students follow, while a *curriculum vitæ* maps the course of one's life to date. (Dame) Muriel Spark gave the title *Curriculum Vitae* to her autobiography.

cwt

Hundredweight

Here "c" denotes *centum*, the Latin for "hundred". "C" was the Roman numeral for 100. *Cf. "**dwt**" infra.*

As its name suggests, the original hundredweight was 100 lb, but to counteract the habit of tradesmen of giving short weight, the authorities were led to decree in the sixteenth century that the measure should be increased by a factor of one-eighth to 112½ lb, which was then rounded down to 112 lb.

D

Da mihi animam, caetera tolle

Give me the soul and take away the rest

[Christ *loquitur*] "… all legs are equal. Moreover, they are not My business. I am interested in souls. *Da mihi animam, caetera tolle*. I leave the bodies on earth."

Giovanni Guareschi, *The Little World of Don Camillo*.

Da mihi castitatem et continentiam, sed noli modo

—St. Augustine

Grant me chastity and continence—but not just yet

This is not our own St. Augustine of Canterbury "with his feet of snow", but a more flamboyant St. Augustine of Hippo in what is now Algeria, who lived two centuries earlier (354-430) and who wrote *inter alia "De Civitate Dei"*, *q.v. infra*. The prayer, quoted in his *Confessions*, was uttered while he was engaged to be married but was still enjoying the comforts afforded first by a concubine and then by a new love. Shortly after this however he was converted to Christianity and became a (celibate) priest.

Data

Given facts

Facts which are accepted, which are acknowledged to be true. The word "data" is plural; its singular is *datum*.

"If we indulge… we must take the *data* which we have, and not those which we desire or imagine." W.Bagehot, *Literary Studies*, "Letter VII". Note that in Bagehot's day (1852) "data" was still recognized as being Latin and hence was italicized as a foreign term.

"But we are not really starting with the *datum* 'Both are poetical' and thence arguing 'Therefore both are false'."

C. S. Lewis, "Is Theology Poetry?"

A "datum-line" is a "given" horizontal line from which heights and depths are measured. Until 1921 the datum line for Great Britain was the mean sea level at Liverpool. Since 1921 it has been the mean sea level at Newlyn, Cornwall.

Deo Data—"Things (plural) given to God" was the motto of the Lords Arundell of Wardour.

De Civitate Dei
Concerning the city of God

The title of a book written *circa* A.D. 427 by St. Augustine of Hippo.

> "… for what saith the blessed Saint Augustin (*sic*), in his treatise *De Civitate Dei* —' 'What saith the devil,' interrupted Front-de-Bœuf;…'"

Sir Walter Scott, Ivanhoe.

*Vide "**da mihi castitatem…**" supra.*

De facto
In fact

It is not uncommon in troubled times for a country to have two governments, the *de jure* (*q.v.*) government, properly elected by law but forced to function in exile, and the *de facto* government, not elected but firmly *in situ* in the country and running its day-to-day affairs and collecting taxes.

"Like her he took a deprecating attitude: the job was a job like any other, and *de facto* boring:…" Philip Larkin, "A New World Symphony". (Larkin's use of *de facto* here could be questioned, since it seems unlikely a job could be *de jure* boring. Perhaps *ipso facto* might have been a better choice.)

In Australia a *de facto* wife is equivalent to what we know in Britain as a Common Law wife.

Defunctos ploro, vivos voco, fulmina frango
The dead I mourn, the living I call, the thunderbolts I break

This is a common inscription on many a church bell, quoted by Iris Murdoch in *The Bell*, as being on this occasion "contributed by that zealous antiquarian, the Bishop:… Upon the shoulder of the bell there was also written,… *Gabriel vocor.*" ["I am called Gabriel."]

(The bell tower of a church was/is usually furnished with a lightning conductor.)

De gustibus non est disputandum

There is no arguing about taste

Jeremy Taylor in "Reflections upon Ridicule" quotes this as an old Latin proverb, and Henderson prints it on page 77 of his "Latin Proverbs". Robert Browning wrote a poem under the title "De gustibus..."

> "Mrs Knox, of Aussolas, was told that I had taken Mrs McRory for a run in the car at one o'clock in the morning, and on hearing it said, '*De gustibus non est disputandum*'.
>
> "Someone, unknown, repeated this to Mrs McRory, and told her that it meant 'You cannot touch pitch without being disgusted'."
>
> E. Œ. Somerville and Martin Ross,
Further Adventures of an Irish R.M.

An extended version of the proverb exists, designed perhaps to confound the critics of contemporary art: *De gustibus et coloribus non est disputandum*—"There is no arguing about taste or colours."

In Chekhov's *The Seagull*, Shamraev says: "But of course, it's a matter of taste. *De gustibus aut bene aut nihil.*" Whether deliberately or not, Shamraev appears to be conflating the present phrase *De gustibus...* with another of uncertain authorship, *De mortuis aut bene aut nihil,*—"Of the dead (speak) either well or not at all". *Cf. "de mortuis nil nisi bonum" infra.*

Dei gratia (D.G.)

By the grace of God

It has to be conceded that British monarchs were on the whole creditably modest about their claims to greatness and majesty, and the letters D.G. impressed on the coinage advertised their acute and grateful awareness that, but for the grace of God, they would be no more than common citizens or worse. *Per contra*, when pressed they could also claim that by the grace of God they were invested as monarchs with a Divine Right.

De jure

By law, legal

> "Unknown to their doting parents, David and Sybilla had for many months been joyfully 'anticipating marriage', and the glitzy ceremony in St. Sidwell's Church, with the bride practically

translucent in virgin white, merely made *de jure* bed-wise what had for long been *de facto.*"

P. J. Dorricot, *Beyond the Nursery Slopes.*

(*Vide* "***de facto***" *supra.*)

Delenda est Carthago
Carthage must be destroyed

Cato the Elder was very much anti-Carthage and took every opportunity to express his antipathy towards her, slipping into each of his speeches the words *Ceterum censeo delenda est Carthago* (or according to another view, *Carthaginem esse delendum*)—"In my opinion Carthage, etc."

> "He was especially great in his hatred of *l'infâme Angleterre. Delenda est Carthago* was tattooed beneath his shirt-sleeve."
>
> W. M. Thackeray, *The Newcombes.*

Delirium tremens (the DTs)
The trembling fever

The DTs are a symptom of one of the final stages in the drunkard's steady progress towards an early grave.

Delirium Tremens is the name of a Belgian Strong Pale Ale, promoted by the *Confrèrie van de Roze Olifant*—"The Brotherhood of the Pink Elephant".

> "We could never be quite sure if Father's agitation was due to righteous indignation at the referee's decision, or if it was just another attack of the d.t.'s."
>
> P. J. Dorricot, *Tales out of the Nursery.*

De minimis non curat lex
—Francis Bacon, *Letter* cclxxxii
The law does not concern itself with trivialities (or trifles)
Literally "with the smallest things".

> Whenever a fellow called Rex
> Flashed his very small organ of sex,
> He always got off,
> For the judges would scoff,
> "De minimis non curat lex."—Anon.

It is reported that such a defence was not accepted when offered by a serial flasher convicted by Teesside Crown Court in 2007.

De mortuis nil nisi bonum (dicendum est)

Let naught but good be said of the dead

Diogenes Laertius (*c.* A.D. 200-250) mentions this phrase in *The Lives and Opinions of Eminent Philosophers*, attributing it to Chilon, one of the "Seven Sages" of Greece.

> "… there was praise without reservation for the victim, as if *De mortuis* was engraved on every county heart."
>
> John Fowles, "The Enigma".

Dr Johnson was all in favour of being generous to the dead in writing their epitaphs. "In lapidary inscriptions a man is not upon oath." On the other hand Mark Anthony in *Julius Caesar* takes a jaundiced view of humanity's humanity to the dead.

> "The evil that men do lives after them,
> The good is oft interred with their bones."

The phrase does *not* mean, as suggested in the schoolboy howler, "When you're dead, there ain't nothing left but bones".

Denarius (d)

Penny

In 1086 the only coin in circulation in Britain was the silver penny. "Penny", like "pfennig", is a Germanic word: the Latin name "denarius", shortened to "d" as in "3d" for "threepence", stuck until 1971. The denarius mutated into "dinar", in use today in Algeria, Bahrain, Iraq, Jordan, Kuwait, Libya, Macedonia, Serbia and Tunisia.

In Marlowe's "Jew of Malta", Act 2, appears the line *Hermoso placer de los dineros*—"The lovely thrill of coins!" The language is Spanish and "dineros" is still the Spanish for "money". The equivalent Portuguese word is "dinheiro": so "denarius" has given both the Spaniards and the Portuguese the name for their whole monetary system.

The French also adopted the *denarius* under the eventual name "denier" for a small coin of little value, twelve of which were worth one sou (*q.v. s.v. solidus*), just as twelve British pennies were worth one shilling. Shakespeare knew of the coin; Richard II says (Act I, scene iii): "My dukedom to a beggarly denier". The denier, like the penny (*vide "**dwt**" infra*), was also used as a measure of weight, and the term is still used to measure the weight of fine thread, such as silk and nylon. For instance, 15-denier nylon stockings are made from thread which weighs 15 grams per 9000 metres.

Deo gratias

—The Mass

Thanks be to God

The closing words of the Mass, used also at various points during the service, such as after the Epistle and after the last Gospel.

In 1605 William Byrd wrote a Sacred Motet with this title.

> "Brother Nick has at last decided to mend the lorry. *Deo gratias*."
>
> Iris Murdoch, *The Bell*.

> "One can only conclude that we are coursing through space all alone. Deo gratias."
>
> Letter to *The Observer*.

Deo optimo maximo (D.O.M.)

To God, most good, most great.

At last the real meaning of the letters D.O.M. which appear on bottles of Benedictine. *Deo optimo maximo* is the motto of the Benedictine Order.

Goodness and greatness have long been attributes of the godhead. The national god of the Roman state was Jup(p)iter Optimus Maximus, and it is clear that Christians at some point adapted and adopted this title for their own God. It seems however that although *optimo* and *maximo* are both superlatives, when applied by the Romans to persons (or to gods) they meant no more than simply "good" and "great".

Deo volente (D.V.)

God willing

My parents took great care to acknowledge the fact that God would determine what happened in the future, and were free at all times with their D.V.'s. An alternative phrase they used was "all being well", again guarding against the malevolence of fate. I like "all being well", and still use it in the face of constant pressure nowadays to say "hopefully" instead. *Cf.* "***dis aliter visum***" and "***homo proponit, sed Deus disponit***" *infra.*

> "'And,' said Caroline, 'you will promise to come to my table, and to sit near me, Mr Hall?' 'I shall not fail, Deo volente,' said he."
>
> Charlotte Brontë, *Shirley*.

The phrase "*Deo volente*" is used by Virgil in *Aeneid*, i, 307. It is the motto of the Palliser family.

De profundis
Out of the depths
The first two words in Latin of Psalm 130: *"De profundis clamavi ad te, Domine: Domine, exaudi vocem meam"*—"Out of the depths have I cried unto thee, O Lord: Lord, hear my voice."

In 1905, while imprisoned in Reading Gaol, Oscar Wilde wrote an *Apologia (q.v. supra) pro sua vita* called *De Profundis*. Both Robert Browning and Elizabeth Barrett Browning wrote poems with this same title, as did C. S. Lewis and Garcia Lorca. A collection of essays by Thomas de Quincey bore the title *Suspiria de Profundis*, "Sighs from the Depths".

> "'Dearest Elinor,' he wrote. '*De profundis clamavi*, from the depths of this repulsive hotel bedroom,… I call to you.'"
> Aldous Huxley, *Point Counter Point*.

De Profundis is the name of a UK based genre-defying metal group.
De Profundis is the motto of the Urban District Council of Bedlington in Northumberland, in a former coal-mining area; and also of the Norwegian Sector of the North Sea Divers Alliance.

De Rerum Natura
On the nature of things
Circa 59 B.C., Lucretius wrote a long poem with this title, stretching to six "books". The poem can be seen as a sort of *apologia* for Epicureanism, a philosophy which aimed at giving man happiness *inter alia* by making him self-sufficient and by persuading him to live a simple life. *Vide "medio de fonte…" infra.*

Desiderata
Things to be desired
> "This something the corporal… supplied by an entire new system of his own… as one of the great *desiderata* of my Uncle Toby's apparatus."
> Laurence Sterne, *Tristram Shandy*.

Desiderata is the title of a poem, "Go placidly…", written by Max Ehrmann and recorded by, *inter alios*, Richard Burton and Dave Allen.

The singular is *desideratum*. Woody Allen in his story "Retribution" describes "Connie Chasen" who through, *inter alia*, "the lewd, humid eroticism her every curve suggested… was the unrivalled desideratum of each young man at the party."

Desideria
Longing, grief

Queen Desideria of Sweden, who also went under the name of Desirée, had once been engaged to Napoleon Bonaparte, but eventually married Maréchal Jean Bernadotte, who became King Charles XIV of Sweden in 1818. "Desideria" is also the name of a (*soi-disante* "multi-faceted") professional belly-dancer operating out of Danbury, Connecticut.

In *The Oxford Book of English Verse*, the heading *Desideria* is given to Wordsworth's "Surprised by joy..." The word appears to be the plural of *desiderium*, so perhaps "longings" might be a better translation.

*Vide "**quis desiderio...**" infra.*

Detur digniori
Let it be given to the more deserving

The slogan of the meritocrats.

> "We could get but one bridle here, which, according to the maxim *detur digniori*, was appropriated to Dr Johnson's sheltie."
> James Boswell, *The Journal of a Tour to the Hebrides.*

> "As long as promotion cometh from any human source,... will not such a claim as this (*viz* fourteen hungry children to feed) hold good, in spite of all our examination tests, *detur digniori*'s, and optimist tendencies?"
> Anthony Trollope, *Barchester Towers.*

There was a time when ladies were considered to be deserving: as the schoolboy howler has it: "A gentleman is one who gives up his seat to a lady in a public convenience."

Deus ex machina
A god from the machine

In Greek drama this was a god lowered by a pulley from above the stage to take an unexpected hand in the action, and was a device much favoured especially by Euripides. In a less mechanical form it is still a very handy device for resolving an *impasse* in a drama, where a quite independent agent acts arbitrarily in an unpredictable and often improbable way.

In John Fowles'"The Enigma", Isobel Dodgson talks of the need for a story to have a credible ending. "I propose to dismiss the *deus ex machina* possibility. It's not good art. An awful cheat, really."

"There are those like Dr Larivière who make a single, splendid cameo appearance: three pages of existence as a *deus ex machina…*"

Julian Barnes, *Something to Declare.*

Section 10 of Fougasse and McCullough's book *You Have Been Warned* has the title "*Dea in Machina*" ("a goddess in the machine"). It records the emotions of a driver who offers a lift in his car to a strikingly beautiful girl ("an exquisite vision of loveliness") and against all hope has the offer accepted.

Dies irae, dies illa,...
—Zephaniah, i. 15
That day is a day of wrath,…

In his prophecy, Zephaniah warned that the great day of the Lord was near, a day of wrath, of "trouble and distress", of "wasteness and desolation", and sundry other forms of discomfort.

In the thirteenth century Thomas of Celano put this idea into verse of some seventeen or more stanzas:

> "*Dies iræ, dies illa,*
> *Solvet sæclum in favilla,*
> *Teste David cum Sybilla…*"
> "In the day of wrath, in that day,
> man shall transmute into ashes,
> by the word of David with the Sybil."

For many years this poem was part of the Requiem Mass for the Dead, but in 1970 it was removed from the Mass, for fear no doubt that its message of doom and despair might frighten the faithful. It may now however be used *ad libitum* in the Liturgy of the Hours.

In *The Bell*, Iris Murdoch quotes the tenth verse of the poem, "the egotistical and helpless cry of the Dies Irae."

> *Quaerens me, sedisti lassus;*
> *Redemisti, Crucem passus;*
> *Tantus labor non sit cassus.*
> "Seeking me you sat exhausted;
> you redeemed (me) by suffering the Cross;
> let so much toil not be in vain."

W. J. Irons translated the poem as a hymn: "Day of wrath! O day of mourning, / See fulfilled the prophets' warning! / Heaven and earth to ashes turning!..." (*Hymns Ancient and Modern* 466).

Dis aliter visum
—Virgil, *Aeneid*, ii. 428
The gods decided otherwise, the gods had other ideas
A more succinct way of saying *Homo proponit, sed Deus disponit, q.v. infra.* Some versions of the original have the full phrase *Dis aliter visum est*, which literally means "To the gods it appeared better otherwise".

> "'It's ext-traordinary', said Brian,... 'that you shouldn't ever have met her.' '*Dis aliter visum*,' Anthony answered...."
> > Aldous Huxley, *Eyeless in Gaza*.

> "But none of these methods [of disposing of the body] had found favour. *Dis aliter visum*."
> > Colin Dexter, *The Daughters of Cain*.

Robert Browning wrote a long poem called *Dis aliter visum*, while Bartłomej Jurkowski gave the same title to a digital painting.

Disjecta membra
Dismembered limbs
Ovid in his *Metamorphoses* wrote of *disjecta membra*—"scattered limbs", and Horace wrote metaphorically of *disjecti membra poetæ*, "the limbs of the dismembered poet", *viz* the remaining fragments of his work, any one or two of which selected at random would be enough to allow you to assess the poet's degree of greatness. *Disjecta membra* are the scattered fragments themselves.

Byron wrote to his publisher, John Murray, about *Don Juan*: "Cut me up root and branch—quarter me in the *Quarterly*—send round my *disjecti membra poetæ* like those of the Levite's concubine –...—but don't ask me to alter it."

The phrase can be used in a literal sense.

> "I can hardly see what use the *disjecta membra* of my late acquaintance [*viz* the bones of a goose] are going to be to me."
> > Sir Arthur Conan Doyle, *The Adventures of Sherlock Holmes*,
> > "The Adventure of the Blue Carbuncle".

Domine, dirige nos
Lord, lead us

The word *dirige* is the first word of an antiphon sung in the Office for the Dead, taken from Psalm v. 8: "Lead me, Lord, in thy righteousness". It gave the English language the word "dirge" for a sad musical tribute to the dead.

Domine Dirige Nos is the motto of the City of London, and also of numerous regiments connected with the City, as well as of the City of London Freemen's School in Surrey.

Dirige me, Domine—"Lead me, O Lord"—is the motto of the Le Mee-Power family.

Dominus illuminatio mea
—Psalm 27
The Lord is my light

These words are the motto of the University of Oxford and appear on the colophon of that city's University Press.

In *The Oxford Book of English Verse*, the title *Dominus illuminatio mea* is given to R. D. Blackmore's poem, "In the hour of death, after this life's whim."

Dominus vobiscum
—The Mass
The Lord be with you

This, from the Ordinary of the Mass of the Roman Catholic Church, has the response: *Et cum spiritu tuo*—"And with thy spirit". The English version of the two phrases appears in the Book of Common Prayer *passim*.

Dominus Vobiscum is the name of a beer brewed in Quebec.

Cf. **"pax vobiscum"** *infra.*

Donat habere viro decus et tutamen in armis
—Virgil, *Aeneid*, v. 262
(Aeneas) gave to this man a beauteous safeguard in battle

Decus et tutamen is inscribed around the edge of the English pound coin, as it once was on the larger (gold and silver) coins of Charles II. For these latter coins the inscription was indeed a safeguard, being a protection against clipping, while few in their right minds would wish to clip the present coinage. Around the edge of the Scottish pound coin, which bears the imprint of the thistle, is inscribed *Nemo me impune lacessit* (*q.v.*); while the Welsh coin announces around its edge "Pleidiol wyf i'm gwlad"—"I'm loyal to my country", a line of the chorus of "Mae hen wlad fy nhadau"—"Land of my Fathers".

The "beauteous safeguard" referred to was a coat of mail "in triple woven gold", seized by Aeneas from Demoleus in single-handed combat and given now to Mnestheus as a reward not for heroic deeds in battle but merely for gaining second place in a boat race.

Decus et Tutamen is the motto of the Borough of Gravesend in Kent, and of the West Essex Yeomanry, while *Decus et Tutamen in Armis* is the motto of the Feltmakers Company.

Dramatis personae
The characters of a play
The traditional heading of a cast list. "Persona" was the name given to the mask worn by a Roman actor.

The drama need not be played out on a stage. Writing in *The Guardian*, Robert Peston says: "… these mind-bogglingly wealthy non-doms… are a cartoon come to real, gilded life. They are among the *dramatis personae* of my new book:…"

> "There wants only the *Dramatis Personæ* for the performance: the play is wrote (*sic*), the Scenes are painted, and the Curtain ready to be drawn up. The whole Piece waits for thee, my Eliza."
> Laurence Sterne, *Journal to Eliza*.

Dulcedo
Desire, fondness
> "I assured [Johnson] that… I felt all the *dulcedo* of the *natale solum*."
> James Boswell, *The Life of Samuel Johnson, LL.D.*

As does the *dulce* of *Dulce Domum*, *dulcedo* expresses the love of and attachment to the place of one's birth and upbringing, one's *natale solum*, "native soil". (*Libertas et natale solum*—"Liberty and my native soil"—is the motto of several families including that of Hawkins-Whitshed.)

Dulce domum
Sweet (is the sound of) home
The title of a school song which originated at Winchester College and was set to music by John Reading who also composed the music for the hymn *Adeste Fideles*—"O come all ye faithful" (*q.v.*). The phrase also has nostalgic connotations of homecoming since *domum ire* means "to go home".

For several years "Dulcie Domum" (*alias* Sue Limb) wrote a "Bad Housekeeping" column in the *Weekend Guardian*.

Dulce est desipere in loco
—Horace, *Odes*, IV, xii. 28

It is pleasant to let one's hair down on proper occasions

"You haughty Southerners little know how a jolly Scotch gentleman can *desipere in loco*, and how he chirrups over his honest cups."

W. M. Thackeray, *The Newcomes*.

Dulce et decorum est pro patria mori
—Horace, *Odes*, III, ii. 13

It is sweet and proper to die for one's country

Tempora mutantur, and Wilfred Owen, writing nearly two thousand years after Horace, took an understandably different view of death in battle. He describes in his poem "Dulce et Decorum" the effects of mustard gas in the trenches in France in the Great War.

> "If you could hear, at every jolt, the blood
> Come gargling from the froth-corrupted lungs…
> My friend, you would not tell with such high zest
> To children ardent for some desperate glory
> The old Lie: Dulce et decorum est
> Pro patria mori."

Pro Patria Mori is the motto of the Wolfe family.

Dum spiro spero

While I have breath I have hope

For centuries this defiant motto has dropped from the lips of members of the MacLennan clan, and has also been adopted in the course of time by several dozen prominent families, including those of Bannatyne of Newhall, Coryton of Pentillic Castle, and Jackson of Putney Hill. It is also the motto of St. Andrews in Scotland. In 1776 the line *"Dum spiro, spero"* was incorporated into the Great Seal of the state of South Carolina, and it is also the proud boast of the Kingdom of Sarawak.

The variant "Dum Spiro Agnew" (Spiro who?) is not attested, but it is inconceivable that no one at least muttered the phrase *sotto voce* during the reign of Mr Agnew as U. S. Vice-President from 1969 to 1973.

Dux ludorum

Leader of games

My ambition when at school was to win the senior athletics championship. I was no good at all at moving ball games, and little better at still ball games, but I was a fair runner and jumper and in my last year at school I became, against mediocre opposition, "Dux Ludorum", and still possess a small silver-plated cup commemorating the achievement.

*Cf. "**victor ludorum**" infra.*

dwt

Pennyweight

Here "penny" is denoted by "d", standing for *denarius* (*q.v.*). It was the Troy weight of a silver penny, twenty-four grains. (*Cf. "**cwt**" supra.*)

> "My grandfather's clock... was taller by half than the old man himself but it weighed not a pennyweight more."
>
> C. Russel Christian.

It is customary to use a similar abbreviation to measure the weight of a ship, so that we should not be surprised to read that a particular vessel is 324,000 dwt. Here the abbreviation stands for "dead weight tonnage".

E

Ecce homo
Behold the man

Under this title Guido Reni, among other artists, painted Christ crowned with thorns. "Then came Jesus forth, wearing the crown of thorns, and the purple robe. And Pilate saith unto them, Behold the man!" John xix. 5.

Ecce signum
Behold the proof

> SIR JOHN FALSTAFF: "I am a rogue if I were not at half sword with a dozen of them two hours together…. I am eight times thrust through the doublet, four through the hose, my buckler cut through and through, my sword hack'd like a hand-saw, *ecce signum*…."
>
> Shakespeare, *Henry IV Part 1,* II, iv.

Eheu fugaces, Postume, Postume, labuntur anni…
—Horace, *Odes*, II, xiv. 1,2
Alas, O Posthumus, the fleeting years are slipping by

Or, as R.H.Barham expressed it:

> "What Horace says is –
> Eheu fugaces
> Anni labuntur, Postume, Postume!
> Years glide away and are lost to me, lost to me!"

The second verse of Barham's poem is slightly more contrived but carries on the same line of thought:

> "Now, when the folks in the dance sport their merry toes,
> Taglionis and Ellslers, Duvernays and Ceritos,
> Sighing I murmur, 'O mihi praeteritos!'"

The last line borrows from Virgil's *Aeneid*, viii. 560: *O mihi praeteritos referat si Iuppiter annos*—"O, would Jupiter restore to me [*sc*. Evander, king of Arcady] the years that are fled!"

A little later, Hilaire Belloc wrote in his "Dedicatory Ode":

> "*Eheu Fugaces! Postume!*
>   (An old quotation, out of mode);
> My coat of dreams is stolen away,
>   My youth is passing down the road."

Part of the verb from which *labuntur* comes is *lapsus*, so that the English "so many years have elapsed" is equivalent to "so many years have slipped by".

Cf. "*pereunt et imputantur*" *infra*.

Ei mihi
Ay me!, Alas!

A possibly useful alternative to "Oy veh", whatever that may mean.

Elizabeth Regina (ER)
Queen Elizabeth

Queen Elizabeth II's monogram appears on post boxes and elsewhere as EⅡR. The combination "ER" is a godsend to crossword compilers who at the drop of a hat will clue the presence of "er" in a solution by a reference to royalty.

Elixir vitae
The elixir of life

The alchemists strove to find the elixir of life, a substance which would confer immortality, or something close to it, on whoever partook of it. (One essential ingredient of any effective elixir was reckoned to be alcohol in one form or another—*Vide* "*aqua vitæ*" *supra*.) The word *elixir* is not originally Latin but derives from the Arabic for a curative powder to sprinkle on wounds.

A Mr Ralph Schauss of Wyoming gave the name "Elixir Vitae" to a thick purple-coloured herbal mixture which he claimed was a cure for cancer. His claim does not yet appear to have been substantiated.

In 2003 the rock band *Low Flying Owls* made its national album debut on Stinky Records with *Elixir Vitae*.

Emeritus

Having earned one's retirement

Especially, nowadays almost exclusively, a retired professor, who, through the title of "Emeritus Professor", is allowed to retain a little of the glory attaching to his previous post.

It is said that Rupert Murdoch dubbed a sacked editor as "emeritus"— "E means you're out, meritus means you deserve it."

E pluribus unum

From many [comes] the one

The motto of the United States of America from 1782 until 1956 (replaced then by "In God We Trust"), this phrase was adapted from one used by Virgil in his *Moretum*, l04: *E pluribus unus*. Whether the motto means that many individual states combined to form the Union, or that millions of people from all over the world came together as "America" might be open to discussion.

> "Give me your tired, your poor,
> Your huddled masses, yearning to breathe free;
> The wretched refuse of your teeming shore.
> Send these, the homeless, tempest-tost, to me.
> I lift my lamp beside the golden door."

These beckoning lines from a sonnet (1883) by Emma Lazarus appear on a plaque in the reception hall at John F. Kennedy Airport. The whole sonnet of 14 lines appears on a plaque on the pedestal of the Statue of Liberty.

"E pluribus unum" is at the time of writing the heading given to a weekly puzzle in *The Guardian* in which the letters of two or more words have to be reassembled to make a single word. *Unum e pluribus* was the motto of Wokingham Rural District Council.

Variants on this motto are popular. *E duobus unum*—"One from two"— is the motto of the Welding Institute, and also of the Corinthian Casuals Football Club, formed in 1939 by the amalgamation of the Corinthians and the Casuals football clubs. *E tribus unum*—"One from three"—is the motto of the Norfolk Joint Police Authority.

Ergo

Therefore

"War happens when people stop talking, ergo, pick up a BT phone."

> A British Telecom advertisement.

FIRST CLOWN: Tell me, neighbour Clodpony, why is a codpiece like a candlemaker?

COARSE ACTOR: Nay, I know not.

FIRST CLOWN: Mass, thou makest light of the jest; and in making light thou art a very candlemaker indeed. Ergo, thou art a codpiece.

COARSE ACTOR: Marry.

> Michael Green, *The Art of Coarse Acting.*

Shakespeare's own First Clown, digging Ophelia's grave, manages to contort *ergo* almost out of recognition. "… if I drown myself wittingly, it argues an act; and an act hath three branches; it is, to act, to do, and to perform: argal, she drowned herself wittingly." *Hamlet*, V, i.

There is a theory that all the world's great men have been marked by an absence of neck. Since greatness consists in the harmonious functioning of the faculties of the head and heart, "the shorter the neck, the more closely these organs approach one another; *argal…* It was convincing." Aldous Huxley, *Chrome Yellow.*

Errata

Errors

The singular is *erratum*.

Patrick Ness, writing in *The Guardian* of a copy he had bought of a first edition of Alasdair Gray's *Unlikely Stories, Mostly*, rejoices that "most bibliophilically delightful of all, it still contains Gray's famous fake *erratum* slip ('This slip has been inserted by mistake')."

*Cf. "**corrigenda**" supra.*

Esse quam videri

—Cicero, *De Amicitia*, §26

To be, rather than to seem to be

This is the motto of a large number of families, eager to acquire a solid existence rather than an illusory one, and the motto also, *inter alia*, of Bedford College, London, Truro School, the State of North Carolina, the British Standards Institute, and the General Dental Council.

Non Videri, sed Esse—"Not to seem, but to be"—is the motto of the Hare family.

Est modus in rebus
—Horace, *Satires*, I, i. 106
There is a measure (or mean or middle course) in everything
Est modus in rebus, translated as "There is measure in all things", is the motto of the Royal Institute of Chartered Surveyors.

Et alii (et al.)
And others
Not to be confused with *inter alia (q.v.)*, where *alia* is neuter and refers to things rather than to people. Usually written (and spoken) as *et al.*, it could stand not only for *et alii* (masculine) but also for *et aliæ* (feminine). The neuter would be *et alia* but for this *et cetera (q.v.)* is preferred.

Et cetera (etc.)
And the others, and the rest
I have seen this spelled "ect" by a professional signwriter.
"I want a proper wedding, with a vicar and bridesmaids and a cake and all the etceteras." Any bride to any mother.
An alternative form of etc. is "&c." where the "&" is in fact "et" written in a rather florid style. The technical term for & is "ampersand", which is a corruption of "and, *per se*, and", this phrase arising from the writing of & at the end of an alphabet, as it might be: "... X, Y, Z, and, on its own, &." (*Vide "**per se**" infra*.)

Etiam sapientibus cupido gloriae novissima exuitur
—Tacitus, *Histories*, IV, vi
Even with philosophers the thirst for fame is the last infirmity to be shaken off.
Cf. Milton in *Lycidas*:

> "Fame is the spur that the clear spirit doth raise
> (That last infirmity of noble mind)
> To scorn delights and live laborious days;..."

(The translators supply "infirmity"—no mention of *infirmitas* appears in the text, and we assume that Roman readers recognized the desire for fame as a weakness, and did not need to have it spelled out.)

Et in Arcadia ego

I too [have lived] in Arcadia

This inscription appears on the tomb in Poussin's painting of "The Arcadian Shepherds", as well as in paintings by Guercino and Bartolomeo Schidoni. An alternative reading is: "Even in Arcady will you find me [*sc.* Death]".

Evelyn Waugh gives the heading *Et in Arcadia ego* to the first part of his *Brideshead Revisited*, in which we meet a table decoration in the form of a human skull which "bore the motto '*Et in Arcadia ego*' inscribed on its forehead".

Arcadia was a district of the Peloponnesus inhabited largely by shepherds and other rustics, and according to Virgil was an area noted for its pastoral simplicity and happiness. In short, the ideal place in which to live, or at least in which to have a second home.

Robert Louis Stevenson wrote a poem with the title *Et tu in Arcadia vixisti*—"You too have lived in Arcadia".

Et sequens (et seq.)

And following

A term (sometimes just "*seq*") used especially with a page reference, noting that the pages following are also relevant, e.g., "Bennett, *op. cit.*, p. 209 *et seq.*"

Et tu, Brute

And you as well, Brutus?

Reported by Suetonius to have been said by Julius Caesar to Brutus in the Forum when Brutus, along with the other conspirators, stabbed him. Just to add a bit of confusion to the scene and in keeping with the spirit of the present compilation, he is said to have scorned to use the vernacular and to have spoken in Greek: και συ, τεκνον; (*kai su, teknon?*)—"And you, my child?"

Shakespeare uses the phrase in Caesar's last words:

"Et tu, Brute? Then fall, Caesar." [Dies]

Later, Anthony rubs it in with a forceful double superlative:

"Through this the well-beloved Brutus stabbed...
This was the most unkindest cut of all..."

"While I watched, her eyes lifted to me a gaze more reproachful than haughty—more mournful than incensed. 'Oh, Moore!' said she—it was worse than 'Et tu, Brute!'"

Charlotte Brontë, *Shirley*.

Ex Africa semper aliquid novi
There is always something new out of Africa
   A proverb derived from Livy. Pliny the Elder, *Historia Naturalis*, II, viii. 42, says: *Semper aliquid novi Africam adferre*, which means much the same as the proverb quoted. Africa is a big place and has always been treated by Europe as an inexhaustible Santa's grotto of novelties: the profusion of curiosities coming from Africa was remarked on by Aristotle. The South African Museum adopted the motto *Semper aliquid novi Africa affert* or "Africa is always producing something new".
   The announcement *Ex Africa semper aliquid novi* appears prominently on the wine boxes shipped out by the South African Vergelegen vineyard.

   "I thought you'd like to see something new," he said, adding, not without pride, "*Ex Africa surgit semper aliquid novo—novi*, eh?"
   Patrick O'Brian, *The Mauritius Command*.

   It seems reasonable to suppose that Karen Blixen found in this quotation the title for her *magnum opus*, *Out of Africa*.
   Semper aliquid novi is the motto of the Commission for the New Towns.

Ex astris scientia
Knowledge from the stars
   This was the motto of Starfleet Academy in the television series *Star Trek: Voyager*.

Ex cathedra
From a chair, with authority
   An *ex cathedra* announcement or judgement is one against which there can really be precious little hope of argument or appeal, such is the overwhelming authority of the person making the statement. In the Roman Catholic Church the author of *ex cathedra* announcements is the Pope, wearing his traditional cloak of infallibility.

   "To hear the grave Dr Samuel Johnson, 'that majestic teacher of moral and religious wisdom', while sitting solemn in an arm-chair in the Isle of Skye, talk, *ex cathedrâ*, of his keeping a seraglio, and acknowledge that the supposition had *often* been in his thoughts, struck me so forcibly with ludicrous contrast, that I could not but laugh immoderately."

James Boswell, *The Journal of a Tour to the Hebrides*.

"'That's only due to lack of opportunities,' Spiller replied in his most decisively scientific, *ex cathedra* manner."

Aldous Huxley, "The Monocle".

"The moral thumpiness is heightened by the use of organ and backing choir, not to mention the spoken *ex cathedra* pronouncement."

Julian Barnes, *Something to Declare*.

Excelsior
Higher
This is both the motto of New York State and the title of a poem by Longfellow in which the protagonist, carrying a banner with the strange device "Excelsior", climbs ever higher and higher in the Alps to be found eventually by a faithful hound, not surprisingly frozen to death. "Excelsior" is also the name of the wood shavings used to stuff, *inter alia*, teddy bears, and research needs to be done to discover whether or not the thriving economy of New York State was based on the teddy-bear-stuffing industry or not: and if so, whether the state motto gave its name to the teddy-bear-stuffing or *vice versa*.

"'All right, but don't encourage him, you're always urging him to go on, *avanti, avanti, excelsior, excelsior.*'"

Iris Murdoch, *The Message to the Planet*.

("*Avànti*" is Italian—"Forward!")
Luigi Manzotti's ballet *Excelsior* staged in Italy in 1881 had a cast of 600, including twelve horses, two cows and an elephant.
(N.B. *Excelsior* is higher even that *in excelsis, q.v.*)

Exceptis excipiendis
With proper exceptions
Used to cover one's back when making all-inclusive statements.
"Goodness is naught unless it tends towards old age and sufficiency of means. I speak broadly and *exceptis excipiendis*."

Samuel Butler, *The Way of All Flesh*.

"'Two masses daily, morning and evening, primes, noons, and vespers, *aves, credos, paters* –'

'Excepting moonlight nights, when the venison is in season,' said his guest.

'*Exceptis excipiendis*,' replied the hermit."

Sir Walter Scott, Ivanhoe.

Cf. "**mutatis mutandis**" *infra.*

Exeat

Let him go out

Permission granted to a priest by his bishop to leave his diocese, or to an undergraduate to leave university during term. Boundaries often assume a surrealistic quality. When I was a very junior Government Officer in pre-independence Kenya I was reprimanded by my superior officer for travelling one weekend to visit friends who lived in a neighbouring Province. It appeared I should have obtained his permission (*exeat*) to travel out of my own Province, something of which I was quite unaware, and the reason for which I do not understand to this day.

My grammar school was a day school. Had it been a boarding school, we should no doubt have been given "exeats" allowing us to go off premises at evenings and weekends.

Exegi monumentum aere perennius

—Horace, *Odes*, III, xxx. 1

I have completed a monument more lasting than brass

Quintus Horatius Flaccus, better known to us as "Horace", had just completed his third book of Odes, and decided that the work he had so far completed would be enough to win him immortality. Judging from the number of quotations from Horace in this or any other collection, his optimism was firmly based.

"Be pleased to accept of my best thanks for your 'Journey to the Hebrides',… I… exulted in contemplating our scheme fulfilled, and a *monumentum perenne* [a lasting monument] of it erected by your superior abilities."

James Boswell, The Life of Samuel Johnson, LL.D.

G. K. Chesterton, in "A Defence of Rash Vows", says of the man who made a vow: "Short as the moment of his resolve might be, it was, like all great moments, a moment of immortality, and the desire to say of it *exegi monumentum aere perennius* was the only sentiment that would satisfy his mind."

"The name of Stoyte would be remembered... for ever; for the Auditorium was a *monumentum aere perennius*, a Footprint on the Sands of Time—definitely a Footprint."

Aldous Huxley, *After Many a Summer*.

Exegi Monumentum is the title of a poem (1836) by Alexander Pushkin, based broadly on Horace's original ode, while *Aere perennius* is the motto of the Norman family of Moor Place.

Exempli gratia (e.g.)
For example

Literally "by way of example". "Gratia" was a Latin word of several uses, generally connected with doing someone a favour: *vide e.g.*, *"ex gratia"*, *"gratis"*. The phrase *exempli gratia* was used by Cicero in the sense we recognize today.

Via Media Exempli Gratia—"A Middle Way for the Sake of Example"—is the motto of the Building Surveyors Institute.

Exempli Gratia is the name of a music group from Seattle who claim that they "could loosely be considered math-punk".

Exeunt (omnes)
They (all) go out

A common stage direction. *Exeunt* is the plural of *exit*.

Ex gratia
By kindness

The victim of a mishap may have no legal claim for damages against the author of the mishap, who may nonetheless, purely out of the goodness of his heart, or for other undisclosed motives, make an *ex gratia* payment in compensation to the victim, without thereby admitting any liability.

Curiously, no music group world wide seems to have chosen *Ex Gratia* as its title. "Excrement" yes (twice): *Ex Gratia*, no.

Exit
He goes out

Sometimes hastily, as in act III, scene iii of Shakespeare's *The Winter's Tale*, where a well-known stage direction reads: "Exit pursued by a bear". The plural is "exeunt (omnes)".

Ex libris
From the books (or library) of

The usual inscription on book plates, a book plate pasted on the inside cover of a book and displaying one's name being a safeguard against losing one's books by lending them to forgetful friends.

It was once the practice for children to write after their name inside the front cover of each of their school books a Latin poem: *Hic liber est meus, Testis est Deus. Si quis furetur, Per collem pendetur*—"This book is mine, A witness is God. If anyone steals this, By the neck he shall be hung." The whole was usually finished off tastefully by a sketch of a body on a gallows.

There is a website called www.xlibris.com which offers help to desk-top publishers.

Ex luna scientia
Knowledge from the Moon

This was the motto of the Apollo 13 Moon mission.

Ex nihilo nihil fit
Nothing comes of nothing

This is a distillation of a statement of Lucretius in *De Rerum Natura*, i. 155, *Nil posse creari de nilo*—"Nothing can be created out of nothing".

Karen Armstrong, in *A Short History of Myth*, notes that the Babylonian creation myth *Enuma Elish* begins with a theogony showing how the gods themselves first came into being. "There is no creation *ex nihilo* but an evolutionary process…."

Ex officio
By virtue of office

Our village Primary School is a Church of England School, and the reigning vicar is *ex officio* chairman of the governors.

> "… the camp cook—a most important member of the outfit—had straddled his bronco and departed, being unable to withstand the fire of fun and practical jokes of which he was, ex-officio, the legitimate target."
>
> O. Henry, "The Marquis and Miss Sally".

Ex parte
From one side

An *ex parte* statement presents only one side of an argument. It is the opposite of impartial.

"I wish merely to caution you against the whole tone of 'L'Etoile's' *suggestion* by calling your attention to its *ex-parte* character at the outset."

Edgar Allan Poe, "The Mystery of Marie Rogêt".

"Her grandmother's comments, although *ex parte*, threw a very favourable light on the character and morals of Miss Penkervis."

Q. Q. Enwright, *Mistress and Maid*.

The phrase can be given a concrete meaning. J. Fenimore Cooper in *The Last of the Mohicans* introduces a horse rider who had a spur on one boot only: "… in consequence of the ex parte application of the spur, one side of the mare appeared to journey faster than the other…"

There is a strong case to be made for preserving this phrase and extending its use. To call an account of an event "impartial" is unambiguous: to call it "partial" is not. *Per contra*, the partiality of an *ex parte* account can be in no doubt.

Ex post facto
From what is done after, retrospectively

Or "as a consequence of what has happened later". In particular an *ex post facto* law allows the conviction and punishment retrospectively of someone who commits an act before it becomes an offence in law. It seems rather unfair and underhand, not least in the eyes of the offender.

CHAS. SURFACE: "… here's the family tree for you…. you may knock down my ancestors with their own pedigree."
SIR OLIVER: (aside) "What an unnatural rogue!—an *ex post facto* parricide!"

R. B. Sheridan, *School for Scandal*, IV, 1.

Ex Post Facto was the title of an episode in *Star Trek: Voyager*, in which Tom Paris is convicted of murder.

Extempore
Made up "at the time"

That is, made up on the spur of the moment, spoken "off the cuff" (in the days when gentlemen orators wore starched white shirt-cuffs on which they could jot down notes a minute or so before they rose to their feet to speak). In this sense (*ex tempore*—"without preparation") the term was used by Cicero.

Ex voto

In consequence of a vow

The heading of a poem by Swinburne: "When their last hour shall rise…"

Jonathan Jones, writing in *The Guardian*, described "the little congregation huddled in front of the marble tabernacle with its silver treasures, ex-voto offerings, and smoky candles".

F

Facilis descensus Averno;
Noctes atque dies patet atri janua Ditis:
Sed revocare gradum superasque evadere ad auras,
Hoc opus, hic labor est.—Virgil, *Aeneid,* vi. 126

The descent is easy to Avernus;
Night and day stands wide the portal of black Dis:
But to retrace your footsteps and regain the light of day,
This is true toil, this is labour indeed.

Aeneas is looking into the possibility of visiting the shade of his dead father Anchises in the Underworld, and the Sybil here is warning him of the difficulties of making the return trip.

Rixi Marcus, writing on Bridge for *The Guardian* a little while before her death, used phrases from this quotation as a commentary on successive stages in the bidding and playing of a disastrous hand. The response to an opening bid elicited *Facilis descensus Averno*; the final slam contract was marked with *Noctes atque dies,* and the actual play was prefaced by *Sed revocare gradum…*

Hoc opus est was the motto of Pedro the Cruel of Castile and Leon (*fl. c.* 1360).

Facsimile
Make the same

At one time a hyphenated word, "fac-simile", this term denotes an exact copy of handwriting, or of a coin or similar object. The "facsimile transmission" of documents electronically is now known popularly as "fax".

Facta non verba
Deeds not words

The motto of Constantine Technical College, Middlesbrough, and of a number of families including those of Dawson of Edwarebury, De Rinzey, Eager, and Huntingdon of the Clock House.

*Cf. "**acta non verba**" supra.*

Factotum
Do everything

A Jack-of-all-trades, a general handyman. Figaro was the factotum of all the town. (In Latin the two words are separate—*fac totum. Cf. "facsimile" supra.*)

Factotum is the title of a novel by Charles Bukowski, made into a film in 2005 by Bent Hamer.

> "He found her in tears in the kitchen. 'What's wrong?' he asked. 'It's all this,' she sobbed. 'I can't stand it any more. I do everything in this house. I'm just a drudge, a skivvy.' He put his arm around her shoulders. 'Darling, I don't think of you as a skivvy. I think of you as a very skilled and resourceful *factotum*.' For no reason at all, this made her feel slightly better."
>
> Q. Q. Enwright, *Mistress and Maid.*

Faex populi
The dregs of the people

One level lower than the plebs. The plural of "fæx" is "fæces". *Faex Populi* is the title of a poem by "Ballerina with Fins".

Fatigatus et aegrotus
Tired and sick

Or plain "sick and tired".

> "A wife who can behave irreproachably when her husband is by his own confession *fatigatus et ægrotus* of her, must be… 'either a goddess or a beastess'; and poor Elizabeth… Sterne appears to have been a very human creature."
>
> G. Saintsbury, Introduction to Everyman edition of Laurence Sterne, *A Sentimental Journey.*

Saintsbury's "either a goddess or a beastess" echoes a Greek phrase from Aristotle's *Politics*, ἢ θηρίον ἢ θεός (*è thēríon è theós*)—"either a beast or a god". *Vide "aegrotat" supra.*

Fauna
Wildlife

Usually the wildlife of a region, but excluding the plant life (*cf. "flora" infra*). The word "fauna" is Latin for a tutelary deity, i.e., a guardian god, of shepherds, which we have taken into English as "faun" and which the French have as "faune", as in "L'après-midi d'un".

"She was named Flora, but one time in the Mission a gentleman bum… said, 'Flora, you seem more like a fauna-type to me.' 'Say, I like that,' she said. 'Mind if I keep it?' And she did. She was Fauna ever afterward."

John Steinbeck, Sweet Thursday.

"Charismatic megafauna" include the elephant, the giant panda and the blue whale.

Favete linguis
—Horace, *Odes*, III, i. 2
Be favourable in your speech
Literally, "be favourable with your tongues", i.e., don't say anything inappropriate to the (sacred) occasion. Since the best way of doing this was not to speak at all, the phrase came to be equivalent to a request for silence.

"My good friends, *favete linguis*—To give you information, I must first, according to logicians, be possessed of it myself; and, therefore, with your leaves, I will retire into the library to examine these papers."

Sir Walter Scott, The Antiquary.

In *Winnie Ille Pu*, the Latin version of *Winnie-the-Pooh*, Alexander Lenard translates Rabbit's "Now don't talk while I think" as "Nunc, dum cogito, favete linguis".

Fecit
He made
An author might sign off at the end of his work: *Adolphus Smith fecit*. The work in question could be written or it could be composed in some other medium: e.g., the Blarney Stone commemorates the builder of Blarney Castle, and is inscribed: Cormac Mac Carthy *fortis me fieri fecit* a.d 1446— "Cormac Mac Carthy had me built strong".

I possess a geometry set which belonged probably to my great-grandfather (born *c*. 1816), or even possibly to his father before him. It includes an ivory ruler 4½ inches long, engraved on both sides with intricate scales whose use has probably long been forgotten, and inscribed "I. Bennett fecit".

Cf., **fieri curavit**, **pinxit**, **sculpsit**.

Feliciter audax

Happily daring

The word "happy" is one with many shades of meaning, and here it means more "fortunate" than "cheerful" or "carefree". Coleridge in his "Notes on Shakespeare" uses the phrase to epitomize the style in which *Anthony and Cleopatra* is written, and his opinion is now generally accepted.

"*Feliciter audax* is the motto for its style comparatively with that of Shakespeare's other works, even as it is the general motto of all his works compared with those of other poets." In the next sentence Coleridge speaks of "this happy valiancy of style".

In using this phrase Coleridge may have had in mind the judgement of Quintilian when writing of Horace in *De Institutione Oratoria*:… *verbis felicissime audax*, "a most happy daring in writing".

Felix qui potuit rerum cognoscere causas

—Virgil, *Georgics*, ii. 490

Happy is he who has been able to find out the causes of things

Because knowledge helps dispel fear of the unknown, even though it may *per contra* be offset by heightened fear of the known.

I am an *alumnus* of the London School of Economics, whose motto is *Rerum cognoscere causas*. The college was always among the *avant-garde* (*acies prima*) of its day, especially in ladies' fashion, and before the second world war it was known to its sister colleges of London University as:

> "*Rerum cognoscere causas*,
> The place where women wear trousers."

Felix qui potuit is the motto of Sir William Carew of Devon, and *Rerum cognoscere causas* is also the motto of Sheffield University and of the Institute of Brewing, with hints of mystery ingredients in beer. (Sometimes however it is better perhaps not to know what you are drinking.)

Felo de se

Suicide

This is the "felony against oneself". It does not mean, as suggested in the schoolboy howler, "found drowned" ("fell in the sea").

On the other hand, The Ratcatcher's Daughter "made an 'ole in the Riviere Thames" but:

> "'Twas a haccident they all agreed,
> And nuffink like self-slaughter;

So not guilty o' fell in the sea
They brought in the ratcatcher's daughter."

K. Hamilton Jenkins in *Cornwall and the Cornish*, describes how the corpse of a murdered man was discovered on a road near Penryn. The body was buried next day near the junction of two roads in a corner of the common, since it was thought to be "a case of felo de se, in which burial in consecrated ground was, of course, prohibited."

Felo De Se is the title of a poem by James Elroy Flecker.

Ferae Naturae

Of a wild nature

Sometimes by extension used to mean "wild animals".

> "Or were pheasants *feræ naturæ*, under no one's control, like the snails thrown over the garden fence in A. P. Herbert's classic Misleading Case, 'Is a snail a wild animal?'"
>
> Katherine Whitehorn, writing in *The Observer*.

Just for the record and solely by way of illustration, Dryden in "The Mock Astrologer" avers that "women are not comprised in our Laws of Friendship: they are *Feræ Naturæ*."

Festina lente

—Suetonius

Hasten slowly

Presumably because "More haste, less speed". It advises caution rather than procrastination. We are told that in its Greek form, Σπευδε βραδεως *"Speude bradeos"*, this was a favourite saying of Augustus Caesar. We are also told it was a favourite of Erasmus.

> LORD CHANCELLOR: Recollect yourself, I pray,
> And be careful what you say—
> As the ancient Romans said, *festina lente*,...
> W. S. Gilbert, *Iolanthe*, Act 1

> "'Come on, get a move on,' said Wilfred. 'Don't be in such a hurry,' replied Ronald. '*Festina lente*, you know.' 'Yes, but not that damn' *lente*!'"
>
> Q. Q. Enwright, *Mistress and Maid*.

The Festina Lente Foundation is based at Bray in Hampshire and offers training in equestrianism and horticulture, both of these being skills which presumably cannot be learned in a hurry.

Festina lente is the motto of a number of families including those of Colquhon, Dunsany and the Earls of Onslow, and also of Audenshaw Urban District Council in Lancashire.

Fiat
Let it be

In *Villette*, Charlotte Brontë mentions blanks in her heroine's life, the "result of circumstances, the fiat of fate, a part of my life's lot…."

> "My grandmother's fiats, delivered *ex cathedra* in staccato tones of an awful majesty, earned her, among us devotees of Rider Haggard, the soubriquet of 'Ayesha', 'She who must be obeyed.'"
> P. J. Dorricot, *Nursery Tales.*

Fiat lux
Let there be light

"And God said, Let there be light: and there was light." Genesis, i. 3.

Fiat lux is the motto of the Moorfields Eye Hospital in London. It is also a popular title with film-makers and with firms producing lighting equipment.

Fidei defensor (fid. def., F.D.)
Defender of the faith

Henry VIII was very flattered to be designated "Defender of the Faith" by Pope Leo X in 1521, in recognition of his diatribe against Luther in *Assertio Septem Sacramentorum*—"A Defence of the Seven Sacraments", although later, following a small disagreement in 1533 over the marital status of Queen Catherine of Aragon, the then current pope, Paul III, revoked the title. The king continued to use it, however, and set up his own version of the faith, becoming head of the Church of England. Parliament later conferred the title "Defender of the Faith" on Henry's son, Edward VI, and to this day his successors to the crown have so described themselves on the coinage of the realm and elsewhere.

On a seal of Henry's daughter, Elizabeth I, appear the words: *Elisabeth D.G. Angliae Franciae et Hiberniae regina Fid. Chr. Prop.* The last three abbreviations stand for *Fidei Christiani Proprietrix*, so that the inscription translates as: "Elizabeth, By the Grace of God Queen of England, France and Ireland, Guardian of the Christian Faith". *Vide* also "**Dei gratia**" and "**Britt. Omn. Rex.**"

Fieri curavit
Caused to be done
   Cf. "**fecit**" *supra and* "**poni curavit**" *infra.*

Finem respice
Look to the end
This is the motto of Godstowe School, High Wycombe, and of several families, including those of Bazley, Bligh and Hall of Grappenhall.
   Cf. "**respice finem**", *infra.*

Finis
The end
Books are still published whose last word on the last page is *Finis*.

> "A swift left hook wrote *finis* to Kid Connelly's hopes of succeeding to the World Bantamweight crown."
>
> Boxing report

In *The Oxford Book of English Verse,* the title "Finis" is given to William Landor's poem, "I strove with none, for none was worth my strife..." Note the word "strove" which seems now to be in danger of being replaced by "strived". "I strived with none..."?

Flebilis occidit
He died mourned
This (often true) testimony appears in many memorials on the walls of our cathedrals and parish churches. In Horace, *Odes*, I, xxiv, we find *multis ille bonis flebilis occidit, nulli flebilior quam tibi, Vergili,*—"to many good men he [*sc.* Quinctilius Varus] died [a cause] of weeping, but none [was] more grief-stricken than you, Virgil".
"Flebilis Occidit" is the title of an "Elegy upon the Death of Queen Mary" by Henry Parker (1604-1652), set to music by Purcell.

Flora
The goddess of flowers
Flora started life as a nymph, Chloris, who was ravished by Zephyr, the spring breeze, and being thus automatically disqualified from continuing as a nymph, was transmuted into the goddess. The whole episode is

succinctly presented by Botticelli on the right hand side of his painting *La Primavera* ("Spring").

> "O, for a draught of vintage! that hath been
> Cool'd a long time in the deep-delved earth,
> Tasting of Flora and the country green...."
>> John Keats, "Ode to a Nightingale".

"Flora" is used generally to denote the plant life of a region. *Cf. "fauna" supra.*

Floreat
May it flourish

This is the first word of the motto of Eton College—*Floreat Etona*—"May Eton flourish". Other perhaps less illustrious establishments use the same formula for their mottoes, and *inter alia* we have *Floreat Actona* (London Borough of Acton), *Floreat Kew*, *Floreat Swansea*, and *Floreat Salopia* (Shropshire).

Floruit (*fl.*)
Flourished

When the date of birth of a painter or author or other creative artist is not known for certain, this label is used to indicate the period in which he was known to be pursuing his art. Giovanni di Paolo (*fl.* 1420-1485) is a case in point.

Focus
Hearth

Until we all invested in central heating and television, the fire burning on the hearth was the centre of any household. Whereas in English we talk now only of the "focus of attention" or of "focusing" a lens, *focus* gives the French their word not only for the hearth, *foyer*, but also for the fire within it, *feu*: the focus of a lens in French is also *foyer*. The Italians use *fuoco* to mean both fire and focus; the Spaniards use *fuego* for fire and *foco* for focus.

Fons et origo
The source and origin

Literally *fons* is a fountain or spring. *Fons et Origo* is the motto of the La Fontaine family.

"… you have the privilege of knowing one of the most complete young blackguards about town, and the *fons et origo* of the whole trouble."

E. W. Hornung, Raffles.

"The *fons et origo* of this view [that a woman should not resist attack by a man] seems to be Chief Inspector B—.H—."

John Naughton, writing in The Observer.

"I'm being good. I am aping the *fons et origo* of domestic virtue. If we had twins I'd call them Lares and Penates (*qq.v.*)."

Julian Barnes, Talking It Over.

Forsitan et nostrum nomen miscebitur istis
—Ovid, *Ars Amatoria*, iii. 399
Perhaps too our/my name may be joined with these

Ovid had been reflecting on great poets of the past—Sappho, Propertius, Tibullus, Virgil—and wondering and hoping. He had not the confidence of Horace, but he need not have worried. (*Cf.* **"exegi monumentum"** *supra.*)

"I remember once being with Goldsmith in Westminster Abbey. While we surveyed the Poets' Corner, I said to him,
Forsitan et nostrum nomen miscebitur istis.
When we got to Temple Bar he stopped me, pointed to the heads upon it, and slily whispered me,
Forsitan et nostrum nomen miscebitur istis."

James Boswell, The Life of Samuel Johnson, LL.D.

(N.B. The heads of Fletcher and Townley, executed for the Jacobite rising of 1745, were placed on Temple Bar.)

(It was not uncommon for Romans to speak using the "royal we", so that *nostrum (pl.) nomen*—"this name of ours"—could well mean "my name". In English also it has been the custom for centuries for the sophisticated as well as the unsophisticated to use the plural for the singular, as in such phrases as "Give us a bite of your apple", i.e., "Give *me* a bite of your apple" and "Let's have a look.")

Fortiter in re

Determined in action

Part of the antithetical phrase: *Fortiter in re, suaviter in modo*—"Determined in action, polite in manner".

> "The bishop was very anxious to be gracious, and, if possible, to diminish the bitterness which his chaplain had occasioned. Let Mr Slope do the *fortiter in re*, he himself would pour in the *suaviter in modo*."
>
> Anthony Trollope, *Barchester Towers*.

> SARTORIUS. That is not true, sir. I –
> COKANE. Gently, my dear sir. Gently, Harry, dear boy. Suaviter in modo; fort-
> TRENCH. Let him begin, then. What does he mean by attacking me in this fashion?
>
> George Bernard Shaw, *Widowers' Houses*, Act II.

Fortiter in Re is the motto of, *inter alia*, H.M.S. Sussex and 42 Squadron of the R.A.F. *Suaviter in Modo, Fortiter in Re* is the motto of the families of Beevor and Wynn. *In Modo Suaviter, Fortiter in Re* is the motto of the Longsdon family.

Fragrat post funera virtus

Virtue smells sweet after death

One of many *dicta* or *sententiæ* making the virtuous feel happier about dying.

> "The glories of our blood and state
> Are shadows, not substantial things;...
> Only the actions of the just
> Smell sweet and blossom in the dust."
>
> James Shirley.

*Vide "**vivit post funera virtus**" infra.*

G

Gallia est omnis divisa in partes tres
—Caesar, *De Bello Gallico*, I, i
Gaul as a whole is divided into three parts

In Caesar's day the *Belgae* occupied the north-east of Gaul (which included present-day Belgium), the *Aquitani* squeezed themselves into a small corner in the far south-west, but the greatest part by far was occupied by the *Celtae*, the forebears of the modern Celts, whom the Romans called *Galli* or Gauls.

Vide "Introduction", the passages devoted to pronunciation.

Gallus in sterquilinio suo plurimum potest
—Seneca, *De Morte Claudii*
A cockerel is most vociferous on his own dunghill

This was a scurrilous comment by Seneca on the character of the emperor Claudius.

Gaudeamus igitur, juvenes dum sumus
Let us rejoice therefore, while we are still young

The opening words of a song which I found first in *The Scottish Students' Songbook*. It has been sung by students throughout Europe over the centuries and is also known under the title *De Brevitate Vitae*—"On the Shortness of Life". It is set to music composed *c*. A.D. 1267 by Strada, Bishop of Bologna. Brahms quotes the tune in his *Academic Festival Overture*.

It is sadly unlikely that this phrase gave rise to the term "Gaudy", an academic and frequently rowdy entertainment at certain universities, but the verb *"gaudire"*—"to rejoice" is the common source of the two "g" words.

Generosus
A gentleman

Now a dying, if not already defunct, breed.

"… we were agreeably surprised with the appearance of the master [of the house], whom we found to be intelligent, polite, and much a man of the world. When Dr Johnson and I were by ourselves at night, I observed of our host, '*aspectum generosum habet*'; '*et generosum animum*' he added."

James Boswell, *The Journal of a Tour to the Hebrides*.

(That is to say, 'He looks like a gentleman' and 'He has the mind of a gentleman'. Johnson and Boswell frequently conversed in Latin, often with the aim of puzzling eavesdroppers in strange lodgings.)

*Vide "**armiger**" supra.*

Generosus nascitur non fit

A gentleman is born, not made

This is the motto of the Wharton family, and is a variant of *Poeta nascitur non fit, (q.v. infra). Vide "**armiger**" supra.*

Genius loci

The spirit or god of a place

In a bygone era and in a place where every natural feature of the land had its own tutelary deity, this would have been a local god. Virgil in the *Aeneid* vii. 136 says: *Geniumque loci invocat*—"He prays to the god of the place".

"I shall sit in that room and see if its atmosphere brings me inspiration. I'm a believer in the *genius loci*."

Sir Arthur Conan Doyle, *The Valley of Fear*.

"We had a comfortable supper, and got into high spirits. I felt all my toryism glow in this old capital of Staffordshire. I could have offered incense *genio loci*."

James Boswell, *The Life of Samuel Johnson, LL.D.*

In *The Oxford Book of English Verse,* the title "Genius Loci" is given to Margaret Woods' poem, "Peace, Shepherd, peace!"

Genius Loci is the name of a professional creative consultancy based in Cornwall.

Genus
A group of closely related species (q.v.)

A *genus* is general but a *species* is special, and a *species* is a sub-division of a *genus*. For example, modern man is *Homo sapiens (q.v. infra)*, *Homo* being the genus and *sapiens* the species (the only extant species, all other species such as *neanderthalensis* and *erectus* now being extinct). "Genus" and "species" are the final elements of the taxonomy or classification of living creatures. Thus man is a member of the animal kingdom (Animalia), of the phylum Chordata, of the class Mammalia, of the order of Primates and of the family Hominidae, before being finally defined by his genus and species.

> "I took these sketches in the second-class schoolroom of Mdlle. (*sic*) Reuter's establishment, where about a hundred specimens of the genus *jeune fille* collected together offered a fertile variety of subject."
>
> Charlotte Brontë, *The Professor.*

Vide also "***sui generis***" *infra.*

Gloria in excelsis Deo
—The Mass
Glory be to God on high

This continues: *Et in terra pax, hominibus bonæ voluntatis*—"And on earth peace to men of good will". Compare this with the heavenly chorus in Luke ii. 14: "Glory to God in the highest, and on earth peace, good will toward men", which in the Vulgate Bible is "*Gloria in* altissimis *Deo*", etc.

Known as "The Gloria", this hymn of praise is part of the Communion service in the Book of Common Prayer.

Gloria in Excelsis Deo is the motto of Trinity College of Music.

Gloria Patri, et Filio et Spiritui Sancto
—From the Mass
Glory be to the Father, and to the Son, and to the Holy Ghost

This *Gloria* is sung after the Psalm.

Gradus ad Parnassum
Steps to Parnassus

> "Here is your book.... In fact... it was my cribbing book, and I always kept it by me when I was writing at Athens, like a gradus, a *gradus ad Parnassum*, you know."
>
> Benjamin Disraeli, *Venetia.*

The first Latin "Gradus" was published in 1702. In Fielding's *Tom Jones*, published in 1748, the barber lists *Gradus ad Parnassum* as one of the books he owns, along with *inter alii* Ovid's *De Tristibus* and *Robinson Crusoe*. My own *Gradus* is dated 1883 and was edited by a Dr Carey. The book is a Latin dictionary aimed to help anyone tasked with writing Latin verse, and I understand that the "Steps" in the title refer to the metres of the "feet" used in Latin verse, of which there are 28. Now $28 = 16 + 8 + 4$; there are 16 feet of four syllables, eight feet of three syllables and four feet of two syllables. As mathematicians we see at once that this must be correct, since two syllables, each either long and short, can be put together in four different ways—short, short; short, long (iambus); long, short (trochee); and long, long (spondee): if we replace "short" with 0 (zero) and "long" with 1 (one), then we can label each foot with a binary number: 00, 01, 10 and 11, which is from 0 to 3 inclusive or 4 in all. In the same way we can number the feet of three syllables from 0 to 7 inclusive (8 in all), e.g., long, short, short (dactyl) is 100 or 4; and we can number the feet of four syllables from 0 to 15 inclusive, or 16 in all. (Carey gives names to all 28 feet, names which include the choriamb and the First to Fourth Epitrites.)

Parnassus was a mountain in Bœotia and was sacred to Apollo and the Muses, and as such was the goal of the student of Latin verse-writing, which was very popular (except perhaps among most of the students) in the grammar schools of the nineteenth century. Parnassus was in fact a twin peak, the other peak being sacred to Bacchus, but I cannot suppose Dr Carey or any of his predecessors had this second peak in mind when choosing this title for the book.

Gradus ad Parnassum is the title of a musical treatise on counterpoint published in 1725 by Johann Joseph Fux; and also of 100 pianoforte *Etudes* published in 1826 by Muzio Clementi.

Gratis
Free

As in the phrase, "free, gratis and for nothing".

Shylock said he hated Antonio because "in low simplicity he lends out money gratis and brings down the rate of usance … in Venice."

> "But my heart is just in privy buildin'. And when I finish a job, I ain't through. I give all my customers six months privy service free *gratis.*"
>
> Charles Sale, *The Specialist.*

"she found you young and handsome, and gave you *gratis*… what to others she would have given for some ox heart and some bits of lung."

Umberto Eco, *The Name of the Rose*.

H

Habeas corpus
Thou mayest have the body

Habeas is the second person singular present subjunctive of *habere*, "to have". The phrase encapsulates the traditional (from the time of Magna Carta) British safeguard against wrongful detention, where the issue of a writ of *habeas corpus* (*ad subjuciendum*) requires the arresting authority to produce the prisoner before a judge, who will then decide whether the prisoner should remain in detention or be released. The Latin is in the present subjunctive, but has the effect of an imperative: "You are to produce the body".

> "The time of the assizes soon came, and I was removed by *habeas corpus* to Oxford, where I expected certain conviction and condemnation;…"
>
> Henry Fielding, *Tom Jones*.

Hic et ubique
Here and everywhere

Shakespeare's *dramatis personæ* spoke very little Latin, although most of them would have been well schooled in the language. Hamlet let slip this phrase in Act I, scene v. line 156. "Hic et ubique? then we'll shift our ground."

Hic et ubique is the motto of 201 Reconnaissance Squadron of the R.A.F.

Hic jacet
Here lies

The traditional first words for an inscription on a tombstone, eloquent in themselves. *Hic Jacet* is the title of a horror story by Oliver Onions; and the title also of poems by Derek Walcott and Louise Chandler Moulton.

> "O, eloquent, just and mighty Death!… thou hast drawn together all the far-stretched greatness, all the pride, cruelty and ambition

of man, and covered it all over with these two narrow words, *Hic jacet*."

> Sir Walter Raleigh, *A History of the World*.

> "May no rude hand deface it,
> And its forlorn *Hic Jacet*."

> Wordsworth, "Ellen Irwin".

Hinc illae lacrimae

—Terence: also Horace, *Epistles* I, xix. 41

Hence those tears

Although Terence used these words in his play "Andria", this is only one sighting of the phrase, and it was commonly used in other works to mean: "So that's what the fuss was really about!"

> "I am too much addicted to the study of philosophy; *hinc illæ lacrymæ*, sir, that's my misfortune. Too much learning hath been my ruin."

> Henry Fielding, *Tom Jones*.

> "Were Freud right and sex supreme, we should live almost in Eden. Alas, only half right. Adler also half right. *Hinc illae lac*."

> Aldous Huxley, *Eyeless in Gaza*.

"Enrapture—*Hinc Illae Lacrimae*" is the title of the first track of the album *Domus Mundi* (Home of the World) by the Austrian symphonic black metal band Hollenthon.

Edgar Allan Poe in "The Mystery of Marie Rogêt" adapts the phrase to *Et hinc illae irae*, or "Hence this anger".

Hoc volo, sic iubeo

This I wish, thus I command

> *Vide "**sic volo, sic iubeo**" infra.*

Homo proponit, sed Deus disponit

—Thomas à Kempis, *De Imitatione Christi*

Man proposes, God disposes

This is the motto of the Barber-Starkey family, perhaps as a consequence early on of a string of thwarted plans for advancement in various directions.

*Cf. "**dis aliter visum**" supra.*

Homo sapiens

Man who can think

This is the species to which all living men belong. Other phrases exist to describe subdivisions or various aspects of humanity, *e.g.*, *Homo faber*, man the toolmaker, and *Homo erectus*, an earlier species of man, including Java man, able to walk upright. I myself, deprived once of the use of a car for several days, recognized my own sub-species as *Homo automobilis*.

It has been suggested that figures like Superman might be classified as a sub-species, *homo sapiens sapiens*, with a double capacity to think.

A group of robotic toys known as "Robosapiens" justify their name by being probably brighter than some of the children who play with them.

*Vide "**genus**" supra.*

Homo sum: humani nil a me alienum puto

—Terence, *Heauton Timorumenos*, I, i. 25

I am a man: I count nothing human to be beyond my concern

In *Heauton Timorumenos* ("The Self-Tormentor") the eponymous Menedemus has driven his son from home for falling in love with an unsuitable (i.e. poor) girl. His neighbour Chremes reproves him for his unkindness on humanitarian grounds, using this phrase to justify his interference in someone else's private affairs. In our day it is the justification for state aid to those who are in need, even if the Nanny State is the result.

> "… he was one who could truly say with him in Terence, '*Homo sum: humani nihil a me alienum puto.*' He was never an indifferent spectator of the misery or happiness of anyone,…"
>
> Henry Fielding, *Tom Jones*.

Homo sum: humani nil a me alienum puto is the motto of The London Hospital.

John Donne in "Devotions upon Emergent Occasions XVII" takes a similarly wide view of the universality of the family of mankind. "No man is an *Iland*, intire of it selfe;… any mans *death* diminishes *me*, because I am involved in *Mankinde*;…"

Honorarium (donum)

An honorary gift

A fee of arbitrary size paid in acknowledgement of services given voluntarily, not always commensurate with the amount of work done.

Honoris causa

As an honour, a token of respect

Literally, "for the sake of honour".

> "A sense of humour may not have been one of the divine attributes which God claimed for Himself, but it was, so to speak, conferred on Him, *honoris causa*, by the Jewish people."
>
> Chaim Bermant, *What's The Joke?*

> "Let us not fail to mention in passing, *honoris causa*, Sir William Hoskins, without whose unflagging efforts this copper mine would never have got off the ground in the first place."
>
> News item.

The phrase can denote the grounds for granting an honorary degree. "In 1853 [Disraeli] went to Oxford to receive a doctor's degree, *honoris causa*." André Maurois, *Disraeli*.

Horas non numero, nisi serenas

I count no hours but those which are serene

William Hazlitt's essay "On a Sun-dial" starts: "*Horas non numero, nisi serenas*—is the motto of a sun-dial near Venice."

The words appear on sun-dials nearer home. *Serenas* means unclouded and hence "sunny"; our own word "serene" fits well here, being a more euphonious word than "sunny".

A common variant is *Horas non numero, nisi aestivas*, where *aestivas* refers to summer hours and summer suns. It appears on a sundial in Petts Wood, Kent, erected to the memory of William Willett, the promoter of British Summer Time.

Cf. "*pereunt et imputantur*" and "*tempus edax rerum*" *infra.*

Horribile dictu

Horrible to relate

Cf. "*mirabile dictu*" *infra.*

Hortus siccus

A dry garden, a herbarium

This could be my lawn languishing under a hosepipe ban, but more particularly a *hortus siccus* is a collection of dried plants arranged in a book, a craft whose first practitioner was Luca Ghini (1490-1550).

Humanum est errare

—Seneca the Younger, *Naturales Quaestiones*, iv. ch. 2

It is human to err

Seneca merely repeats here one of the most widely used of all Latin proverbs, which continues *perseverare diabolicum*—"to persist is of the devil". Alexander Pope extended its scope in a different direction in "An Essay on Criticism", line 525: "To err is human, to forgive, divine".

"'I,' said Peppone,... 'have made one mistake in my life. I tied crackers to the clappers of your bells. It should have been half a ton of dynamite.' '*Errare humanum est*,' remarked Don Camillo."

Giovanni Guareschi, *The Little World of Don Camillo.*

I

Ibidem (ibid., ib.)

In the same place

In, for instance, the *Oxford Book of Quotations*, the first quotation from, say, a poem is labelled with the name of the poem followed by the number of the line. Subsequent quotations from the same poem are then labelled simply *ib.* with the new line number.

I, bone, quo virtus tuo te vocat, i pede fausto.
Grandia laturus meritorum præmia

—Horace, *Epistles*, II, ii. 37

Go, good (lad), where thy courage calls thee, go with propitious step, (certain) to carry away the rich rewards of thy merit.

In fact the "good lad", having won his laurels in an earlier battle, was happy now to rest on them and was very much disinclined to go anywhere near further danger.

I pede fausto is the motto of the Windward Islands and of Oadby District Council in Leicestershire.

Idem (id.)

The same (person)

This word is used particularly in notes on sources or in bibliographies. Thus from the consecutive footnotes:

1. Raymond Thurman, *The Sources of Pleasure*, p. 39
2. *Idem, The Fact of Pain*, p. 192;

we understand that Thurman was also the author of *The Fact of Pain*.

The word may however be used in the same way as *ibidem* (*q.v.*) to mean "in the same place", but this is not to be recommended.

"Not a bush, not an inch, was not searched again, and over a much wider extent; *idem*, where Thurlow was found, and all about, and as closely."

John Fowles, *A Maggot*.

Id est (i.e.)
That is

"Père Simon, it seems, had closely watched me, had ascertained that I went by turns, and indiscriminately, to the three Protestant chapels in Villette—the French, German, and English—*id est*, the Presbyterian, Lutheran, Episcopalian."

Charlotte Brontë, *Villette*.

Vide also "**arcades ambo**" *supra*.

Iesus Hominum Salvator
Jesus the saviour of men

The letters IHS seen frequently on church furniture do not normally represent the initial letters of this phrase, but instead represent the first three letters of the name "Jesus" in Greek (Ἰησοῦς): *iota, eta, sigma*.

Iesus Nazarenus Rex Iudaeorum (INRI)
Jesus the Nazarene, King of the Jews

"And Pilate wrote a title, and put it on the cross. And the writing was, Jesus of Nazareth, the King of the Jews…. Then said the chief priests of the Jews to Pilate, Write not, The King of the Jews; but that he said, I am King of the Jews. Pilate answered, What I have written, I have written."

John xix. 19, 21, 22.

Ignis fatuus
Will-o'-the-wisp, a foolish fancy

"… in among the marshes and the ridges a light sprang up. That is an *ignis fatuus* was my first thought; and I expected it would soon vanish…."

Charlotte Brontë, *Jane Eyre*.

Sir John Falstaff: "When thou rann'st up Gadshill in the night to catch my horse, if I did not think thou hadst been an *ignis fatuus*, or a ball of wild fire, there's no purchase in money."

Shakespeare, *Henry IV Part 1*, III, iii.

(Falstaff was talking to Bardolph, whose carbuncled face was held by his friends to be all but luminescent.)

LIVING LATIN

Jonathan Keates, reviewing *Images of English* by R. W. Bailey in *The Observer*, referred to "The *ignis fatuus* of feminist political correctness".

Ignoramus
We do not know, we are ignorant

This is an ancient law term, written by a Grand Jury on the back of an indictment when they had decided that there was not enough evidence to justify a case proceeding to trial. The accusation was subsequently flung at anyone who doesn't know much.

Impedimenta
Encumbrances, impediments

The singular *impedimentum* is "a hindrance". The plural *impedimenta* referred to the baggage and essential supplies carried by an army, which slowed down its speed of advance and impeded its progress. The term is now firmly associated with holiday makers.

Research needs to be done into the extent to which the Roman definition of "baggage" embraced camp-followers.

Imprimatur
Let it be printed

So giving it the stamp of authority. In particular a licence given by the Roman Catholic Church to print a book. A previous stage in the granting of such a licence is the *Nihil Obstat* ("Nothing hinders"), the finding by the censor of the diocese that the work is free of moral or doctrinal error. The *Imprimatur* indicates that the bishop or other ecclesiastical authority approves the book as well. Thus in 1907 *The Catholic Encyclopaedia* was granted a *Nihil Obstat* by the Censor Remy Lafort S.T.D., and an *Imprimatur* by John Cardinal Farley, Archbishop of New York.

> "What they seek, in essence, is a scientific *imprimatur* for their own metaphysics."
>
> John Naughton, writing in *The Observer*.

Sometimes the word is used as a guarantee of worth. "Julie's initials at the bottom of any letter were the sure imprimatur of a clean and flawless sheet of typing." Colin Dexter, *Last Bus to Woodstock*.

Imprimatur is the motto of the Institute of Printing, Ltd.

(S.T.D. is the abbreviation of *Sanctae Theologiae Doctor*, "Doctor of Holy Theology", equivalent to "Doctor of Divinity" {D.D.}.)

Imprimis

First (of all), for a start

GRUMIO: Now I begin: *Imprimis*, we came down a foul hill...
Shakespeare, *The Taming of the Shrew*, IV, i.

(Caroline and Shirley agree that a woodland stroll would be spoilt by the presence of men.) "[Even] if they are of the right sort, there is still a change—I can hardly tell what change, one easy to feel, difficult to describe." "We forget Nature, *imprimis*." Charlotte Brontë, *Shirley*.

Imprimis also marked the first component of a list; and *Imprimis* is the name of an Airedale Terrier hobby kennel in Wisconsin.

Vide "item" infra.

In absentia

In one's absence

R. Bruce Lockhart, writing in *The Observer*, said: "Higgs was sentenced to death *in absentia*, along with my father and Reilly."

"Under Italian law, defendants can be tried *in absentia*."
Report in *The Guardian*.

The concept of *in-absentia* health care seems to have started with Galen who was proficient in diagnosing diseases by having the symptoms described him by post; by return post he would prescribe the appropriate treatment. The modern equivalent is available on-line.

In Absentia are fully defined as an instrumental jazz fusion hardcore metal band.

In articulo mortis

At the point of death, in the arms of death

"As to the youthful sufferer, he weathered each storm like a hero. Five times was that youth 'in articulo mortis', and five times did he miraculously survive."
Charlotte Brontë, *Villette*.

Sometimes written (for the sake of easier scansion) as *Mortis in articulo*. In his poem "The Song Against Grocers", which begins "God made the wicked Grocer...", G. K. Chesterton writes:

"The evil-hearted Grocer
Would call his mother 'Ma'am',

And bow at her and bob at her
Her aged soul to damn,
And rub his horrid hands and ask
What article was next,
Though *mortis in articulo*
Should be her proper text."

In *Epistolæ ad Quintum Fratrem*, V, 19, Cicero says *in ipso articulo temporis*— "at this point in time". Perhaps not surprisingly there appears to be no phrase in Latin for "at this moment in time".

In camera
In private, behind closed doors
A case heard *in camera* is heard in a closed courtroom or in a judge's private room, with outsiders excluded.

> "Before the case started (the judge) told the jury part of it would be held *in camera* with press and public excluded."
>
> Report in *The Guardian*.

In *Wild Mary*, his biography of Mary Wesley, Patrick Marnham says: "Despite its dramatic nature—the plot straight from Anthony Trollope— the case of the Swinfen Trust went unreported as it was held *in camera*, in the Chancery Division of the High Court."

There is no completely satisfactory English equivalent for the phrase *in camera*, and there is no need for one. If the need for one arose, then it would no doubt be found with no difficulty at all: until then *in camera* is perfectly adequate. The French have their own equivalent, "huis clos", which is succinct and pithy: when a translation of Sartre's play of this name was mounted in London, it was presented under the title "In Camera".

(Note: since the above note was written, the legal authorities have begun to discourage the use of perfectly adequate time-honoured terms, and recent cases have been reported as being heard "behind closed doors"— 17 letters in place of 8.)

Incolumi gravitate
With a straight face, without loss of dignity
Horace uses this phrase in his *Ars Poetica*, line 222.

"[Boswell's father] had a great many good stories, which he told uncommonly well, and he was remarkable for humour, *incolumi gravitate*, as Lord Monboddo used to characterize it."

James Boswell, *The Journal of a Tour to the Hebrides*.

Ind.Imp. (Indiae Imperator, Imperatrix)

Emperor, Empress of India

Victoria was the first Queen Empress, *Regina Imperatrix*, Queen of Great Britain, etc., and Empress of India. The British Crown had taken over the government of India in 1858, but it was not until 1877 that Victoria declared her wish to assume the title of Empress. George VI was the last King Emperor, *Rex Imperator*, relinquishing the title when India and Pakistan became Dominions in August 1947. Coins of the realm struck between these dates carried the letters IND. IMP. Some postboxes from the nineteenth century bear the initials V.R.I: "Victoria Regina Imperatrix". (*Vide "***R.I.***" infra.*)

Indocilis pauperiem pati

—Horace, *Odes* I, i. 18

He has not been taught to suffer poverty

Or "He is not used to being in reduced circumstances". Horace was talking of the trader who, despite shipwrecks and other setbacks, still keeps sending his ships to sea, trying to scrape thereby a decent living. Thackeray uses the same idea in *Henry Esmond*: "When Lady Castlewood found that her great ship had gone down, she began... to put out small ventures of happiness... as a merchant on 'Change, *indocilis pauperiem pati*, having lost his thousands, embarks a few guineas upon the next ship."

Indocilis pauperiem pati is the motto of the Society of Merchant Adventurers of the City of Bristol.

In extenso

At length

"'It's all right,' said the reporter.... 'We never report Sir Thomas *in extenso*. Only the fines and charges.'"

Rudyard Kipling,
"The Village That Voted The Earth Was Flat".

"After hearing an account of the deceased's habit of proclaiming loudly and *in extenso* the virtues of her first husband and in like manner the shortcomings of her second husband (the accused), the jury unhesitatingly returned a unanimous verdict of 'justifiable homicide'."

Q. Q. Enwright, Mistress and Maid.

"I shall ask them to head it 'No Copyright', so that other papers … may reproduce it in extenso and free of charge."

Julian Barnes, Arthur and George.

In extremis

At the point of death, at one's last gasp

In Mark v. 23 Jairus beseeches Jesus to come: "My little daughter lieth *at the point of death…*"—rendered as *filia mea in extremis est* in the Vulgate.

"Addison died there [Holland House], exhibiting his fortitude *in extremis* to [his stepson] the dissolute Earl of Warwick."

E. V. Lucas, A Wanderer in London.

"… could despatch boxes with never-so-much velvet lining and Chubbs' patent, be of comfort to a people *in extremis*, I also would call on the name of Lord John Russell."

Anthony Trollope, The Warden.

Nowadays it is often used in a somewhat devalued sense to mean "at one's wits' end". Katherine Whitehorn, reviewing a book on etiquette in *The Observer*, suggested that ordinary people needing advice would not spend money on such a book but would "ask a friend or, in extremis, write to a magazine". *Vide **"in articulo mortis"** supra.*

Corruptus in Extremis—"Corrupt in the extreme"—is the motto of the Mayor's office in Springfield, home town of Homer Simpson and his family.

In flagrante delicto

In the act

Usually in the act of (illicit) love. The Latin has the implication of a "blazing crime" being committed at the time.

"The number of times my cousin Jethro was caught *in flagrante delicto* earned him the title of 'The Lothario of Bishop's Stortford'."

P. J. Dorricot, Beyond the Nursery Slopes.

In *Close Quarters*, one of William Golding's characters suggests that, had little Marion not detained her "uncle", he would have been "a devil of a sight nearer being detected *in flagrante delicto* than I was!" .

"'Unfortunately for Kemp, however, Cedric Downes discovered the guilty pair *in flagrante delicto*, which as you will remember, Lewis, is the Latin for having your pants down.'"

> Colin Dexter, *The Jewel that was Ours*.

Infra
Below

In the visible spectrum of light, red and violet mark the extremities. Objects not hot enough to glow red emit invisible infra-red rays, rays "below" the red section. The term is apt to cause some bewilderment because in the familiar spectrum which is the rainbow, red appears at the outer or top edge of the bow.

Also used by an author to denote "further on" in the text. *Cf. "supra" infra. Cf.* also "*ultra*" *infra.*

Infra dignitatem (infra dig.)
Beneath (one's) dignity

Dignity gives one a standard at least to aim at in life if not to achieve.

Writing in *The Observer*, Keith Boot was scathing about "suburbanites who think satellite dishes are *infra dig.*"

> "What's self-respect got to do with it? There's nothing *infra dig* about snitching pigs."
>
> P. G. Wodehouse, *Uncle Fred in the Springtime*.

In *The Wench is Dead*, Colin Dexter allows the phrase full exposure when describing the predicament of Morse "who was about to face the slightly *infra-dignitatem* embarrassments of hernias and haemorrhoids…"

In hoc signo (vinces)
By this sign (thou shalt conquer)

In hoc signo was the motto of Constantine the Great and the sign in question was that of the Cross, which Constantine saw in a vision before the Battle of Milvian Bridge in the year 312. (In fact the "cross" was rather a *labarum*, the "Chi-Rho" symbol. These two Greek letters are the first two in Χριστός, the Greek name for "Christ".) *In hoc signo vinces* was also a phrase used by the Knights Templar and by the Freemasons.

Many families share the motto *In hoc signo vinces*, and crosses figure in their coats-of-arms. They include the families of Burke, of Glinsk, of Campbell of Bleaton-Hallett, of Ormsby-Gore. of Taafe and of the Earls of Arran. *Hoc signo vinces* is the motto of the family of Moore of Mayes Park.

"The pink of her face was the *in hoc signo* of a culinary temper and a warm disposition."

O. Henry, "Telemachus, Friend".

In loco parentis
In place of a parent

One of the main drawbacks of schoolteaching is having other people's children constantly getting under one's feet. Being *in loco parentis* one is entrusted with their care and is adjured to treat them as a loving parent would, but is usually quite glad to return them to the care of their true loving parent(s) at the end of the school day. However this quasi-parental rôle has now been replaced by the requirement that a teacher give such care as "can be expected of a competent professional acting within the constraint of circumstances".

"'And why, Colonel Newcombe,' Virtue exclaimed, laying a pudgy little hand on its heart—'why did I treat Clive so? Because I stood towards him *in loco parentis*; because he was as a child to me and I to him as a mother.'"

W. M. Thackeray, *The Newcombes*.

In Loco Parentis is the motto of Cheadle Hulme School, Cheshire, and also somewhat unexpectedly of 200 Squadron of the R.A.F.

In medias res
—Horace, *Ars Poetica*, 148
Into the thick of things

Horace was irritated by Homer's habit of plunging the reader into the middle of a story, assuming that the reader already knows or can somehow divine telepathically what went before.

Writing of C. S. Lewis's novels in *The Guardian*, John Mullan noted that at the opening of *The Voyage of the Dawn Treader*, Edmund, Lucy and Eustace found themselves simply plunged into the sea near King Caspian's ship. "*In medias res* is how most of the novels begin, with children hurried into a story that has already begun."

In Medias Res is the motto of 258 Squadron of the R.A.F., while *Silenter in Medias Res*—"Silently into the thick of things"—is the motto of 177 Squadron of the R.A.F.

There is a good case to be made for using certain Latin phrases rather than the equivalent English ones, on the grounds that the Latin is dispassionate and not loaded with connotations. *In medias res* is a case in point.

"Into the thick of things" brings with it a suggestion of "hurly-burly" whereas *in medias res* is a simple statement that we are entering without fuss into a situation which is already partly developed.

(*Vide* "***ab initio***", "***ab incunabulo***" and "***ab ovo***" *supra*.)

In memoriam
In memory of
Tennyson's poem "In Memoriam", composed in memory of his friend Arthur Hallam, is one of the longest elegies in the language.

During the nineteenth century (when else?) the custom arose of sending "In Memoriam" cards to friends and acquaintances, announcing the death of a family member. In *Household Gods* (*alias* "*Lares et Penates*"? *qq.v.*) Deborah Cohen relates how a Victorian spinster papered her bedroom with "black-bordered In Memoriam cards".

In nomine Patris, et Filii, et Spiritus Sancti
In the name of the Father, and of the Son, and of the Holy Ghost
These words introduce the Ordinary of the Mass in the Roman Catholic Church.

In perpetuum
For ever
In Perpetuum is the name of a Brazilian band mixing Dark, Black and Gothic Metal. It is also the name of a Dutch Black Metal band. *Tenebrae in Perpetuum*—"Shadows for ever"—is the name of an Italian Black Metal band.

In propria persona
In his/her own person
Said of someone acting on his own behalf in person and not through a deputy or agent.

"… under the serene sway of Madame Back, who, *in propriâ personâ*, was giving one of her orderly and useful lessons…" Charlotte Brontë, *Villette*. (The circumflex on the â indicates that it is a "long a", the ablative case of the noun.) The inference here seems to be that Mme Back was often in the habit of entrusting the delivery of her orderly and useful lessons to a subordinate. Scope for research?

> "There was no real need for Aunt Karen to tell us bed-time ghost stories to frighten us into insomnia. She was scary enough *in propria persona*."
>
> P. J. Dorricot, *Nursery Tales*.

Inquisitio post mortem
An inquest

This phrase gave English the word "inquest" as well as the phrase *post mortem* ("after death") for the clinical examination of a body. In the Middle Ages however an *inquisitio post mortem* following the death of a prominent man or woman was a judicial enquiry into the property owned by the deceased, into services owed to an overlord or to the Crown, and especially and understandably into who might be the rightful heirs to the deceased's property. An incredible number of documents recording the results of such enquiries over many centuries is held in the National Records Office, and photocopies may be had on request.

In re
Concerning

"Dear Sir, *In re* your complaint about the curious behaviour of our representative, we have now fully investigated the circumstances, and have come to the rather unexpected conclusion that…" The use of the phrase is nowadays felt to be rather pretentious, but it may well serve its purpose in the right surroundings.

Insignia
Badges

Usually military badges, worn on the uniform. "The Major was wearing the insignia of the Royal Corps of Signals."

In situ
In place

Archaeologically speaking, an artefact is *in situ* if it has not been moved from the place where it was originally deposited. The notion can be applied to any object which has been gathering dust in a particular place for some time. "We decided to paint the Aga *in situ*, rather than try to move it to the garage."

> "Indeed, there was a sense in which Morse was happier to have avoided any *in situ* inspection of the corpse, since the liquid contents of his stomach almost inevitably curdled at the sight of violent death."
>
> Colin Dexter, *The Daughters of Cain.*

> "When we came to fumigate her room, Aunt Enid refused to budge, so we were forced to go ahead with the old lady *in situ*."
>
> Q. Q. Enwright, *Mistress and Maid*

Instanto mense (inst.)

In this month

In a letter written on any day in, say, January, "inst." refers to another day in that same January.

"I refer to your letter of 13th inst." i.e. the 13th of this month. This practice was once widespread but has now generally been discontinued.

Cf. ***"ult.", "prox."***

Instanter

Straight away, instantly

"'They told me you had the gout, Cassilis?' 'So I had; but I found out a fellow who cures the gout *instanter*.'"

Benjamin Disraeli, *Coningsby*.

"Hector, draw off your forces and make your bear-garden flourish elsewhere—and, finally, be all of good cheer till my return, which will be *instanter*."

Sir Walter Scott, *The Antiquary*.

The word crops up *passim* in stories set in public schools, e.g.: "*Cave*, there's a beak coming. We'd better get out of here *instanter*."

In statu pupillari

In the position of a pupil

This is the complement of *in loco parentis, q.v. supra*.

"Philip had a joke about his wife's housekeeping which perhaps may apply to other young women who are kept by over-watchful mothers too much *in statu pupillari*."

W. M. Thackeray, *The Adventures of Philip*.

Julian Barnes in *Talking It Over* admits he could not quite remember the identities of the people under consideration but that were those currently "*in statu pupillare* (*sic*) to be assembled in a *décontractée* atmosphere—rather like, say, a police line-up", he felt that the whole matter could be discussed.

In statu quo (ante)

As it was before

This is an understandable shortening of the full phrase: *In statu in quo ante erat*—"In the state in which it was before".

I possess a letter written on 12th October 1762 by a surgeon in which he describes to a friend a visit by two ladies known to them both: "I saw Mrs Parkinson and Miss the day before they set out for Liverpoole (*sic*), the Mother in statu quo, Broad and Blunt, the Daughter tall and Marketable, provided trade runs brisk...."

> "There had been no robbery, nor is there any evidence as to how the man met his death.... I have left everything *in statu quo* until I hear from you."
>
> Sir Arthur Conan Doyle, *A Study in Scarlet*.

In statu quo may be used as a euphemism for man's initial state of nakedness:

> "All this summer I've slept, if you'll believe me, practically *in statu quo*, and had my morning tub as cold as I could get it."
>
> M. R. James, "Mr Humphreys and his Inheritance".

*Cf. "**status quo**" infra.*

Integer vitae scelerisque purus
—Horace, *Odes*, I, xxii. 1
(He who is) blameless in respect to his life, and has no share in wickedness
Horace modestly ascribes to his own blameless life the fact that a large wolf he met in the woods refrained from attacking him.

> "Who so *integer vitæ scelerisque purus*, it was asked, as Mr Pontifex of Battersby?"
>
> Samuel Butler, *The Way of all Flesh*.

> "'It seems to me the right thing to do, you know, with the Pussums, is to pay them.' 'And the right thing for mistresses: keep them. And the right thing for wives: live under the same roof with them. Integer vitæ scelerisque purus —' said Birkin. 'There's no need to be nasty about it,' said Gerald."
>
> D. H. Lawrence, *Women in Love*.

In *The Oxford Book of English Verse* the heading *Integer vitæ* is given to Thomas Campion's poem:

> "The man of life upright,
> Whose guiltless heart is free

From all dishonest deeds,
Or thought of vanity."

Integer vitæ is the motto of the Christie family of Glyndebourne.

Inter alia
Among other things
Rumour has it that this has been seen abbreviated to i.a., just as *id est* is usually written as i.e. Joanna Slaughter, writing in *The Observer*, reported that over 4000 members of the public had cried foul (on life insurance salesmen), "claiming, *inter alia*, misrepresentation, breaches of polarization, mis-selling, misleading literature and inappropriate advice."

When applied to people rather than things, the neuter *alia* changes to the masculine *alios* or the feminine *alias*.

"It is also the view, *inter alios*, of James Cellan Jones,... Philip Saville,..."
Charles Nevin, writing in *The Guardian*.

"Morse drained his wine, only newly aware of why Eleanor Smith could so easily have captivated (*inter alios*) Dr Felix McClure."
Colin Dexter, *The Daughters of Cain*.

Interim
Meanwhile, in the meantime
Now used to mean simply a space of time between two events, which is after all the "mean time".

"Between the acting of a dreadful thing
And the first motion, all the interim is
Like a phantasma or a hideous dream."
Shakespeare, *Julius Caesar*, II, i.
"There was a delay between the finish of the second race and the start of the third, caused by the invasion of the course by a small herd of wildebeest, so in the interim we had a couple of drinks in the bar."
Q. Q. Enwright, *Mistress and Maid Abroad*.

As an adjective it is equivalent to "stop-gap" or "temporary". In diplomatic circles a *chargé d'affaires ad interim* acts for an absent ambassador. An interim government or administration is usually more or less legitimate (*de jure* as well as *de facto*), and can be expected to give way before long to a permanent, properly constituted body. An interim measure in such cases may simply be the setting up of an interim administration.

Inter pares
Among equals
> "To the end of his career his position *inter pares* was what it had been at the beginning, namely, among the upper part of the less reputable class… rather than among the lower part of the more respectable."
>
> Samuel Butler, *The Way of All Flesh*.

*Vide "**primus inter pares**" infra.*

In toto
In total, altogether
> "He asked leave, therefore, to withdraw the charge *in toto*…"
> Rudyard Kipling, "The Village that Voted the Earth was Flat".

> "The chairs, of uniform style, are upholstered in a material of bottle-green; and the colour combination of the room *in toto* has appealed to many (if not to all) as an unusually happy one."
>
> Colin Dexter, *The Remorseful Day*.

"In-toto Kitchens" is a firm specializing in supplying complete kitchens.

"Toto" is the name of Dorothy's dog in *The Wizard of Oz*, and it has been suggested that his name derives from the fact that he loves Dorothy completely, i.e. *in toto*.

In transitu
In transit

The phrase "in transit", now accepted as entirely English, is derived immediately from the Latin, the loss of the final "u" going almost unnoticed. However in law a "stoppage in transitu" allows a seller to snatch back goods which are on the way to a buyer whom the seller has just found out to be insolvent.

In vacuo
In a vacuum
> "The fault of [this speculative and indeterminate kind of study] is sometimes to produce a sort of lecturer *in vacuo*, ignorant of exact pursuits, and diffusive of vague words."
>
> W. Bagehot, "The First Edinburgh Reviewers".

"It is one thing to discuss *in vacuo* whether So-and-so will join us tonight, and another when So-and-So's honour is pledged to come…"

C. S. Lewis, "On Obstinacy in Belief".

The phrase is also used literally. The M.E.I. Students' Handbook lists the symbol C (= 2.998 x 10^8 m s^{-1}) as representing the speed of light *in vacuo*.

Invictus
Unconquered
Invictus is the heading given in *The Oxford Book of English Verse* to W. E. Henley's poem, "Out of the night that covers me,…"

"Invictus Locks and Security" operate within the hinterland of the Firth of Forth.

The feminine form of the adjective, *Invicta*, is the motto of the Kent Volunteer Fencibles.

In vinculis
Bound, in bondage
(Sir Alan Herbert took on) "bishops who tried to keep married couples *in vinculis*" (i.e. married).

Aubrey Anon, *The Guardian*.

A *vinculum* is a bond, in particular, the marriage bond: *a vinculo matrimonii* means "from the bond of matrimony". In mathematics, it is a horizontal line used in place of brackets: Newton used *vincula* rather than brackets in his mathematical writings. The vinculum survives today in the square root sign, so that $\sqrt{3^2 + 4^2}$ (= 5) is not the same as $\sqrt{3^2} + 4^2$ (= 19). The fraction bar also acts as a *vinculum* in that sometimes when we remove a fraction bar, we must replace it with brackets. For example, if we solve:

$$x = \frac{3}{x} - \frac{x-2}{x}$$

by multiplying both sides of the equation by *x*, we must write

$$x^2 = 3 - (x - 2)$$

as the next step in the solution.

A memorial to Sir Joseph Bazalgette stands in London on the Embankment which he built. It reads *Vincula flumini posuit*, which can be translated as "He set bounds to the river" or simply as "He bound the river".

In vino veritas

—Pliny, *Historia Naturalis*, ii, xiv. 141

In wine, truth, that is, *drunken men speak the truth*

In Vino Veritas is the title of a syndicated wine column by Jonathon Alsop, and the name of a Scottish Black Metal/Ambient band.

Just to keep the record straight, we should note that the phrase is distilled from the longer one which Pliny actually wrote: *volgoque veritas iam attributa vino est*—"truth in the popular mind has come to be credited to wine".

> "[The Greek restaurateur Sonny Boy] probably knows more secrets than any man in the community, for his martinis are a combination of truth serum and lie detector. *Veritas* is not only *in vino* but regularly batters its way out."
>
> John Steinbeck, *Sweet Thursday*.

> "*In vino veritas*, they say,
> Yet lying is so much the custom
> Of certain folk, the safest way
> Is, drunk or sober, not to trust 'em."—Anon.

In vitro

In a glass

In vitro fertilization of the human egg is fertilization outside the womb, leading to the birth of a "test-tube" baby. Generally, *in vitro* experiments are performed in a controlled environment using material removed from a living organism. Experiments made on parts of an organism which are still *in situ* are referred to as being *in vivo*, "in a living (situation)". Experiments made by computer simulation have been termed *in silico*.

We may even now be eating *"in-vitro* cultured meat", grown in laboratories from animal cells and by-passing the problems associated with the birth, nurture and slaughter of real animals.

Io

Joy

When at Christmas we sing the carol, "Ding, dong, merrily on high", we come at length to the lines "Let steeple bells be swungen, and 'Io', 'Io', 'Io', by priest and people sungen." Those singing "Io" are singing "Joy" in Latin. Technically they should be singing "Io!" which is "Joy!", where the exclamation mark is made up of the letters of Io set one over the other.

Cf. "quaestio" infra.

Ipsissima verba
The very same words

"Then Will said, like a barrister: 'I put it to you, that the Voices ordered you to plant things by the wayside *for such as have no gardens.*'… 'My God!' said Wollin. 'That's the *ipsissima verba.*'"

Rudyard Kipling, "Fairy-Kist".

"'She said the flowers were for Professor Vallar and I said surely she'd never met him and she said she hadn't but she –' '*Ipsissima verba*, please.' 'She said, "I've never met him…"'"

Iris Murdoch, *The Message to the Planet.*

Sometimes the phrase may act almost as a substitute for *sic* (*q.v.*).

"… he found himself somewhat surprised… when his Lordship pressed to be introduced to Claiborne's bagnio, since he had always supposed his Lordship insusceptible to the temptations of the flesh … but that his Lordship now appeared determined (*ipsissima verba*) to make up for lost time."

John Fowles, *A Maggot.*

Ipso facto
By that (very) fact

"Catriona was decidedly deficient in looks and brains and breeding, but her father was worth thirteen and a half million, and she was *ipso facto* a very attractive young lady."

Q. Q. Enwright, *Mistress and Maid.*

"Whatever the captain does is right, *ipso facto*, and any opposition to it is wrong, on board ship."

R. H. Dana, *Two Years Before the Mast.*

"The person in question is not a king or queen, because everything about such a person is *ipso facto* exceptional."

Barbara Tuchmann, *A Distant Mirror.*

Item
Also

This word was used originally to mark such components of a list as followed the first component. Subsequently it came to be used for the components (items) themselves.

The inventory of the property of Isaac Elliott of Woodbury in Devon who died in 1722 began with *Imprimis* (*q.v.*).

Imp[rimi]s His waring apparill and money in Hous £5
It[e]m in the chiching [kitchen] 3 brass Pans
2 brass pots and other chiching implements £12

There were twelve more lines in the inventory, each starting with "Item".

> OLIVIA: "… I will give out various schedules of my beauty; it shall be inventoried as, item, two lips, indifferent red; item, two grey eyes, with lids to them; item, one neck, one chin, and so forth…"
>
> Shakespeare, *Twelfth Night*, I, v.

Ius primae noctis
The right of the first night

The French *Droit de Seigneur* included *inter alia* the alleged right of the feudal lord to spend the first night of a vassal's marriage with his (*sc.* the vassal's) wife. Sadly for those to whose minds the story clearly has a certain appeal, there is apparently no firm evidence that such a practice ever existed.

> "There was also something called the *jus primae noctis*, which would probably not be mentioned in a textbook for children. It was the law by which every capitalist had the right to sleep with any woman working in one of his factories."
>
> George Orwell, *Nineteen Eighty-four*.

The "first night" need not be a nuptial one:

> "Simple mortals, accustomed to pay for their pleasures, are always impressed by the sight of a free ticket. The critic's *jus primae noctis* seems to them an enviable thing."
>
> Aldous Huxley, "Two or Three Graces".

J

Jupiter pluvius
Jupiter, the bringer of rain

Some poor devil has to take the blame for a prolonged period of wet weather.

L

Laborare est orare

To work is to pray (work is prayer)

Laborare est orare was the old motto of the Benedictine monks, and is also the title of a painting by John Roger Herbert (1810-1890) now in the Tate Gallery. It is also the motto of Gloucester Training College and of the London Borough of Willesden.

> "But he was damned if he'd do anything. Work, the gospel of work, the sanctity of work, *laborare est orare*,—all that tripe and nonsense."
>
> Aldous Huxley, *Point Counter Point*.

> "'The world has gone well with you, I am glad to hear and see.'
> '*Qui laborat, orat,*' [Who works, prays] said Hatton in a silvery voice, 'is the gracious maxim of our Holy Church, and I venture to believe my prayers and vigils have been accepted, for I have laboured in my time...'"
>
> Benjamin Disraeli, *Sybil*.

Ora Et Labora—"Pray and work"—is the name of a trawler (Z34) registered in Zeebrugge.

Labor omnia vincit

Work conquers all

This was the apt motto of Lord Attlee, Labour Prime Minister from 1945 to 1951. It is also the motto of a number of other families, and of Ashton-under-Lyne and of Bradford and of Cheltenham College and of the Royal Marsden Hospital, as well as of the State of Oklahoma.

In *Barchester Towers*, Anthony Trollope quotes a longer form of the phrase, *Labor omnia vincit improbus*—"Unceasing work conquers all", which appears in Virgil's *Georgics*.

119

Lachrimae Christi
The tears of Christ

Lachryma Christi—"Christ's tear", is the name of a sweet wine made from grapes grown on the slopes of Mount Vesuvius. (N.B. *Lachryma* is a mediaeval spelling of the Classical Latin *lacrima*.)

Lapis lazuli
The "lazulum stone"

A bright blue feldspathoid mineral, often flecked or streaked with gold, the best quality being mined in Afghanistan. The blue colour derives from constituent minerals such as lazurite and sodium aluminium silicate with some sulphur, while the flecks of gold indicate the presence of iron pyrites. The Late Latin word *lazulum* derives from the Persian "lajward", the source also of the word "azure".

Lapsus linguae
A slip of the tongue

"I'm sorry, darling, forgive me. When I called your mother an old *mat*, that was a *lapsus linguæ*. I meant to call her an old *bat*."

"There is nothing more illiberal than the ostentatious correction of an obvious *lapsus linguae*." Patrick O'Brian, *Desolation Island*. (Illiberal or not, the temptation to correct "boomkin nottings" to "bowsprit nettings" is understandable.)

We may also have *lapsus calami*, a slip of the pen, and *lapsus memoriæ*, a slip of the memory, these lapses being just as common in the young as in those in the clutches of *anno domini*.

(Now that so many of us write no longer with a pen but with a computer keyboard, it seems legitimate to add to the above list *lapsus digitis*—"a slip of the finger", or *lapsus claviaturæ*—" a slip of the keyboard". The Vatican has produced a lexicon of Latin words for modern artefacts and institutions, choosing *claviatura* for "keyboard", both for the piano and for the computer. The full list can be found in *Lexicon Recentis Latinitatis*, accessible through Wikipedia, "Ecclesiastical Latin".)

Lares et penates
Household gods

Lares et penates are those personal possessions which make up a "home". To the Romans *lares* were the household gods, often deified ancestors, with a guardian role, while *penates* were also deities, but with the function of bringing prosperity to the home and in particular of bringing into it a regular supply of food.

"They flit from furnished room to furnished room, transients for ever –... they carry their *lares et penates* in a band-box...."

> O. Henry, "The Furnished Room".

"In Grosvenor Square there were no Lares—no toys, no books, nothing but gold and grandeur, pomatum, powder and pride."

> Anthony Trollope, *The Way We Live Now*.

"I'm being good. I am aping the *fons et origo* of domestic virtue. If we had twins I'd call them Lares and Penates."

> Julian Barnes, *Talking It Over*.

Writing in *The Guardian* of the Aga stove, Matthew Fort suggested: "In a way, the Aga has become the contemporary equivalent of the *lares et penates*—household gods—of ancient Rome..."

Latet anguis in herba

—Virgil, *Eclogue* III, 93

A snake lurks in the grass

We may safely assume he or she does not lurk for any benevolent purpose, hence the pejorative flavour of the phrase "a snake in the grass".

Laus Deo

Praise be to God

On the aluminium cap atop the Washington Monument in Washington D.C., *Laus Deo* is written in letters barely six inches high. In Bourton-on-the-Water in Gloucestershire, above a doorway of an old building presumably with ecclesiastical connections in former times, these words appear as LAVS DEO. This doorway is now the entrance to public toilets.

Lente, lente currite, noctis equi

Slowly, oh run slowly, ye horses of the night

In *Doctor Faustus*, Christopher Marlowe puts these words into the mouth of Faustus as he awaits the hour when Mephistopheles will come to claim his soul. Ovid, in *Amores*, I, xiii. 39, wrote: *At si, quem malis, Cephalum complexa teneres, / Clamares: lente currite noctis equi*—"But if you held Cephalus, whom you favour, tight in your arms, you might call out: Run slowly, ye horses of the night". For Ovid's young lover, these words were a prayer to Time that his bliss might be prolonged; for Faustus they were a desperate supplication that his doom might be postponed.

Colin Dexter heads chapter 30 of *The Wench is Dead* with the words, *Lente currite, noctis equi!*

Lex talionis
The law of retaliation

This is the law of "like for like", exemplified in the Old Testament laws: "if any mischief follow, then thou shalt give life for life, eye for eye, tooth for tooth, hand for hand, foot for foot, burning for burning, wound for wound, stripe for stripe." Exodus xxii. 23-25.

Lex talionis is the name of a track on the album *Domus Mundi* by the Austrian symphonic black metal band Hollenthon.

As a sociology student I heard Professor Isaac Shapera describe how the same *lex talionis* held in many communities across the world, although it could be flexible. He had come across a case in which a man had killed another man from a different clan by accidentally falling on him from high up in a tree. Members of the dead man's clan were invited to try to exact revenge by dropping from the same tree while the guilty man walked up and down below. After a brief discussion and a quick vote, the aggrieved clan settled instead, *nem. con.*, for blood money to the value of three iron cooking pots and a goat.

Libra (£)
Pound

The literal meaning of *libra* is "scales", and this is the name of the seventh sign of the Zodiac. The name subsequently transferred to the weights used on the scales.

The £ which we now use as a symbol for the pound sterling is merely a capital L with one or two lines drawn across indicating that it is a unit of currency. Other currency symbols which have similar lines drawn across them are $ (dollars), ¢ (cents), € (euros), and ¥ (yen).

In old documents using Roman numerals, £20 was written as xx[li], and even after the use of modern numerals had become the norm, it was still common for £20 to be written as 20*l*. As late as 1849, Charlotte Brontë's *Shirley* records that: "When asked for money, Shirley rarely held back. She put down her name for 5*l*.: after the 300*l*. she had lately given,… it was as much as she could at present afford."

It was only recently that, seeing the sign £ on a price label on a stall in an Italian market, I realized that "lira" is the same word as "libra". Other countries which still use the pound (£) as their unit of currency, often a legacy of the British Empire (or of British occupation), include Egypt, Lebanon, Sudan, and Syria.

Libra (lb)
Pound

It is clear that "lb" is an contraction of *libra*. A pound in money terms was originally the value of a pound (avoirdupois) of silver.

Lingua franca
A general language

A *lingua franca* comes into being to make commerce possible between peoples whose native tongues are mutually unintelligible. The phrase is only superficially Latin, being coined in mediaeval Italy as a label for a trade jargon used in the Levant, but it is included here because *lingua* is Latin for "tongue". *Franca* referred to the Franks, a German tribe who founded France, and whose name became a synonym among the peoples of the Near East for Western Europeans, such as the Crusaders.

Latin itself was a *lingua franca* among scholars throughout Europe from the founding of the first universities until well into the nineteenth century.

For some modern authors the phrase is almost synonymous with "jargon":

> "Without ever leaving England, [Marco Pierre White] absorbed enough French kitchen *lingua franca* to convince Michelin he was the peer of Bocuse, Guérard, Robuchon, *et al.*"
>
> Book review in *The Guardian*.

A *lingua franca* does not have to be a spoken language. The website www.w3c.org contains the statement that "HTML [Hypertext Markup Language] is the *lingua franca* for publishing hypertext on the World Wide Web."

Litt.D. (Litterarum Doctor)
A Doctor of Letters or of Literature.

Many of our university degrees are still commonly expressed in Latin, and so their abbreviations read backwards. *Cf. M.B., M.D., Mus.Bac.*

Litterae humaniores
Human letters or literature

This phrase has given us the term "Humanities", as opposed to the "sciences", in schools and colleges. (*Humaniores* is in fact "more human".)

> "… people getting so excited about [words] they'll murder their neighbours for using a word they don't happen to like. A word that

probably doesn't mean as much as a good belch…. I don't know how you *litterae humaniores* boys manage to stand it."

Aldous Huxley, *After Many a Summer*.

Loco citato (loc. cit.)
In the place cited

In the course of writing, say, a magazine article, it may be necessary to quote from another article or book, giving the author, title, and page reference. A second reference to the same source can be given simply by mentioning the author's name followed by *loc. cit.* and the appropriate page number.

Vide also *"opere citato"* *infra*.

Locum (tenens)
A temporary replacement, someone "holding a place"

For most of us a locum is a doctor who stands in for our G. P. when he is on holiday, but the term may occasionally be applied to a stand-in for a clergyman or for a member of any other profession. (The teaching profession still sticks with "supply teacher".)

Locum tenens is the origin of the French phrase *lieu tenant*, and is used in Latin inscriptions, especially in epitaphs, for the military rank of Lieutenant.

Locus
A place

Not just a place, but a special place.

> "The movement of newspaper offices away from Fleet Street has given the Garrick [Club] new importance as a locus."
>
> *The Observer*.

Locus classicus
The stock example, the classic example

> "Our *locus classicus* (of the 'second wife' kind of affair) here was Sara Keays and Cecil Parkinson."
>
> Simon Hoggart, writing in *The Observer*.

> "On the night of the murder she [*sc.* the dead woman, but before she was murdered] had a client in bed with her, and if ever there was a *locus classicus* for what they call *coitus interruptus* [*q.v.*], this was it, because someone interrupted the proceedings."
>
> Colin Dexter, *The Remorseful Day*.

The phrase *splendide mendax*—"nobly untruthful" (*q.v. infra*) is held to be the *locus classicus* of an oxymoron; while it has been claimed that the *Huang Di Nei Jing* ("The Yellow Emperor's Inner Classic") is the *locus classicus* of Chinese medical theory and especially of acupuncture and moxibustion.

Locus standi

A place for standing, a right to interfere

> "Before he engages in further criticism of the organization's actions, he ought to take a very close look at his *locus standi*."
>
> Financial report.

Sometimes it appears to be used to mean status:

> "It's bad for one's *locus standi* to live on a woman's charity."
>
> Iris Murdoch, *Under the Net*.

Also the right to bring an action or an appeal before a court.

Locus standi has been proposed as the most fitting Latin translation for a "car parking space".

Loquitur

Speaks

> "'If,' he was told, 'you could be alarmed into the semblance of modesty, you would charm everybody; but remember my joke against you,' (Sydney Smith *loquitur*)…"
>
> W. Bagehot, "The First Edinburgh Reviewers".

Under the pseudonym of "Brunette Coleman", Philip Larkin wrote a poem called "Fourth Former *loquitur*".

Lucifer

The light-bearer

"Lucifer" is the planet Venus when it is the morning star. (As the evening star it becomes "Hesper".) Also one of the names of Satan, acquired allegedly by a mistaken translation in Isaiah xiv. 12; "How art thou fallen from heaven, O Lucifer, son of the morning!"

A "lucifer" was a pre-safety match, referred to in the First World War song "Pack up your troubles in your old kitbag": "While you've a lucifer to light your fag, smile, boys, that's the style!"

Lustrum
A period of five years

A *lustrum* was a purificatory sacrifice made on behalf of the Roman people every five years, the use of the term being extended to indicate the lapse of the equivalent amount of time. The Roman people purified themselves in the interim by frequent washing, as did our own Queen Elizabeth I, who is said to have taken a bath once a year whether she needed it or not.

> "The sacred flame of curiosity burns dimmer and dimmer as lustrum is added to lustrum in human life, but it is never extinguished."
>
> > "The Circus at Olympia", *Manchester Guardian*, November 1889 (*sic*).

Lustrum was anglicized to "lustre". In *Roundabout Papers*, Thackeray says: "Was there not a Lord Orville in your case too? As you think of him eleven lustres pass away." ("On a Peal of Bells".)

Lusus naturae
A freak of nature

A famous *lusus naturæ* was the "vegetable lamb", said by Sir John Mandeville to be rooted to the ground by a thick stem growing from its belly.

"*Lusus naturæ*" could be a useful phrase to use when one wishes to circumvent the many restrictions on describing in pejorative terms anyone who is clearly not 100% *compos mentis*, but please note that this publication is nothing if not politically correct.

> "A 'woman of intellect' it appeared, was a sort of 'lusus naturæ', a luckless accident, wanted neither as wife nor worker."
>
> > Charlotte Brontë, *Villette*.

> "'But dwarfs,' he read, 'he held in abhorrence as *lusus naturae* and of evil omen.'"
>
> > Aldous Huxley, *Chrome Yellow*.

Lusus is a fourth declension noun, as is *apparatus* (*q.v.*), and takes the ending *–us* in both the singular and the plural (nominative). Its literal meaning is "sport" or "a game", and *lusus naturæ* is one of nature's little jokes.

Lux Mundi

The light of the world

The light of the world manifests itself in a multitude of persons. But although we read in St. Matthew's Gospel, v. 14: *Vos estis lux mundi*—"Ye are the light of the world", it is more usual to assign the title "The Light of the World" to Christ himself since in John viii. 12 we have: *Ego sum lux mundi*—"I am the light of the world".

"The Light of the World" is the title of a painting of Christ by William Holman Hunt.

Lux Mundi is the name of an American firm producing oil-burning rechargeable candles for use in churches.

M

Macte nova virtute puer, sic itur ad astra
—Virgil, *Aeneid*, ix. 641
God speed thy youthful valour, boy, in this way one attains to the stars
Or "Go on as you have begun, etc."

The Trojans led by Aeneas are camped near the mouth of the Tiber and are being taunted by Numanus, one of the besieging force, who casts doubts on their manhood. Aeneas' son, Ascanius, draws his bow from within the camp and transfixes Numanus through the skull with the arrow. Apollo, who has witnessed the feat from a passing cloud, speaks the above words in congratulating Ascanius on his marksmanship.

Had the film "The Way to the Stars" been made in ancient Rome, it might well have been called *Sic itur ad astra*.

Macte Virtute is the motto of the families of Hollins and Murray-Graham, and of the 3rd Battalion, 16th Field Artillery, while *Macte Virtute Esto* is the Lowndes family motto. *Sic Itur ad Astra* is the motto of Essex Girls' High School and of the families of Carnac, Kerry and MacKenzie of Glen Muick.

Magna Carta
The Great Charter

Otherwise known as Magna Charta, this was obtained, some say extorted, by the barons from King John at Runnymede in 1215. Its aim was to shield the customary privileges and interests of the baronial class from attack by the Crown, the implication being that there was a law to which even the monarch was subject. Later the name came to embody the idea that everyone was entitled to the protection offered by the law of the land.

Addressing his fellow-jurors in the television episode of "Hancock's Half Hour" called "Twelve Angry Men", Hancock famously asked, "Does Magna Carta mean nothing to you? Did she die in vain?"

Magna cum laude
With great praise

This is slightly less praiseworthy than *summa cum laude* (*q.v.*) but definitely more praiseworthy than just plain *cum laude*.

> "The tour leader was pleased with the way the session had gone. Lots of good questions, with both Sheila Williams and Cedric Downes acquitting themselves *magna cum laude...*"
>
> Colin Dexter, *The Jewel that was Ours*.

Magna est veritas et praevalet
—I Esdras iv. 41
Great is Truth and mighty above all things

Magna est veritas et praevalet is the title of a 2002 painting, oil on canvas, by Don Lewallen.

Magna est Veritas is the Magnay family motto, while *Veritas Magna est* is the motto of the Jephson family. It is not clear and in any case doesn't in the least matter whether the mottoes are part of the above quotation or of the one below.

Magna est veritas et praevalebit
—T.Brooks: *The Crown and Glory of Christianity* (1662)
Great is truth and shall prevail

> "'But what did the poor devil believe himself? Truth shall prevail—don't you know. *Magna est veritas et...* Yes, when it gets a chance.'"
>
> Joseph Conrad, *Lord Jim*.

Coventry Patmore called one of his short poems "Magna est Veritas"; it ends:

> "For want of me the world's course will not fail:
> When all its work is done, the lie shall rot;
> The truth is great, and shall prevail,
> When none cares whether it prevail or not."

Magnificat
It (my soul) praises

> *Magnificat anima mea Dominum*—"My soul doth praise the Lord"
>
> —Luke i. 46 *et seq.*

The words of the Virgin Mary *in re* the annunciation by the archangel Gabriel, and addressed to her cousin Elisabeth who was herself then six months pregnant with John the Baptist.

Magni nominis umbra
The shadow of a great name

Or perhaps possibly "the black sheep of the family". This is the name of a track on the album *Domus Mundi* by the Austrian symphonic black metal band Hollenthon. It is also the name of a group of young people in the Philippines devoted to community service, and the motto of the King Edward VII School in Taiping, Perak.

Magnum
Large

Used chiefly in tandem with *opus* (*q.v. infra*), but also used to indicate the particular size, traditionally two quarts, of a bottle of wine or spirits. It is most familiarly linked to champagne. Two magnums make a "tappit hen", a "jeroboam" is two tappit hens, and a "rehoboam" is two jeroboams and so holds four gallons.

Magnum in parvo
Much in a small space
*Cf. "**multum in parvo**" infra.*

Magnum opus
A great work

"The writing and the printing of this *Magnum Opus* had been going on as long as she could remember. All her childhood long Uncle Henry's History had been a vague and fabulous thing, often heard of and never seen."

Aldous Huxley, *Chrome Yellow.*

Note that the plural of *opus* (*q.v.*) is *opera*, which has its own special meaning in English writing and speech. The plural of *magnum opus* in Latin is *magna opera*, which is at best unwieldy and at worst not clearly linked to its singular form; and so we can really do no better than to speak of "magnum opuses" when referring to more than one.

Malleus Monachorum
The Hammer of the Monks

"Thomas Cromwell (in his youth better known as the *Malleus Monachorum*)…"

Samuel Butler, *The Way of All Flesh.*

Edward I (1239-1307) was known as "The Hammer of the Scots". His tomb in Westminster Abbey reads: "*Edwardus Primus Scotorum Malleus hic est*".

Mandamus
We command
A command issued by a higher court to a lower.

> "It seems that... the Imperor [Nero] had mandamused the Impress wid a divorce suit, and Misses Poppæa, a cilibrated lady, was ingaged, widout riferences, as housekeeper at the palace."
> O. Henry, "The Door of Unrest".

Manet
He remains
A stage direction opposed to *exit*—"he leaves", *q.v.* The plural is *manent*. It is a direction which needs to be strictly adhered to, otherwise the theatre audience may well be left facing an empty stage for an indefinite length of time while rapidly losing the thread of the plot.

Mare nostrum
Our sea
To the Romans the Mediterranean was "Our Sea", since the Roman Empire at its greatest extent included all its coastline. When Italy entered the Second World War in June 1940, Benito Mussolini claimed the Mediterranean Sea for Italy under the title *Il Mare Nostrum*. It was Gabriele D'Annunzio (1863-1938) who had coined this revised phrase, giving it an Italian definite article, in the course of urging the development of the Italian Navy as an instrument of Italian colonial expansion into Africa.

Maritae suae
To his wife
The heading of a poem, "Of all the flowers rising now", by William Philpott in *The Oxford Book of English Verse*.

Mater
Mother
Familiar to all readers of (public) school stories as the usual word for referring to or addressing one's mother: "I must write to the mater tonight"—*passim*. My wife uses a number of Devon dialect words in her everyday speech and very little Latin, but she frequently addressed her mother as "Mater".

> Vivie: "How do, mater. Mr Praed's been here this half-hour, waiting for you."
> G. B. Shaw, *Mrs Warren's Profession*, Act 1.

"Mater is not 'frantic'. Only the prospect of the decanter running dry could make Mater frantic."

David Mitchell, *Cloud Atlas*.

Mater dolorosa

The sorrowing mother

Specifically Christ's mother standing at the foot of the cross.

In *The Oxford Book of English Verse* William Barnes' poem "I'd a dream tonight / As I fell asleep" is given the heading *Mater Dolorosa*.

Mater Dolorosa is the title of a painting (oil on oak) from the workshops of Dirk Bouts, *c.* 1470, now in the National Gallery.

Vide also *"stabat mater dolorosa..." infra.*

Materfamilias

Mother of a family

The better half of the *paterfamilias* (*q.v.*), and who was in charge of the domestic side of Roman family affairs. She had not the legal powers of her husband but it is unthinkable that she was not still a force to be reckoned with.

"Ian Talbot has attracted a famous personage to his company. Yes, Jerry Hall plays the materfamilias, Mother Lord,... She is tall, elegant, nice, and smiles big smiles."

Theatre review of *High Society* in *The Times*.

Matre pulchra filia pulchrior

—Horace, *Odes* I, xvi. 1

Fairer daughter of a fair mother

(Horace in fact begins his ode by addressing the daughter—*O... filia pulchrior...*)

"Faith, the beauty of *filia pulcrior* (*sic*) drove *pulcram* (*sic*) *matrem* out of my head! and yet as I came down the river, and thought about the pair, the pallid dignity and exquisite grace of the matron had the uppermost, and I thought her even more noble than the virgin."

W. M. Thackeray, *Henry Esmond*.

Maxima debetur puero reverentia

—Juvenal, *Satires* xiv. 47

The utmost reverence is due to a child

That is to say, a child's innocence (whenever it can be found) is to be respected at all times.

"'*Maxima debetur pueris*', says Jones (a fellow of very kind feeling…), and writing on his card to Hoskins, hinted to him that a boy was in the room, and a gentleman who was quite a greenhorn; hence that the songs had better be carefully selected."

W. M. Thackeray, *The Newcombes*.

(The speaker uses the plural *pueris*, "to children".)

M.B. (Medicinae Baccalaureus)
Bachelor of Medicine

A physician who is a Bachelor of Medicine is nonetheless entitled to call himself "Doctor". Clearly the word *Baccalaureus* gives the French their word "Baccalaureat", which however is an educational qualification at a lower level than our Bachelor's degree.

M.D. (Medicinae Doctor)
Doctor of Medicine

Mea culpa
—from the Mass
Through my fault

This phrase, repeated, comes in the Public Confession in the Mass, following the words: *Peccavi nimis cogitatione, verbo, et opere*—"I have sinned exceedingly in thought, word and deed". Then: *Mea culpa, mea culpa, mea maxima culpa*—"through my fault, through my fault, through my most grievous fault."

Richard Brooks wrote in *The Observer* of a former government economic adviser who had suspicions that his advice in the past had helped create unemployment: "Budd's *mea culpa*, admirable in principle, may not go down so well with the jobless".

"But Oliver used to be called Nigel. *Mea culpa, mea maxima culpa.* Or rather, not. Or rather, Thanks, Mum."

Julian Barnes, *Talking It Over*.

The negative of *mea culpa* is *mea non culpa* or "Don't blame me!" "Slater's *mea non culpa* was ghosted by an Australian rock journalist, Jeff Apter, and reads at times like one of those self-mortification memoirs beloved of showbiz figures, lacking only a visit to the Betty Ford Clinic." Gideon Haigh, *Silent Revolutions*.

In *The Bell*, Iris Murdoch, no doubt with St. Augustine or Book XII of Paradise Lost or the Catholic service for Holy Saturday in mind, uses the phrase *felix culpa*—"joyous fault": "… the joys of repentance,… the delicious pleasure of… grovelling in the dust. *O felix culpa!*"

Media vita in morte sumus
—The Book of Common Prayer
In the midst of life we are in death
This is part of the service for the burial of the dead, recited at the graveside. *Media Vita in Morte Sumus* is the name of a Mass by Nicholas Gombert (*fl.* 1540), and also the title of a Danish horror film of 1993 directed by Nina Powers-Bates.

Medio de fonte leporum
Surgit amari aliquid quod in ipsis floribus angat
—Lucretius, *De Rerum Natura*, iv. 1133
From the depths of this fountain of delights wells up some bitter taste which chokes them even amid the flowers
S. T. Coleridge uses the first seven of these words as the preface to his cautionary poem of "Julia", in which a too-ardent lover kneels heavily before Julia, not noticing that her lap-dog is at her feet.

> "'A pity that Bingley is flourishing like a green what-is-it, but one can't have everything.'
> 'No, sir. *Medio de fonte leporum surgit amari aliquid in ipsis floribus angat.*'"
> P. G. Wodehouse, *Much Obliged, Jeeves.*

> "Yes, indeed, it was a delightful little holiday; it lasted a whole week. With the exception of that little pint of *aliquid amari* at Rotterdam, we were all very happy."
> W. M. Thackeray, *Roundabout Papers.*

> "It was more than he had ever had… so why was there something as yet undefined beneath his exultation, the *aliquid amari* of his schooldays?"
> Patrick O'Brian, *Master and Commander.*

Byron worked the lines into "Childe Harold's Pilgrimage":

> "Full from the fount of Joy's delicious springs,
> Some bitter o'er the flowers its bubbling venom flings."

Amari Aliquid is the name of the Viskr Aspect of the Kumoti (Wyld) Faction of the Ananasi werespiders.

Membrum virile

The "virile member", the penis

"... there are times when it seems to me that nothing short of a radical ablation of the *membrum virile* would answer, in this case."

Patrick O'Brian, Master and Commander.

"'[Doctor Swain]'s considered quite a competent quack, they tell me.' 'To be honest, I thought he was a bit of a...' 'Bit of a *membrum virile*? You're not always wrong, you know,...'"

Colin Dexter, The Jewel that was Ours.

Membrum virile (pronounced as three syllables (vi–ri–le, *cf. recipe*) might be a useful euphemism to add to the vocabulary of anyone who, like Morse in the extract above, (and like the present author), hesitates through a certain (prudish?) delicacy to use the word "pr–ck".

Memento

A keepsake, a reminder

This is often misspelled "momento", through a failure to associate it with the word "memory". *Memento mei*—"Remember me"—is the motto of the L'Estrange family.

Memento hominem te

Remember (thou art) a man

That is, mortal rather than immortal or divine. When a Roman General was enjoying his triumphal parade, he was accompanied by a slave whose duty it was to whisper in his ear from time to time: *Respice post te: hominem memento te*—"Look behind you: remember you're a man."

Kate Kellaway, writing in *The Observer* and reviewing the work of Allen Kurzweil, in particular, "A Case of Curiosities", says of a glass box and its contents: "It's a *memento hominem* which, 'rather than proclaiming mortality, registers a life'".

Hominem et esse memento, meaning much the same as *hominem memento*, is the motto of the Wybergh family.

Memento mori

Remember you must die

A "memento" is now simply a reminder, perhaps of a friend or of a holiday. A *memento mori*, a reminder of death, often took the form of a skull or skulls on the border of a memorial to a dead person. *Memento mori* has no obvious plural: consider the following extract as an example of how the phrase is used as its own plural: "Hundreds of tiny skeletons, skulls and bones are on show… These *memento mori* are bought and displayed throughout Mexico on All Souls' Day…." Dr C. Helman, writing in *The Observer Magazine*.

In the midst of life we are occasionally in death:

> "(Bidlake) could not remember having spoken to her more than three or four times in all the quarter of a century which had turned Mary Betterton into a *memento mori*."
>
> Aldous Huxley, *Point Counter Point*.

Memento mori is the motto of the Trappists, and the title of a novel by Muriel Spark.

Memorabilia

Things easy to remember

Specifically things which belonged to or were written about or which referred to a person, by which he or she is remembered. The person need not be dead:

> "The sigh of midnight trains in empty stations,
> Silk stockings tossed aside, dance invitations.
> These foolish things remind me of you."
>
> Eric Maschwitz

Robert Browning wrote a poem called *Memorabilia*.

In fact the "person" may not even actually have lived. A television game contestant was described as a "collector of Winnie-the-Pooh memorabilia", and the collectors of railway memorabilia are legion.

Memorandum

(Something) to be remembered

Often shortened to "memo". The plural is "memoranda".

Mens sana in corpore sano
A sound mind in a sound body
  *Vide "**orandum est**" infra*

Meum et tuum
Mine and yours
  A gentle reminder that one should not steal.

> "This friend was the gamekeeper, a fellow of a loose kind of
> disposition, and who was thought not to entertain much stricter
> notions concerning the difference between *meum* and *tuum* than the
> young gentleman himself."
>
> Henry Fielding, *Tom Jones*.

> "We know from Marlborough's story that the bravest man and
> greatest military genius is not always brave or successful in his
> battles with his wife; that some of the greatest warriors have
> committed errors in accounts and the distribution of *meum* and
> *tuum*."
>
> W. M. Thackeray, *Philip*.

> "To the old such plots and plans, such matured schemes for
> obtaining the goods of this world without the trouble of earning
> them, such long-headed attempts to convert 'tuum' into 'meum',
> are the ways of life to which they are accustomed."
>
> Anthony Trollope, *Barchester Towers*.

Miles gloriosus
The braggart soldier
  Miles Gloriosus was a stock character in drama from ancient Greek times
through to the Commedia dell'arte. It is the title of a comedy by the Roman
playwright Plautus (*fl.* 210-200 B.C.), almost certainly based on a Greek
original. Plautus' hero/villain was called Pyrgopolynices, and was the
prototype for any one of the blustering blackguards to be found on, for
example, the Elizabethan stage.
  Writing in *The Guardian* of any incompetent author who wishes to be taken
seriously, James Fenton says: "… we quietly refuse to grant him his wish.
We put him in some other less welcome category: that of the comic show-
off, the *miles gloriosus* or boastful soldier of the old drama."

Minutiae
Details, the small print
"He fancies that you are acquainted with all which is great and important, and he dwells... upon that which is small and unimportant. The curious *minutiæ*, so elaborately set forth, are quite useless...."

W. Bagehot, "Lady Mary Wortley Montague".

"It may be worth remarking, among the *minutiæ* of my collection, that Johnson was once drawn to serve in the militia,..."

James Boswell, *The Life of Samuel Johnson, LL.D.*

Mirabile dictu
Wonderful to relate
The phrase can be used to indicate surprise, or to mean "surprise, surprise".

"In the first place, *mirabile dictu*, there were one or two even greater duffers than I on the Abbey cricket field."

E. W. Hornung, *Raffles*.

"And in any case, 5C weren't all that bad, really, and she, Julia Stevens, *mirabile dictu*, was one of the few members of staff who could handle that motley and unruly crowd."

Colin Dexter, *The Daughters of Cain*.

John Naughton, writing in *The Observer*, says: "Here she entertains her brutal lover who—*mirabile dictu*—turns out to be one of the [Ministry of Defence] battle-order chappies." The reverse side of the coin is *horribile dictu*—"terrible to relate".

In *The Guardian*, John Crace reported that "Stephen Fry... managed to casually bump into both Sting and Morgan Freeman—*mirabile dictu!*—on his potter around the US".

Miserere mihi!
Woe is me!
This phrase may possibly (and understandably) be confused with *Miserere mei*—"Have mercy on me", the opening words of Psalm li, which is the text of Gregorio Allegri's well-known "*Miserere*". "*Miserere Mihi*" is the title of a motet for six voices composed jointly by William Byrd and Thomas Tallis.

Cf. "**ei mihi**" *supra.*

Missa

Missa brevis. *A short Mass*

Missa solemnis, *High Mass*

Mobile vulgus

The common herd, the rabble

Or, in cut-down form, "the mob". Equivalent to the Greek *hoi polloi*— "the people", but still a cut above *faex populi* (*q.v.*). *Vulgus* designates the common people, *mobile* implies that they are swift to shift their affections, as do the Roman mob in *Julius Caesar*, III, ii.

Mobile Vulgus is the title of a book by Christian Nold which looks at how corporate action by the people can be made effective in the face of total state policing.

Modus operandi (M.O.)

The way of working

Inter alia, a well-known guide to the identification of a criminal, who betrays himself by the manner in which he commits his crimes, although the use of the term is not restricted to the criminal classes.

> "The corpse was missing an arm, a leg, and an ear, and the words "Watford United" had been carved on its back *post mortem* with a sharp instrument. It did not take Detective Superintendent Cartwright long to recognise the *modus operandi* of the East Basingstoke serial killer".
>
> Q. Q. Enwright, *Mistress and Maid*.

> "What it did throw light on was my fascination with a woman whose characteristics and whose *modus operandi* were precisely the opposite of those which delineated Angela."
>
> Anita Brookner, *Altered States*.

> The plural of *modus* is *modi*. "I sit at the piano, Ayrs on the divan, smoking his vile Turkish cigarettes, and we adopt one of our three *modi operandi*."
>
> David Mitchell, *Cloud Atlas*.

The phrase can also be used impersonally. Joanna Slaughter, writing in *The Observer* of the Access fund to help students with no money, said: "… the arithmetic of this exercise has always been suspect and its *modus operandi* appears close to disastrous."

Modus vivendi

A way of living (together)

Any two people who choose to live together have to arrive at a mutual accommodation which takes into account inevitable differences in personal taste and opinions. In short, they establish (with luck) a *modus vivendi*. Any two or more political parties attempting to form a coalition have to sink their differences and establish a common ground: they also have to find a *modus vivendi*."

David Bell, reviewing a biography of François Mitterand in *The Guardian*, said that Mitterand "implemented austerity policies [and] sought a *modus vivendi* with French business…"

> "It was not exactly that he had pressed and she had invited. They had simply simultaneously discovered a relaxed and cheerful *modus vivendi* together."
>
> Iris Murdoch, *The Message to the Planet*.

Anthony Burgess, writing in *The Observer*, says: "(Angus) Wilson's novels are all about the need to construct a *modus vivendi* in a moral vacuum."

However, the phrase has been used in a different sense. In Colin Dexter's *The Remorseful Day*, we read of Morse's "resumption of his erstwhile *modus vivendi*", making the phrase synonymous with "life style".

Modus Vivendi is the name of a Greek manufacturer of men's underwear.

Mons Veneris

The Mount of Venus

There are three Mounts of Venus on the human (female) body. Two are on the hands, at the base of each thumb; the third (and the one which probably most commonly springs to mind) is a fatty elevation on the pubic symphysis.

> "People will insist," [Mary] used to say, "on treating the *mons Veneris* as though it were Mount Everest. Too silly."
>
> Aldous Huxley, *Eyeless in Gaza*.

Mons Veneris became "Venusberg" in German, and although presumably still a mountain of sorts, was the subterranean home of Venus. Tannhäuser found his way there and spent a year *in situ* worshipping the goddess.

Mons Veneris is the name of a Portuguese Black Metal band.

Mors janua vitae

Death is the gateway of life

This encouraging phrase appears in John Buchan's *The Thirty-Nine Steps*. The narrator, Richard Hannay, has just met Digby, *alias* Scudder, who observes that his friends hadn't yet played their last card. They had the ace up their sleeves, and unless Digby could keep alive for a month they were going to play it and win. "'But I thought you were dead,' I put in. *'Mors janua vitae,'* he smiled."

Janua is a word for "door" associated with Janus, the god of beginnings, whence our word "January". *Vide* "***facilis descensus Averno***" *supra.*

Mors janua vitae is the title of a tomb by Alfred Gilbert in the Royal College of Surgeons in London, and is also the motto of H.M.S. Valhalla.

Multum in parvo

Much in a small space

An example which comes to mind is a Swiss Army penknife.

O. Henry, in "The Hand that Riles the World", speaks, tongue in cheek, of "a combination steak-beater, shoe-horn, marcel-waver, monkey wrench, nail file, potato masher and Multum in Parvo tuning fork".

Multum in Parvo is the motto of Rutland, the smallest county in England (smallest except at high tide when the Isle of Wight is fractionally smaller). It is also the name of an 1880's lawn mower made by the firm of Green.

A bronze sculpture of a pug dog by Louise Peterson has the title *Multum in Parvo*. The Connecticut firm of Pugsplace offer items of clothing such as a "*Multum in Parvo* Pug Hoodie" for humans and a "*Multum in Parvo* tee-shirt" for dogs.

Mus.Bac. (Musicae baccalaureus)

Bachelor of Music

Mutatis mutandis

With necessary changes

> "[The couplet is said to refer to Queen Elizabeth having got over her grand climacteric safely.] The dictionary-meaning has, as nearly always, *something* to do with the real meaning, but not more than the 'anecdote' of a picture has to do with its design. And it is the same with prose, *mutatis mutandis*."
>
> George Orwell, "New Words".

"A young girl… in a dark serge skirt… disclosing a pair of work-manlike rubber boots, which, mutatis mutandis, were very like those Davies was wearing."

Erskine Childers, *The Riddle of the Sands*.

The writer of the piece below refers to a comment that it was no matter that a group of artists had an insufficient grasp of the rules of their craft— indeed that many of them really did not know much about painting at all.

"Imagine this observation applied, *mutatis mutandis*, to a bricklayer or an airline pilot."

N. Jarrett, *Observer Magazine*.

Mutatis Mutandis is the name of a "collaborative online roleplaying environment" and of a theatre company run by David Whiteley in Ottawa.

Mutato nomine de te fabula narratur
—Horace, *Satires*, I, i. 69
Change the name and the story applies to yourself

Mutato nomine is an "ablative absolute" like *mutatis mutandis* (*supra*), and translates as "The name having been changed". The phrase in Horace is prefaced by the words: *Quid rides?*—"Why do you laugh?" The amused listener to the tale could well himself be the butt of the joke therein.

The tale need not be humorous. "'*De te fabula narratur*,' I said to myself, and I wondered if those pages did not already contain the story of future events in store for me." Umberto Eco, *The Name of the Rose*.

N

Nemine contradicente (nem. con.)

No one contradicting

Used in the House of Commons, and in any number of lesser gatherings, to signify that a vote was carried unanimously. The corresponding phrase in the House of Lords was/is *"Nemine dissentiente"* (*Nem. diss.*)—"No one dissenting".

"The motion is that as directors we all accept a productivity bonus of thirty per cent of our stipends. All those in favour?… All those against?… Thank you. Carried nem. con." (Minutes of any board meeting.)

Nemo me impune lacessit

None shall provoke me with impunity

This is the motto of the kings of Scotland and of all Scottish regiments. It is the motto of the Order of the Thistle, and also of the Nettles family, which if one thinks about it seems appropriate. The phrase is engraved around the edge of the Scottish pound coin, the coin itself bearing the impression of a thistle.

Nemo me impune lacessit appeared as the motto of a seal on a $20 bill issued in Georgia in 1778, although here the threat was not from a mere plant but from a rattlesnake.

Cf. ***"donat habere viro decus et tutamen…"*** *supra.*

Ne plus ultra

No more, no further, the ultimate

Literally "no more beyond"—*vide* **"ultra"** *infra*. It can be argued that Marilyn Monroe was the *ne plus ultra* of twentieth-century pin-up girls, with Betty Grable just failing to keep abreast of her.

J. Sams, writing in *The Observer*, says: "*Semiramide* is the *ne plus ultra* of *opera seria*, a great, neo-classical edifice built of everything that Rossini had learned."

"'Well, if this isn't the fair nefus ultra!' articulated the sergeant."
Ernest Bramah, "The Holloway Flat Tragedy".

Tradition has it that the twin Pillars of Hercules, situated at the Straits of Gibraltar and marking the westward boundary of the classical world, were joined by a scroll bearing the legend *Ne Plus Ultra*. An issue of a Spanish silver dollar in 1563 displayed the two pillars linked by such a scroll, and it is said that this design was simplified to give the familiar symbol for a dollar, $ (now drawn with one or with two vertical lines).

Nescit vox missa reverti
—Horace, *Ars Poetica*, 390
The published word can never be recalled
Literally, "a voice sent forth knows not how to return". Horace addressed his *Ars Poetica* to Piso and his family, and is here advising Piso's eldest son to refrain from rushing too precipitously into print (or, in those days, into manuscript). A safe interval in which to give full opportunity for second thoughts between writing and publishing would be something like nine years.

"He was gone; and Morse knew, within a second of his going, that he would not be forgiving himself easily for such monumental ingratitude. But the damage was done: *nescit vox missa reverti*."
Colin Dexter, *The Wench is Dead*.

In his edition of A. E. Housman's collected poems and selected prose, Christopher Ricks notes that in 1955 Tom Burns Haber published some of Housman's manuscript poems in violation of Housman's will and with a number of mistranscriptions. "The dust, as is its way. has since settled. And here too *Nescit vox missa reverti*, the voice sent forth can never be recalled."
Nescit vox missa reverti is the motto of the Halsey family.
A variant of this *sententia* is *Nescit semen missum reverti*, which prompted the search for an effective morning-after pill.

Ne sit ancillae tibi amor pudori
—Horace, *Odes*, II, iv. 1
Do not be ashamed of your love for a serving-maid
Serving-maids are a *sine qua non* of any happy household and my regret is that my own family has never been able to afford one, not even part-time. They were frequently and unashamedly held by their masters to be a

legitimate object of affection. Robert Louis Stevenson wrote a poem ("There's just a twinkle in your eye") with the title *Ne sit ancillæ tibi amor pudori*, addressed to a "graceful housemaid, tall and fair".

> "Well, if I asked you to stay *here*, I should never hear the last of it from Rhoda. She's a little cracked, of course, but the soul of devotion and capable of anything. *Ne sit ancillae*, you know."
>
> Rudyard Kipling, "My Son's Wife".

Ne supra crepidam sutor iudicaret

—Pliny, *Historia Naturalis*, II, xxxv. 85

The cobbler should not judge above his sandal

Or "The cobbler should stick to his last". The renowned Greek artist Apelle was happy to be guided by a cobbler as to the correct representation of a shoe in one of his paintings, but issued this mild rebuke (in Greek) when the cobbler began to offer advice on details of the painting which concerned bits of anatomy other than feet.

Nil admirari

—Horace, *Epistles* I, iv. 1

To wonder at nothing

Horace says that finding that nothing is to be wondered at, is the only thing that can make a man happy and keep him so. This is nonchalance carried to extremes.

> "'It's pretty, Miss Harriet,' said Mick, looking up at the ceiling with a careless, *nil admirari* glance."
>
> Benjamin Disraeli, *Sybil*.

> "Very many men nowadays... adopt or affect to adopt, the *nil admirari* doctrine; but nevertheless to judge from their appearance, they are just as subject to sudden emotions as their grandfathers and grandmothers were before them."
>
> Anthony Trollope, *Barchester Towers*.

> "The Empress of Blandings was a pig who took things as they came. Her motto, like Horace's, was *nil admirari*."
>
> P. G. Wodehouse, *Uncle Fred in the Springtime*.

Nil admirari is the motto of, *inter alias*, the Bolingbroke and Carew families.

In 2003 Dorothy Farson gave the title *nil admirari* ("to be excited about nothing") to a picture in watercolour and charcoal on Sennelier paper.

Nil desperandum Teucro duce et auspice Teucro
—Horace, *Odes*, I, vii. 27
We must not despair, with Teucer to lead us and under Teucer's star
The speaker was Teucer himself, desperately trying to cheer up his friends following his banishment from Salamis by his father. It can be loosely translated as "Have no fear, Teucer's here".

A horse called *Nil Desperandum* was placed sixth in the Aintree Grand National of 2005. *Nil Desperandum* is also the title of a 1904 poem by Abdullah Quilliam: "Courage, brother! do not falter".

Nil Desperandum is the motto of H.M.S. *Dauntless* and of a number of families including those of Anson, Hedley Dent, Walker of Teignmouth and Williams of Tregullow.

Auspice Teucro is the motto of the Tucker family.

Variants of the phrase such as *Nil carborundum* are of later date. During the Second World War U. S. General Joseph "Vinegar Joe" Stilwell adopted as his motto *Illegitimis Non Carborundum*, translated loosely as "Don't let the bastards grind you down".

Nil satis nisi optimum
Nothing but the best is good enough
This is the motto of Everton Football Club.

Nisi
Unless
Familiar from the (now obsolete) legal term "decree nisi", implying that "all will be well unless…" In divorce cases this usually meant that the party wanting the divorce in the first place had to behave properly and circumspectly for the next six months if the decree was to be made "absolute": once this was done, the new happy couple could get together and celebrate freely and in safety. It was in a way the opposite of a cooling-off period.

Noctes ambrosianae
Ambrosian nights, delightful nights
In the 1820's and 1830's *Blackwood's Magazine* printed a series of dialogues under this title and under the authorship of "Christopher North" (John Wilson). The title was given to the dialogues apparently because they had originated in conversations held in Ambrose's Tavern, Edinburgh.

However the phrase seems since to have acquired sybaritic connotations, with the homeliness of Ambrose's Tavern overshadowed by the glamour of "ambrosia".

Ambrosia was the food of the gods on Olympus, conferring immortality on those who ate it. (Nectar was their drink, and, in place of blood, ichor flowed in their veins. It was, incidentally, considered unwise to eat any dead god one might stumble across, since ichor was said to be poisonous to mortals.) Hence "Ambrosian" carries a hint of carefree nights spent talking, eating and drinking, with little awareness of the impermanence of youth.

> "Altogether it was a very different story from the old festive, unsuspected, club and cricket days, with their *noctes ambrosianæ* at the Albany."
>
> E. W. Hornung, *Raffles.*

Nolens volens
Unwilling, willing
Whether he will or not, "willy-nilly".

> "Events have put NATO in a position where it is the policeman of Europe and beyond, *nolens volens.*"
>
> Article in *The Daily Telegraph*, 1999.

Nolens volens is the name of a chamber ensemble comprising two voices, a baroque transverse flute and a harpsichord; and also of an indie/psychedelic/post-punk group from Russia.

Noli me tangere
—John xx. 17
Touch me not
"Jesus saith unto her (*sc.* Mary), Touch me not, for I am not yet ascended to my Father."

The incident has been a popular one for paintings, such as that by Hans Holbein the Younger, now in Hampton Court, and that by Titian in the National Gallery.

> "I did make attempts to overcome that terrible British exclusiveness—that *noli me tangere* with which an Englishman arms himself, and in which he thinks it necessary to envelop his wife…"
>
> Anthony Trollope, "George Walker at Suez".

According to Solinus, white stags found 300 years after Caesar's death had their collars inscribed with "*Noli me tangere, Caesaris sum*", meaning "Do not touch me, I am Caesar's". Sir Thomas Wyatt wrote a poem, "Whoso list to hunt?", acknowledging despondently that his former mistress, thought to have been Anne Boleyn, had abandoned him now that Henry VIII had begun to take an interest in her. The poem concludes with the lines:

> "There is written her fair neck round about;
> 'Noli me tangere; for Caesar's I am,
> And wild for to hold, though I seem tame'."

The wild balsam plant has seed cases which when ripe and when touched spring open and scatter their seeds. A common name for the plant is "Touch-me-not" and its scientific name is *Impatiens noli-tangere*.

Noli Me Tangere is the motto of the families of Wormald and Graeme of Garvock.

Nolle prosequi
To be unwilling to continue

An indication by a plaintiff or by the public prosecutor in a court of law that for some reason he does not want to continue with his case against the defendant. A *locus classicus* was the case of Dr John Bodkin Adams (1899-1983) of Eastbourne, who in 1957 was accused of murdering two elderly patients (out of, some say, 163 *in toto*). He was found not guilty on the first case, whereupon the Attorney-General entered a controversial *nolle prosequi* for the second and seemingly stronger case. A *nolle prosequi* could also be won by plea-bargaining.

> "Vanessa Cook has told me she will marry me…. I couldn't issue a *nolle prosequi*, could I, when she said that?"
> P. G. Wodehouse, *Aunts Aren't Gentlemen.*

> "'What did Waldo do to you?'… 'Stooled on a bank job in Michigan and got me four years. Got himself a nolle prosse.'"
> Raymond Chandler, "Red Wind".

> "May it please your honour, I desire to enter a *nolle pros.* in this case…. The piece of counterfeit coin upon the identity of which the case was built is not now available as evidence. I ask, therefore, that the case be stricken off."
> O. Henry, "One Dollar's Worth".

Nolo Episcopari

I do not wish to become a bishop

The modest and conventional response of a prelate upon first being offered a bishopric. In *Tom Jones*, Henry Fielding uses this phrase to characterize the reaction of a well-brought-up lady when she first receives a proposal of marriage: she remains however fully determined to accept it after a decent interval of demurral has passed.

> "The *nolo episcopari*, though still in use, is so directly at variance with the tendency of all human wishes, that it cannot be thought to express the true aspirations of rising priests in the Church of England."
>
> Anthony Trollope, *Barchester Towers*

Non amo te, Sabidi, nec possum dicere quare, Hoc tantum possum dicere, "Non amo te"

—Martial, *Epigrammata*, I, xxxii

I don't love thee, Sabidi, I can't say why,
All I can say is, "I don't love thee".

Martial put into words what all generations have felt about some of their friends.

> "My concern was to know just what it was offended you in him. Or is it merely *non amo te, Sabidi*?"
>
> Patrick O'Brian, *Master and Commander.*

> "I love him not, but show no reason can
> Wherefore, but this, I do not love the man."
>
> Rowland Watkyns

> "I do not love thee, Doctor Fell,
> The reason why, I cannot tell,
> But this I know and know full well,
> I do not love thee, Doctor Fell."
>
> Thomas Brown (1662-1704).

Non Angli sed angeli

Not Angles but angels

According to tradition, probably based on an account of the incident in Bede's *History of the English Church and People*, these words were spoken *c.* A.D. 600 by Pope Gregory I when told that the golden-haired young slaves in the market were Angles, that is, came from England. The incident happened before Gregory became Pope, but once he succeeded to the Papacy he began the task of converting Britain to Christianity.

Non compos mentis
Not of sound mind, mentally challenged

A legal term, hedged around with doubts about what constitutes sanity. Used by Cicero: *In Pisonem*, Ch.20, §48.

In *Handley Cross*, R. S. Surtees talks of "a lunatic, or one *non compos mentis*, who hath understanding, but who, from disease, grief, brandy-and-water, or other accident, hath lost the use of his reason".

> "Shakespeare was really a Literary Syndicate. Rainproof [Nogg] is demonstrably *non compos mentis* on that subject, and his infirmity is spreading."
> Ernest Bramah, "The Ingenious Mind of Mr Rigby Lacksome."

> "It was the clown's doing, and the clown, poor creature, was *non compos*, not entirely there, and couldn't be called to account for his actions."
> Aldous Huxley, *Antic Hay*.

The phrase *non compos mentis* spawned a noun "non-composser", a useful and exotic (since it does not appear in most modern dictionaries) alternative label for anyone who is intellectually challenged. "If you are not then knocked on the head, your being a non-composser will protect you." J. Fenimore Cooper, *The Last of the Mohicans*.

Non est inventus
He cannot be found

When a writ is served on a person and that person cannot be found, the phrase *Non est* (for *non est inventus*) is or was written on the writ by the sheriff or bailiff.

> "Would that it were not my unhappy duty to inform Your Grace that my journey… has met… with defeat in the greatest matter. *Non est inventus*."
> John Fowles, *A Maggot*.

Non est inventus is the name of a motet by Manuel Leitão de Aviles.

Non est vivere, sed valere vita est
—Martial, *Epigrammata*, VI, lxx
Life is not just being alive but being in health

Too true, and the motto of various eminent health-encouraging institutions such as the Royal Society of Medicine and the Boyce Hill Golf Club at South Enfleet.

Non nobis, Domine
—Psalm cxv
Not unto us, O Lord

The first verse of the psalm is: *Non nobis, Domine, non nobis: sed nomini tuo da gloriam*—"Not unto us, O Lord, not unto us, but unto thy Name give the praise."

King Henry V is said to have adopted "Non nobis Domine" as his motto after the Battle of Agincourt.

> "Do we all holy rites:
> Let there be sung Non nobis and Te Deum;…"
> Shakespeare, *King Henry V*, IV, viii.

In *The Oxford Book of English Verse*, the heading *Non Nobis* is given as we might expect to Henry Cust's poem "Not unto us, O Lord…"

Non omnis moriar
—Horace, *Odes*, III, xxx. 6
I shall not wholly die

This is a later and equally cheerful thought in the Ode which begins: *Exegi monumentum… q.v. supra.*

> "*Non omnis moriar*—if dying I yet live in a tender heart or two."
> W. M. Thackeray, *Henry Esmond*.

> "He… assured himself that a great part of him would escape oblivion. '*Non omnis moriar*', in some language of his own, was chanted by him within his own breast,…"
> Anthony Trollope, *The Way We Live Now*.

Non Omnis Moriar is the motto of the Wimberley family, and is also the name of a track on the album *Domus Mundi* by the Austrian symphonic black metal band Hollenthon.

Non sequitur

It does not follow

A *non sequitur* is a statement which does not seem to follow logically from anything that has been mentioned before.

> "'It's all one and the same, for every man who curses the cloth would curse the king if he durst; so for matter o' that, it's all one and the same thing.' 'Excuse me there, Mr Sergeant,' quoth Partridge, 'that's a *non sequitur*.' 'None of your outlandish linguo (*sic*),' answered the sergeant, leaping from his seat."
>
> Henry Fielding, *Tom Jones*.

> "'What a lovely baby!' I said to the young(ish) mother in the supermarket. 'You can 'ave 'im,' she replied. 'I got thirteen more at 'ome.' 'Thirteen!' 'Well, me 'usband snores, don't 'e?' 'Your husband snores, so you've got thir—fourteen children.' My puzzlement at this *non sequitur* must have shown in my face. 'Well, I gotta wear ear-plugs in bed, ain't I? I puts 'em in and 'e comes to bed and says, "Right, are we goin' to go to sleep or wot?" And I says, "Wot?"'"

Non sufficit orbis

—Juvenal, *Satires* X. 168

The world is not enough

The World is not Enough is the title of a James Bond film, and it just so happens that *Non sufficit orbis* is the motto of the Bond family.

Nota bene (N.B.)

Note well

The Weekend Book published a culinary hint for those with a taste for exotic food: "N.B. Mice in honey should be imported from China and not prepared at home."

Nota Bene is the not inapposite name of a vocal group based in Exeter, and is also the name of innumerable choirs elsewhere in Britain and in the United States and Canada. It is also the motto of the Handling Squadron of the R.A.F.

Nova Scotia

New Scotland

The cultured and erudite Caledonian emigrants to the New World favoured a more classical-sounding name for their settlement than that chosen by the Sassenachs who had settled in New England.

Nulla dies sine linea

—Pliny, *Historia Naturalis*, II, xxxv. 91

No day without a line

A saying attributed to the Greek artist Apelles. The line could be a drawn line or a written line—the important thing for an artist or a writer was to keep your hand in.

Nulli secundus

Second to none

This is the motto of the Lombard Banking Company and of the Coldstream Guards. As "The Lord General's Regiment of Foot Guards" the latter were placed as the second senior Regiment of Foot Guards in 1661, and they adopted this motto as a protest at being thus placed. They became the "Coldstream Regiment of Foot Guards" in 1670.

Nulla domus tales umquam contexit amores, Nullus amor talis coniunxit foedere amantes

—Catullus, *Carmina*, lxiv

No other house was ever home to lovers such as these,
No other lovers were ever joined in such a bond.

These lines and their translation above appear in Joanna Hines' *The Lost Daughter*. In Catullus' poem the words were spoken by the Fates (Parcae) on the occasion of the marriage of Thetis and Peleus, the parents of Achilles. Peleus, though a mortal, was a great hero, and as such was accorded the special privilege of marriage to a goddess.

Numero (Nº)

In number

The abbreviation "no." or "Nº" is now used widely as an abbreviation of the word "number" but the Latin provenance explains the "o".

Nunc dimittis (servum tuum, Domine,... in pace)
—Luke ii. 29

Lord, now thou lettest thy servant depart in peace

Simeon had waited all his life to see the Lord's anointed, and when he came into the temple and found the infant Jesus, he took him in his arms and spoke these valedictory words, followed by "for mine eyes have seen thy salvation".

Nunquam se minus otiosum esse quam cum otiosus, nec minus solum quam cum solus esset
—Cicero, *De Officiis*, III, i. 1

Never less idle than when wholly idle, nor less alone than when wholly alone.

It is possible that Cicero acquired this meandering thought (*via* Cato) from Scipio Africanus, who wrote *circa* 200 B.C. Abraham Cowley quotes a shortened version in his essay "Of Solitude":

"*Nunquam minus solus, quam cum solus*, is now become a very vulgar saying. Every man, and almost every boy, for these seventeen hundred years has had it in his mouth."

Hazlitt quotes the same shortened version, *anglice*, in his essay "On going a Journey", clearly confident that every reader will recognize its provenance. "... out of doors, nature is company enough for me. I am then never less alone than when alone."

Nunquam solus ambulabis
You'll never walk alone

This is offered to Liverpool A.F.C. as an alternative to their current motto, although they may have problems in setting it to music.

Nunquam ubi sub ubi
Never where under where

A piece of pseudo-Latin which only makes sense when the English is spoken aloud. It heads chapter 45 in Colin Dexter's *The Remorseful Day*, which contains the following passage: "With his own right hand he refastened the top three buttons of the dress he'd specifically requested her to wear above no underwear."

O

Obiit
He (or she) died

To be seen on old tombstones and memorials, along with *ætatis suæ* and *A.D.* (*qq.v.*), and often shortened to "*ob.*".

Obiter dicta
Sayings by the way, comments in passing

Strictly speaking an *obiter dictum* was a comment made by a judge in court which was not to be counted as forming part of his judgement, an "aside" as it were. *Dicta* is the plural of *dictum*.

> "(James) Wood has a trick of coining grand aphoristic *obiter dicta* in a way that suggests no one had ever thought of the idea before."
>
> Book review in the *Independent on Sunday*.

Obiter dicta can be any concatenation of casual remarks.

> "...the worrying suspicion that amongst the evidence already accumulated, the statements taken, the people interviewed, the personal relationships observed, the *obiter dicta*, the geography of North Oxford..."
>
> Colin Dexter, *The Jewel that was Ours*.

Obolus (Ob.)
A small coin, a halfpenny

From the Greek "obol". This was the standard fare to be paid to Charon for ferrying departed souls over the River Styx to the shores of Hades. Since there ain't no pockets in a shroud, the requisite coin was placed in the mouths of the dead in ancient Greece before they were buried.

"Item	Sack, two gallons	5s 8d
Item	Anchovies and sack after supper	2s 6d
Item	Bread	Ob.

Prince: O monstrous! but one halfpennyworth of bread to this intolerable deal of sack?"

Shakespeare, *Henry IV Part 1*, III, i.

Octavo

Eighth

A term used in printing, sometimes written "8vo", where a sheet of paper has been folded so as to make eight leaves of the book. *Cf. "quarto".*

Odi et amo

—Catullus, *Carmina*, lxxxv.

I hate and I love

The full couplet describing this early love-hate relationship reads:

Odi et amo: quare id faciam, fortasse requiris.
Nescio, sed fieri sentio et excrucior.
I hate and I love: why do I do this, you may ask.
I don't know, but I feel it to be so and I suffer (excruciatingly).

Robert Graves, in *The White Goddess*, suggests that the poet is in love with the White Goddess, with Truth. She is the Flower-goddess Blodeuwedd; but she is also Blodeuwedd the Owl, with her foul nest in the hollow of a dead tree. "*Odi atque amo*: 'to be in love with' is also to hate." (Graves misquotes slightly but excusably, with echoes perhaps of *Ave atque vale* sounding in his ears.)

(*Odi* is technically the first person singular perfect tense of the verb, "I have hated", but is used with a present tense meaning—"I hate".)

Odi et Amo is the motto for some undisclosed reason of the family of Viscount Norwich. It is also part of the title of a series of television drama programmes, "Odi et Amo—Of Love and Hate", produced in Vancouver and dealing with the "adult" themes of sadism and masochism.

Odi profanum vulgus et arceo

—Horace, *Odes*, III, i. 1

I hate the vulgar throng, and exclude them

Elitism is no modern phenomenon.

Charles Valentin Alkan wrote *c.* 1861 a piece for piano in E flat minor with this title. It is also the name of a (music) album by Miss Violetta Beauregarde.

Odi profanum—"I hate everything profane"—is the motto of the families of Hare and O'Hehir.

O et praesidium et dulce decus meum
—Horace, Odes, I, i. 2
O both my protector and my honoured friend

James Boswell writes of Dr Johnson that he had numerous friends, one of whom was "Sir Joshua Reynolds, who was truly his *dulce decus*, and with whom he maintained an uninterrupted intimacy to the last hours of his life." The literal translation of *dulce decus* as "a sweet honour" clearly will not do here: Horace addresses Maecenas as *et præsidium et dulce decus meum*, which can be translated loosely as it is above.

St. Venantius Fortunatus, "the last of the Roman poets", wrote a poem (Carmen 11.5) *c.* A.D. 580 to Agnes, abbess of the Convent of the Holy Cross at Poitiers, addressing her as *Dulce decus nostrum, Christi sanctissima virgo*—"My sweet beauty, most holy virgin of Christ." For the use of *noster*, literally "our", to mean "my", *vide* **"Forsitan et nostrum nomen..."** *supra*.

Dulce Decus is the title of a poem by Phil MacCabe.

O fons Bandusiae, splendidior vitro
—Horace, *Odes*, III, xiii
O fountain of Bandusia, more sparkling than crystal

This phrase is the source of F. Sidgwick's "O fons Brent Reservoir" in his "The Bankolidaid", quoted in Appendix II.

O fons Bandusiae is the name of various pieces of choral music by composers such as Randall Thompson and Douglas Lilburn; and Horace's ode has been cast in its entirety into English verse by such iconic poets as A. H. Clough, James Joyce, and W. E. Gladstone.

Omne ignotum pro magnifico est
—Tacitus, *Agricola* 30
Everything unknown appears stupendous

Or "tends to be exaggerated". Tacitus fathers these words on Galgacus, leader of the Britons, as a comment on the current (and mistaken) view in Rome of Britons as being wild and fierce. The next line notes that most of Britain has however now been explored. The words also appear in Robert Bland's *Proverbs* of 1814.

> "I begin to think, Watson," said Holmes, "that I make a mistake in explaining. '*Omne ignotum pro magnifico*' you know, and my poor reputation... will suffer shipwreck if I am so candid."
>> Sir Arthur Conan Doyle, "The Red-headed League".

John Fowles in *A Maggot*, speaks of "ignorant, fearful people, more apt (*omne ignotum pro magnifico est*) for the most part to see the Devil's hand in all than to weigh with reason."

Omnia vincit Amor: et nos cedamus Amori

—Virgil, *Eclogue*, x. 69

Love conquers all, and we ourselves, let us bow to Love

Many a girls' school must boast *Omnia Vincit Amor* or else *Amor Omnia Vincit* as a motto—word order does not much matter—although few perhaps subscribe openly (if indeed they know it) to the rest of the quotation. *Amor Omnia Vincit* is the motto of the Ussher family, while *Cedamus Amori* is the submissive motto of the Blunden family.

Chaucer tells us about the Prioress who spoke French "after the scole of Stratford atte Bowe":

> "Of smal coral aboute hire arm she bar
> A peire of bedes, gauded al with grene,
> And theron heng a brooch of gold ful sheene
> On which ther was first write a crowned A,
> And after *Amor vincit omnia*."

Omnia Vincit Amor is the title of a 1599 engraving by Agostino Carracci. Mae West suggested that love conquers all things except poverty and toothache.

Omnibus

For all

The "bus" was not the invention of M. Omnibus, a mythical Frenchman, in 1828, but was designed "for the use of all". The original horse-drawn bus gave way in the twentieth century to the motor-bus, a name that prompted A. D. Godley's poem "What is this that roareth thus? / Can it be a Motor Bus? / Yes, the smell and hideous hum / Indicat Motorem Bum...." (*Vide Appendix III.*)

Omnium consensu

By common consent

Gallus was emperor of Rome for eight months in A.D. 68-69 until he met the inevitable fate of so many emperors and was assassinated. Tacitus said of him: *Omnium consensu capax imperii nisi imperasset*: "All would have pronounced him worthy of empire had he never been emperor".

"Denis Cornford, *omnium consensu*, was a fine historian…"

Colin Dexter, *Death is now my Neighbour*

Omnium gatherum

A comprehensive collection

A joke expression, in which *omnium*, "of all", is Latin, while "gather(ing)" has been given a Latin ending in place of the English one.

One of Anthony Trollope's characters in the Barsetshire novels was the Duke of Omnium, and inevitably the name of his ducal seat was Gatherum Castle.

> "We… looked for a while at Woodgate's bric-à-brac shop, which I never can pass without delaying at the windows—indeed, if I were going to be hanged, I would beg the cart to stop, and let me have one look more at that delightful *omnium gatherum*."
>
> W. M.Thackeray, *Roundabout Papers*.

Omnium Gatherum is the name of an acclaimed black/death metal band from Finland.

Onus probandi

The burden of proof

> "It is… quite certain that rural and provincial institutions won't so alter and adapt all national characters, as to fit all nations for a Parliamentary Constitution; consequently, the *onus probandi* is on those who assert it will so alter and mould the French."
>
> W. Bagehot, *Literary Studies*, "Letter VII".

Opere citato (op. cit.)

In the work cited

In the course of writing, say, a magazine article, it may be necessary to quote from a book or other publication, giving the author, title, and page reference. A second reference to the same book can be given simply by mentioning the author's name followed by *op. cit.* and the page number.

*Vide "**loco citato**" supra.*

Opus

Work

This term is used to cover the whole of the output of an artist or composer or other creative soul, and has its equivalent/derivative in the French term "œuvre". On the other hand it is also used in the phrase "opus number" as a label for a single piece of music. The plural of *opus* is "opera" which now has its own meaning in music. The masterpiece of an artist's output is his *magnum opus*, *q.v.*

Opus Dei
God's work
  Opus Dei is a Catholic institution founded by Saint Josemaria Escrivá. Its declared mission is to help people turn their work and daily activities into occasions for growing closer to God, for serving others, and for improving society.

Orandum est ut sit mens sana in corpore sano
  —Juvenal, *Satires*, viii. 356
You must pray for a sound mind in a sound body
> "I have said that that sojourn of mine in the T[urkish] bath had done much to re-establish the *mens sana in corpore* what-not."
> P. G. Wodehouse, *The Code of the Woosters*.

> "My predestinated lot in life, alas, has amounted to this: a mens not particularly sana in a corpore not particularly sano".
> Viscount Mumbles, *A Reflection on My Life*.

  (Quoted by Colin Dexter in *Daughters of Cain* but, being an invention of Dexter himself, Mumbles is not to be found in Debrett.)
  Two cobblers had shops on opposite sides of the village street. One was an educated man, the other was not. One day there appeared in the window of the educated cobbler the sign: "Mens sana in corpore sano". The following day the other cobbler riposted with the sign: "Mens and womens sana in corpore sano".
  Mens Sana in Corpore Sano is the motto of the Chelsea College of Physical Education, Eastbourne, and of the Carlton (Australian rules) Football Club.

Ora pro nobis
Pray for us
  The "Anthem of Our Lady" known as *Regina Cæli* (*q.v.*) attributed by some to Pope Gregory V, *c*. A.D. 998, contains the phrase *Ora pro nobis Deum*, a request to the Virgin to "pray (to) God for us".

Oratio obliqua

Indirect speech

Or reported speech—"He said he was fed up"—as opposed to direct speech or *ipsissima verba*—"'I'm fed up!' he said."

> "When Trim is required to read a Sermon we are not surprised to find that he does read it, at length and without any device of summary or *oratio obliqua*."
>
> T. C. Livingstone,
> Introduction to Laurence Sterne, *Tristram Shandy*.

> "Since we're finding Chapter 3 a bit heavy in B'ham, would it help to transfer the Ursula story into *oratio obliqua* for Kitty's benefit?"
> Philip Larkin, Notes for "A New World Symphony".

Oremus

Let us pray

> —Non, répliqua Bernard, je ne vais pas vous dire, mais je suis en train de me demander, si au premier oremus, la fontaine se mettait à couler.
>
> Marcel Pagnol, *Manon des Sources*.

Oremus is the name of the magazine, published monthly, of Westminster Cathedral; and also of a vineyard in Hungary producing classic Tokaji wines.

O tempora, o mores

—Cicero, *In Catilinam*, I, i. 1

O what times! O what conduct!

This was Cicero's reaction to his suspicion that Catilina might be planning some sacrilegious crime. It could loosely be translated as "Fings ain't what they used to be".

Writing in *The Guardian*, Tom Holland used these words in bemoaning the fact that the OCR examination board had decided to abolish the A-level papers in Ancient History.

O tempora, o mores is the title of a juvenile poem by Edgar Alan Poe: "O Times! O Manners!"

Ogden Nash in "The Baffled Hermit" extended the sentiment: "O tempora, O mores, O Montreal!"

P

P (Princeps)
Prince

The Latin *Princeps* gives us our word "Prince", but as applied to Roman Emperors meant "first (among equals)". Just as his mother signs herself "Elizabeth R", the Prince of Wales is entitled to sign his name as "Charles P".

Pabulum
Food, fodder

A somewhat derogatory but usually well-deserved label given to prepared food. Traditional school meals, whether served up in the private or the public sector, were often, to be frank, unappetizing. We referred in my school to a particular type of pudding as "mattress". Generations of children (and their teachers) however took consolation from the thought that the contents of their plates were nevertheless *pabulum*, and, if nothing else, served to ward off starvation.

The blurb on the 1973 dust cover of *Noblesse Oblige*, edited by Nancy Mitford, states that Miss Mitford's discussion of U-usage "provided conversational pabulum at dinner tables in English-speaking Paris and New York".

Pabulum is the considered choice of name of a commercial firm based in the Isle of Wight, producing tasty and nutritious meals for schools, colleges and business enterprises.

Plautus in his *Casina* speaks of *Acherontis pabulum*, "food for Acheron", our common destiny, Acheron being a river in Hades.

Pace (tua)
By leave of, with (your) permission

Pace is the ablative of *pax*; and *pace*, with or without the *tua*, is a polite but firm way of indicating dissent from someone else's views.

> "Meanwhile, *pace* the tabloids, that other continuity prospers."
> M. Church, writing in *The Observer*.

Pallida Mors aequo pulsat pede pauperum tabernas regumque turres

—Horace, *Odes*, I, iv. 13,14

Pale Death kicks with impartial foot at the cottages of the poor and at the palaces of kings

The Romans did not knock at doors, they kicked.

> "'Saw your trap Tottenham Court Road way,' says the slang parson, nodding to the physician.
>
> 'Have some patients there. People are ill in Tottenham Court Road,' remarks the doctor.
>
> '*Pallida mors æquo pede*—hey, doctor?...'"
>
> W. M. Thackeray, *The Adventures of Philip.*

Pallida Mors is the name of a track on the album *Domus Mundi* by the Austrian symphonic black metal band Hollenthon.

These lines are followed directly in the Ode by *"vitae summa brevis..." q.v. infra.*

Panem et circenses

—Juvenal, *Satires*, X, 81

Bread and circuses

Juvenal suggested that the two things the Roman populace most valued were free food and entertainment.

> "The masses are unalterable. It is one of the most momentous facts of social science. Panem et circenses! Only today education is one of the bad substitutes for a circus."
>
> D. H. Lawrence, *Lady Chatterley's Lover.*

Both *panem* and *circenses* are in the accusative case which is fine if they are the object of the verb. The nominative is "panis et circenses".

Panis angelicus

Angelic bread, the bread of angels

The phrase *panis angelicus* occurs in the hymn *Sacris solemniis* (translated as "At this our solemn feast") written for the feast of Corpus Christi (*q.v.*) by St. Thomas Aquinas. The verses the phrase introduces were set to music by César Franck as part of his Messe Solonnelle, Op. 12.

Somewhat intriguingly, the phrase "Angel cake" translates into Latin as *Placenta angelica.*

Par

Level, equal

A term adopted in finance as well as in golf and in medicine—"I'm feeling a little below par today". It is a level with reference to which other achievements or situations are measured. "This book is on a par with his previous works." It is comparatively rare however to find anything categorized as "above par". In golf, of course, scoring below par is every player's aim.

Pari passu

With equal pace, together

"Consider recent history. Industrialism has grown *pari passu* with population."

Aldous Huxley, *Eyeless in Gaza.*

"Arthur was gone so far away, and his regret and himself were moving towards Arthur, or towards annihilation, *pari passu,...*"

A. S. Byatt, *Angels and Insects.*

Thomas de Quincey, considering Murder as one of the Fine Arts, calls for an improvement in the style of criticism of masterpieces of murder. "Practice and theory," he says, "must advance *pari passu.*"

Parturient montes, nascetur ridiculus mus

—Horace, *Ars Poetica*, 139

The mountains shall labour and shall spawn a laughable little mouse

There has been at least one sighting of this creature in modern literature. W. S. Gilbert, in his poem "Etiquette", ("The *Ballyshannon* foundered off the coast of Cariboo"), has this line: "One day, when out a-hunting for the *mus ridiculus,...*"

In *Eyeless in Gaza*, Aldous Huxley conflates two quotations, this one and *Si monumentum requiris, circumspice (q.v.).*

Passim

Throughout, in many places

An indication that a particular subject is referred to in some passage of writing not once or twice but many times.

Pater
Father

Familiar to all readers of (public) school stories from the early part of the twentieth century as the usual word for referring to or addressing one's father: "The pater won't be pleased when he hears about it."

Paterfamilias
Father of a family

A "Victorian paterfamilias" was traditionally one who kept his wife and children firmly under his thumb. Nevertheless he might well have envied the powers of his Roman counterpart, the senior male member of a family, who could on a whim decide in the interests of eugenics or economy to condemn a new-born child to death by exposure and sell any other superfluous children into slavery.

The species, although endangered, is not wholly extinct. "Certainly there was Humphrey, who took on some kind of importance now as a latter-day paterfamilias." Anita Brookner, *Altered States*.

Paterfamilias is usually written as one word. However a report in *The Guardian* about a publishing takeover splits it up. "Pater familias Toby Blackwell is reported to be £100 million richer thanks to Wiley,..."

(The literal meaning of *"pater familias"* is "father of the family", and *"familias"* is an archaic genitive of *"familia"*, the later, classic, genitive being *"familiae"*.)

*Vide "**materfamilias**" supra.*

Pater filio
A father to (his) son

In *The Oxford Book of English Verse*, the heading *Pater Filio* is given to Robert Bridges' poem "Sense with keenest edge unusèd...."

Pater, Filius et Spiritus Sanctus
Father, Son and Holy Ghost

Paternoster
Our Father

Pater noster are the first two words of The Lord's Prayer in Latin. Paternoster Row runs along the north side of St. Paul's Cathedral.

Every tenth (or eleventh?) bead on a rosary is a paternoster bead, at which point in telling the rosary the Lord's Prayer is repeated.

Sometimes the rosary itself is called a paternoster, and this practice gave rise to the naming of a fishing line with hooks and weights (and, with luck, fish) at intervals as a "paternoster-line". The name extends to other artefacts: a paternoster-wheel or paternoster-pump contains buckets on a chain, and the Bodleian Library's paternoster is a conveyor belt carrying books from the stacks to the main library and back.

Patria
Motherland, fatherland, homeland
Essentially the place one would like to return to for comfort and security, full of happy childhood memories, the next best place to the womb.

> "Despite his new-found passion for the lowlands, Mabey's latest book… has returned him to his 'patria', the beech groves that rise above his former hometown of Berkhamsted."
> Book review in *The Guardian*.

*Cf. "**pro patria**" infra.*

Pax
Peace
When I was at my grammar school, playground chases could be halted when exhaustion set in by the cry of *Pax* or "Paxes". Only later did I realize that, as with *cave* (*q.v.*), I was speaking Latin. (Only much later still did I discover, through the Opies' books on children's games, lore and language, that when at primary school in the same situation I had called out "fainites" or "fains", I had been using words which children for centuries past in our village had been using in their own play.)

Pax is the motto of the families of Foulis, Hatfeild (*sic*) and Hatton.

Pax Britannica
British peace
For a long time, between 27 B.C. and c. A.D. 180, the Roman army, with the authority invested in them by the Senate and people of Rome (*vide* **S.P.Q.R.**), kept the *Pax Romana*, the Roman peace, in the Empire, stamping down on rebellion and damping down internecine strife within its bounds. In the same way the British navy and army kept, with varying degrees of success, the *Pax Britannica* throughout the British Empire.

Pax Britannica is the title of a trilogy by Jan Morris.

In a book review in *The Guardian*, Veronica Horwell mentions the *pax consumeria*, the peace which descends on the world when all potential combatants are busy shopping.

Pax vobiscum

Peace be with you

Joseph's steward reassures Joseph's panic-stricken brothers with these words (Genesis xliii. 23) when they return, bringing with them the money which Joseph had caused to be placed in the sacks of corn they had carried home on their previous visit to Egypt.

In the Mass, the priest addresses the congregation singly, with the singular form of the greeting: "*Pax tecum*" –"Peace be with thee". The reply, "*et cum spiritu tuo*"—"and with thy spirit", is the same as the reply to "*Dominus vobiscum*" (*q.v.*).

> "I rose, thanked the father for his hospitality and his tale, [and] was benignantly answered by a 'pax vobiscum'...."
>
> Charlotte Brontë, *Villette*.

[The Latin for "with" was *cum* (*q.v.*) and was an independent preposition, but was specially combined with personal pronouns as a suffix, so that, e.g., *cum me*—"with me"—was written as *mecum*, and likewise with *cum te* and *cum vobis* (*supra*).]

Peccavi

I have sinned

> "'I shall say peccavi,' said Elizabeth, with the air of doing something exceedingly noble. 'I shall myself resign.'"
>
> E. E. Benson, *Mapp and Lucia*.

Where did Elizabeth Mapp find *peccavi*? It is possible, though not probable, that she had attended Latin Mass and confessed: *Peccavi nimis cogitatione, verbo et opere*—"I have sinned exceedingly in thought, word and deed." However, it is more likely that she knew the story of how Sir Charles Napier is said to have sent this single-word despatch back to H.M. government in 1843 after he had conquered the Indian state of Sindh.

Pede claudo

With halting foot

The phrase is extracted from Horace, *Odes*, III, ii. 31,32:...*Raro antecedentem scelestum / deseruit pede Poena claudo*—"Rarely has retribution failed to overtake the guilty, though with halting foot and long after the crime". It comes from the same stable as the later maxim translated by Longfellow from von Logau: "Though the mills of God grind slowly, yet they grind exceeding small."

"[Kew] hung down his head. He thought of the past and its levities, and punishment coming after him *pede claudo*."

W. M. Thackeray, *The Newcombes*.

"Ay, it must be that: the ghost of some old sin,... punishment coming, *pede claudo*, years after memory has forgotten and self-love condoned the fault."

R. L. Stevenson, *Strange Case of Dr Jekyll and Mr Hyde*.

"The tramp of the Bobbeian boots may readily be recognised full half a mile away; and *Bill Sykes* has ample time to put his crowbar in his pocket, and vanish round the corner, ere the Peeler, *pede claudo*, can manage to come up to him."

Punch, 1873.

Per
By, each

Latin had no simple word for "week", borrowing for the purpose the Greek *hebdomas*; hence, in addition to *per diem*, *per annum*, etc., we have by extension "*per* week".

"Per" also enables us to label rates succinctly: miles per hour (m.p.h.) is perhaps the most familiar example. It is an invitation mathematically to divide. Other examples are metres per second, miles per gallon, children per family, and words per minute (shorthand, typing or speech).

It will be remembered that the late Stanley Holloway told of how Mr and Mrs Ramsbotham and young Albert, their son, chose to walk across the Mersey at Runcorn rather than pay the exorbitant fare on the ferry.

> "'Y'not charging tuppence for that little lad?'
> Said Mother, her eyes flashing wild.
> 'Per tuppence per person per trip', answered Ted,
> 'Per woman, per man or per child'."

It may crop up in places where it is used for emphasis, as in "as per usual" or just following a whim, as in "as per instructions".

Per annum (p.a.)
Each year

Used almost exclusively to give a time scale to the charging of rates of interest. "New low-cost mortgages at only 6.3% p.a."

Per ardua ad astra
Through toil to the stars
The motto of the Royal Air Force, and before that of the Royal Flying
Corps, possibly adapted from an early Latin tag, *Ad astra per aspera*—"To
the stars through difficulties", which itself is the motto of the State of
Kansas. To me as an ex-R.A.F. man (A.C.1), the modern version sounds
an improvement. It might be considered that No. 27 (Bomber) Squadron
went one better with their own motto, spurning delays: *Quam celerrime ad
astra*—"As quickly as possible to the stars".

Per capita
By heads, for each head or person
> "Finland broadcasts the news in Latin on national radio to a
> claimed 75 000 listeners, which on a per capita basis [of the total
> population] is reported to be more than some BBC Radio 4
> programmes get."
>> Leader in *The Guardian*.

> "[More affordable alcohol] has been accompanied by escalating
> *per capita* alcohol consumption and alcohol-related deaths."
>> Letter in *The Guardian*.

> "These days the Irish buy more Mercs *per capita* than do the
> Germans."
>> Book review in *The Guardian*.

Caput, "head", of which *capita* is the plural, was used in Classical times to
mean "person". *Vide "**quis desiderio...**" infra*.

Per centum (per cent)
Out of 100
The symbol % is said by some to derive from the rearrangement of the
digits of 100. It is also a reminder that, say, 12% can be written for purposes
of calculation as the fraction 12/100.

Per contra
Conversely, on the other hand
> "Thinking in terms of first principles entails acting with machine-
> guns... *Per contra*, if you never consider principles and have no plan,
> but deal with situations as they arise, piecemeal, you can afford to
> have unarmed policemen, liberty of speech, and *habeas corpus*."
>> Aldous Huxley, *Eyeless in Gaza*.

"Per-contra accounts" are occasional payments made to set off a debt:

"(The transaction)… was further entangled by *per-contra* accounts
of cribs of turf, scores of eggs, and a day's work now and again."

E. Œ. Somerville and Martin Ross,
Further Adventures of an Irish R.M.

Per diem

Each day

Diem is the accusative of *dies*.

"[The county laughed as Bob] abandoned the three-per-diem
meals of the one-horse farm for the discontinuous quick lunch
counters of the three-ringed metropolis."

O. Henry, "The Defeat of the City".

Pereunt et imputantur

—Martial, *Epigrammata*, V, xx

(*The days*) *pass away and are reckoned* (*to our account*)

The full passage reads: *Bonosque soles effugere et abire sentit, qui nobis pereunt et
imputantur*—"And he feels the good days are flying by and vanishing, our
days which are lost and are reckoned to our account." *Soles* are literally
"suns" but are used poetically to mean "days". (*Cf. "**soles occidere et
redire possunt…**" infra.*)

The sundial over the porch of St. Buryan Church near Land's End in
Cornwall offers to passers-by the timely reminder *Pereunt et imputantur*, and
these words also appear on the face of the 15th century clock in Exeter
Cathedral. For a more cheerful sundial message, *vide* "**horas non
numero…**" *supra.*

Pereunt et Imputantur is the motto of *Snakeskin*, the poetry webzine.

Per mensem

Each month

Mensem is the accusative singular of *mensis*, whose plural is *menses*.

Perpetuum mobile

Perpetual motion

For centuries inventors have tried to build perpetual motion machines
which, once set in motion, would continue to work *in perpetuum* without the
help of any further external impulse. One such inventor was Dr Algernon
Porter of North Carolina, father of the writer O. Henry, who in the latter
part of the nineteenth century invented (unsuccessfully), *inter alia*, "a steam-

driven automobile, a washing machine, a flying machine,… and a water-driven *perpetuum mobile*."

Several composers have written pieces of music whose notes, played rapidly, all have the same value, and have given them the title of "Perpetuum mobile". These compositions also have the property that all or part of the piece is intended to be repeated, but without a break in the "motion" of the melody when a repeat begins. A well-known *perpetuum mobile* piece, not labelled as such, is Rimsky-Korsakov's "The Flight of the Bumblebee".

> "…Skrebensky still rocked languidly on the [rocking-] chair….
> 'You look really floppy,' said Gudrun.
> 'I am floppy,' he answered.
> 'Can't you stop?' asked Gudrun.
> 'No—it's the perpetuum mobile.'"
>
> D. H. Lawrence, *The Rainbow*.

Per pro (p.p.)
For and on behalf of

Used traditionally in offices when the person who wrote or dictated a letter is not available to sign it, in which case a secretary or other subordinate signs it "p.p." the author. *Per pro* is also an abbreviation of *per procurationem* or "through the agency of".

Per se
On its own, by itself

Hugh Fearnly-Whittingstall writing in *The Observer* said: "Robbins does not object to the flapjack *per se*: 'As a snack for someone who is short of energy, it's probably marginally preferable to a Mars Bar'." *Vide* also "***etc.***", *supra*.

> "To you, sex is just sex, an unvarying spasm repeated at intervals, worthless *per se* and meaningless *per se*,…"
>
> Philip Larkin, "Round Another Point".

> "Everything is symbolic. There is no such thing as a 'thing' *per se*. It is only a symbol of something else that is itself, and so on."
>
> Mervyn Peake, *Gormenghast*.

Persicos odi, puer, apparatus
—Horace, *Odes*, I, xxxviii, 1
Boy, I hate Persian luxury

> "… his chest of mangoes, chutney and currie-powders: his shawls for presents to people whom he didn't know as yet: and the rest of his *Persicos apparatus*."
>
> W. M. Thackeray, *Vanity Fair*.

In *The Oxford Book of English Verse* the heading *Persicos Odi* is given to W. M. Thackeray's poem which begins: "Dear Lucy, you know what my wish is,— / I hate all your Frenchified fuss:… " *Persicos Odi* is also the title of a poem by Charles Edward Merrill Jr.: "Boy, I detest these modern innovations…"
*Vide "**apparatus**" supra.*

Persona
Person

One's *persona* is the face we present to the long-suffering world at large, and one which may change with the company or the mood we are in. It was the name given to the mask worn by a Roman actor.

> [In *Cactus Flower*] "Goldie Hawn converts her lovable *Laugh-In* kooky bimbo persona into a believable screen character."
>
> *Radio Times* film review.

> "Legendary beauty, surrealist muse, photographer, Lee Miller was all of these and more: model, photojournalist, gourmet cook, alcoholic, child rape victim, beloved daughter, mistress, wife, friend, mother… Carolyn Burke's startling achievement is to document each persona with empathy and insight,…"
>
> Book review in *The Guardian*.

Persona grata
An acceptable person

A phrase technically used to confirm that a member of a diplomatic mission is acceptable to the country to which he is assigned. If for any reason, or for no reason at all, he is not acceptable, he is *persona non grata* (*q.v.*). The plural would be *personæ (non) gratæ*.

> "Don't ever let it straggle out from under your hat that you seen Buck Caperton fraternal with sarsaparilla or *persona grata* with a checker-board, or I'll make a swallow-fork in your other ear."
>
> O. Henry, "The Lonesome Road".

"You've no right to dismiss my husband like that. Bernard is *persona grata* wherever he goes, in *any* company."

Q. Q. Enwright, *Mistress and Maid*.

Persona non grata

An unacceptable person

"He (*sc.* Francis) and Celia would have to withdraw to Paris, *persona non grata* in London." Richard Condon, *Any God Will Do*. (It was only Francis who was *persona non grata* in London, having been declared an undesirable alien following the unfortunate encounter with the belligerent dwarf. In Condon's sentence, it is not made clear which of the two was *non grata*. Had both been so, then the phrase would/should have appeared in the plural, *personae non gratae*.)

Persona non grata is the name of a book by Jorge Edwards, who was made to feel unwelcome in Cuba; and is also the name of a Polish film by Krzysztof Zanussi.

Cf. "**persona grata**" *supra*.

Pervigilium Veneris

The Eve of (St.) Venus

A poem of 21 stanzas composed *circa* A.D. 350, with a refrain beginning *Cras amet...* (*q.v. supra*). The phrase is used by Evelyn Waugh as the heading of a chapter in *Decline and Fall* which partly concerns the lamentably fleeting courtship of Paul Pennyfeather and Margot Beste-Chetwynde.

Petitio principii

Begging the question, arguing in circles.

This is not the same as "asking the question" or "raising the question", although it is often used in this sense by some voices of the media. Begging the question is more or less assuming as true a portion of what you are asked to prove, and adducing this as proof—stealing rather than begging. It can clearly lead to arguing in circles.

A. E. Housman, discussing the editing of Juvenal's works, suggests that an argument such as "Bœotians were stupid, Pindar was a Bœotian, therefore Pindar was stupid," is suspect because whether or not Bœotians were stupid can only be settled by considering the case of every known Bœotian, including Pindar himself, and so in this argument he suggests we "detect *petitio principii*".

Pinxit (pinx.)

He painted
Cf. ***fecit***, ***sculpsit***.

Placebo

I shall please

Used particularly of a medicine which makes you feel better, even though your G.P. may reckon it to have no inherent medical properties or curative powers.

It is also the name given to Vespers in The Office of the Dead. *Placebo Domino in regione vivorum*—"I will walk before the Lord in the land of the living", the implication being that walking before the Lord is one way of pleasing him.

Placens uxor

A pleasing wife, a sweet wife

Horace in *Odes* II, xiv. mentions three things one must leave when one dies: *tellus et domus et placens uxor*—"the world and home and a pleasing wife". The Ode begins: *Eheu fugaces (q.v.)*.

In his *Enemies of Promise*, Cyril Connolly reflects on the fate of a friend, Godfrey Meynell, killed in action in Waziristan, gaining by his bravery a posthumous Victoria Cross, but *linquenda tellus et domus et placens uxor*— "having to leave the world and home and a loving wife". (*Linquenda* is literally "things which must be left behind or *relinquished*" and comes from the same stable as *agenda*, *corrigenda* and *videnda*, *qq.v.*)

> Less tragically: "The Colonel was not so depressed as some mortals would be, who, quitting a palace and a *placens uxor*, find themselves barred into a spunging-house;…"
>
> W. M. Thackeray, *Vanity Fair*.

Plebs

A commoner

In ancient Rome, every free man was a *plebs* unless he was lucky enough to be a patrician or a knight. Now the word, together with its adjectival derivative, "plebeian", is used in a pejorative sense to categorize one of the lower classes.

> "This [single figure who stood raised above them on a chariot, swaying and gesticulating] doubtless was Catiline, inflaming the Roman plebs."
>
> Iris Murdoch, *Under the Net*.

Peers: Distinction ebbs
Before a herd
Of vulgar *plebs*!
Fairies: (A Latin word.)

W. S. Gilbert, Iolanthe, Act 1

Poeta nascitur non fit

A poet is born, not made

The origin of this saying is uncertain, as is that of a linked saying: *Orator fit, poeta nascitur*—"An orator can be made, a poet is born".

Lewis Carroll chose not to agree with the statement and wrote a poem entitled *Poeta Fit, Non Nascitur*, and starting "How shall I be a poet…?"

In *Eyeless in Gaza*, Aldous Huxley adapts the phrase to "A man is not born but is made": "'Swine will be swine.' 'But may become human,' I insisted. '*Homo non nascitur, fit*. Or rather makes himself out of the ready-made elements and potentialities of man with which he's born.'"

A. E. Housman also adapted the phrase to his own purpose. Textual criticism of the classical authors was his trade, and he suggested that "this science and this art require more in the learner than a simply receptive mind; and indeed the truth is that they cannot be taught at all: *criticus nascitur, non fit*."

"Pone seram, cohibe."
Sed quis custodiet ipsos custodes? Cauta est et ab illis incipit uxor

—Juvenal, *Satires*, vi. 347

"Bolt the door, put guards on her." But who shall guard the guards themselves? She's cunning, the wife, and will begin with them

It was at times not only wise but imperative for a Roman husband to place a guard over a flighty wife, and the admonishment to "lock up your daughters" is of antique origin. The speaker has no illusions. He may take the advice of old friends and place guards, but should then also in all prudence place guards on the guards, and so presumably *ad infinitum*. Clearly a great saving in manpower followed the invention of the chastity belt.

Sed quis custodiet ipsos custodes heads Colin Dexter's story about Chief Inspector Morse, entitled "Neighbourhood Watch". Here the problem has been passed from the anxious husband to the Police Watchdog.

"'If a vacancy occurs as head of the family, I should consider your application.' '*Quis custodiet*, Arthur? Who tells the head of the family he is at fault?'" Julian Barnes, *Arthur and George*. (This appears to be an instance of a Latin tag being impressive, without being *prima facie* apposite. It needs perhaps something of "belling the cat" rather than placing guards.)

Qui custodit—"Who guards"—is the motto of no. 399 Signals Unit of the R.A.F.

(N.B. Some versions of the above lines replace *cohibe* with *prohibe*. The two words both mean "restrain".)

Poni curavit (P.C.)

Caused to be placed

This is a phrase frequently to be found on memorials in churches, recording who (usually the grieving spouse) ordered the said memorial to be set in place.

Pons asinorum

The bridge of asses

The diagram accompanying the fifth proposition in Euclid's Geometry looked a little like a bridge. Beginners found the fifth proposition difficult to understand, and hence this was the bridge that asses failed to cross. Readers may themselves care to take the asses' test.

ABC is an "isosceles" triangle, with AB = AC. We are asked to prove that the angle of the triangle at B (∠ABC) is equal in size to that at C (∠ACB).

Proof: Extend AB to D and AC to E with BD = CE. Join B to E and C to D.

The triangles ABE and ACD are the same shape and size (congruent). They have two corresponding sides equal (AB = AC, AE = AD) and they have angle A in common. So BE = CD.

The triangles BCD and BCE are congruent. They have three corresponding sides equal (BD = CE, BE = CD, and they have BC in common), so ∠DBC = ∠BCE (corresponding angles of congruent triangles).

Finally, ∠ABC = 180°—∠DBC and ∠ACB = 180°—∠BCE and so ∠ABC = ∠ACB. Q.E.D. (*q.v. infra.*)

Philip Larkin, in his notes for "A New World Symphony", has a bald entry: "Honeymoon bridge—*pons asinorum*." Is this a pun on "bridge"? Do his characters play bridge on their honeymoon, or is the honeymoon also the downfall of asses?

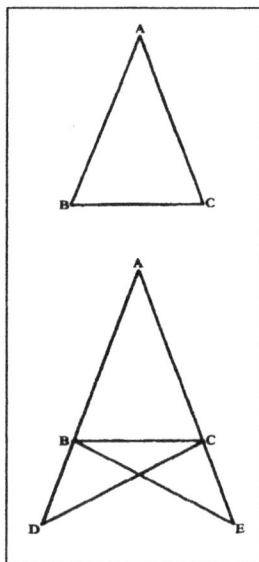

Pontifex maximus
The greatest guardian of bridges

In ancient Rome, the care and maintenance of the bridges, and of the *Pons Sublicius* in particular, was in the hands of the principal college of priests, whose head was the *Pontifex Maximus.* Julius Caesar at one time was *Pontifex Maximus*, as were all the emperors after him. The title, though stripped of the duties of bridge maintenance, was taken over by the Bishop of Rome, the Pope, and was subsequently modified to "Pontiff".

The word "pontifex" is used in the Vulgate Bible to translate the Greek αρχιερευς, "*archiereus*" or "high priest".

It may or may not be significant that Samuel Butler, in *The Way of All Flesh*, gave the surname "Pontifex" to the family with whose fortunes the book largely deals.

Posse
To be able

The *posse comitatus* ("available power") was the temporary police force of the locality which could be called out by the magistrates or by the sheriff when the need arose. The "posse" survived longer perhaps in the American West than it did in its homeland of Great Britain.

> "'Tis a case of disappearance,…' said the Squire…. 'We must offer rewards; we must raise the *posse comitatus*.'"
>
> Benjamin Disraeli, *Venetia*.

> "*In posse*" denotes possibility or potential. "People are excited and regard every neutral as an enemy *in esse* or *in posse*." (i.e., as an actual or potential enemy.)
>
> Ernest Bramah, "The Secret of Headland Height".

> "Mr Crosbie said that Lord Monboddo believed the existence of everything possible; in short, that all which is *in posse* might be found *in esse*. JOHNSON. 'But, Sir, it is as possible that the ouran-outang does not speak, as that he speaks. However, I shall not contest the point. I should have thought it not possible to have found a Monboddo; yet *he* exists.'"
>
> James Boswell, *The Life of Samuel Johnson, LL.D.*

*Vide "**a posse ad esse**" supra.*

Post bellum

After the war

In the United States the post-bellum era is that following on the Civil War of 1861-5.

Post coitum

After coitus

> "The books and lectures are better sorrow-drowners than drink and fornication; they leave no headache, none of that despairing *post coitum triste* feeling."
>
> Aldous Huxley, *Point Counter Point.*

"Triste" is "sad", and the allusion is to Aristotle:

> "… the oily and balsamous parts are of a lively heat and spirit, which accounts for the observation of Aristotle, '*Quod omne animal post coitum est triste.*'" (Every animal is sad after coitus.)
>
> Laurence Sterne, *Tristram Shandy.*

Although this saying is attributed here by Sterne to Aristotle, Galen is also quoted as the source of a longer version: *Quod omne animal post coitum est triste, præter mulierem gallumque*—"For every animal is sad after coitus, except woman and the cockerel". The sadness is most evident perhaps in those species in which after copulation the male is eaten by the female.

> "The absence of the object that had unleashed my desire and slaked my thirst made me realize suddenly both the vanity of that desire and the perversity of that thirst. *Omne animal triste post coitum.*"
>
> Umberto Eco, *The Name of the Rose.*

Post equitem sedet atra Cura

—Horace, *Odes,* III, i. 40

Behind the horseman sits black Care

Throughout the ages the man on a horse was a wealthy man. The poor walked.

> "Anxiety? Pray Heaven he never may suffer the sleepless anguish, the racking care which has pursued me! '*Post equitem sedet atra cura*' our favourite poet says."
>
> W. M. Thackeray, *The Adventures of Philip.*

"'Post equitem sedet atra Cura' he quoth / They invite their destruction, these drongos most loth."

> Chris Oakley, "The Destruction of Balliol".

Post Equitem is the title of a bronze roundel by Sir Alfred Gilbert, R.A.

Post facto
Afterwards
Literally "after (something has been) done."

"You were assisting an elopement *post facto?*"
> John Fowles, *A Maggot.*

"… late mediaeval and Tudor (churchwardens') accounts survive… which look like very close *post facto* reporting of the parish audit…"
> Eamon Duffy, *The Voices of Morebath.*

Information posted on the Internet and subsequently edited in the light of comments, favourable or otherwise, upon its content, is said to undergo *post facto* editing.

Post hoc, ergo propter hoc
After this, therefore because of this
Quoted by Richard Whately in *Elements of Logic* (1826), this well-known logical fallacy suggests that if two things happen at different times, the earlier must be the cause of the later.

There was a recent debate about whether or not the MMR vaccine could cause personality disorders in some children. Opponents claimed that many children show symptoms of such disorders after they had been vaccinated. Defenders of the vaccine claimed that there was no firm evidence that it was harmful, and suggested that those who claimed it was harmful were arguing fallaciously along *post hoc, ergo propter hoc* lines.

Post meridiem
After noon, after midday
Cf. **"ante meridiem"** *supra.*

179

Post mortem
After death

A "post mortem" examination is usually carried out to ascertain the cause of death. In earlier times, an *inquisitio post mortem* (*q.v. supra*), which gave us the word "inquest", was an enquiry into the dead man's holdings of land and the duties of service attached thereto.

The phrase can be used adverbially to mean what it says. "The thumbs must have been cut off *post mortem* as there was no sign of extensive bleeding."

The phrase has two possible plural forms. "'Nothing we can do till we get some reports, results of the post-mortems—' 'Somebody once told me the plural should be post-mortes.' 'Bloody pedant!' 'It was you actually, Morse.'" Colin Dexter, *The Remorseful Day*.

Postscriptum (P.S.)
Written after, a postscript

And hence P.P.S. for *post-postscriptum*.

> "A considerable length of time separates the ending of my journal proper and this *postscriptum*."
>
> William Golding, *Close Quarters*.

Praemonitus, praemunitus
Forewarned is forearmed

The Whittemore-Durgin Glass Co. of Rockland, Maine, offer free gifts with their products but warn that "if you try ordering just free stuff alone, you'll still have to pay minimum shipping charges. *Praemonitus, praemunitus*."

Praemonitus, praemunitus is the motto of the Intelligence School of the R.A.F.

Pre
Before

"Pre" is not a Latin word but, as a reduced form of the preposition "præ", it is widely used in English. The American "ante-bellum" becomes our "pre-war": our children go to pre-school and often eat pre-cooked meals: Wales is largely perched on top of pre-Cambrian rocks; and many a young lady shop assistant I meet appears sadly to be in the grip of PMT.

Prima facie
At first sight

Often translated as "on the face of it", and having regard to the evidence so far available.

"There seemed to be a *prima facie* case to make for charging Sir Jasper with tentative but no less indecent assault."

P. J. Dorricot, Tales from the Nursery.

"Prima Facie" is the name of an organization offering, *inter alia*, "Facial Plastic and Reconstruction Surgery through laser resurfacing".

Primus inter pares
First among equals

Gideon Haigh in *Silent Revolutions* points out that although New South Wales is on the surface just one among six Australian states, its people have always regarded themselves "as *primus inter pares*, reflected in the car number plates, which still boast of theirs being 'The Premier State'."

The term *primus inter pares* was used to mollify those members of the Roman Senate who considered the Emperor to be too powerful, and was intended to suggest that he was really just one of the boys. In more recent times the phrase has been used to define the status of the British Prime Minister in relation to his colleagues. It can in fact be applied to the nominal heads of many organizations, implying that they may at any time be eased from office and replaced by others equally well (or ill) qualified to carry out the duties of the post. An exception is the Pope who, as the Vicar of Christ and leader of the bishops and successor to St. Peter, is seen as holding a post senior to the other bishops, who are not his equals.

Pro bono publico
For the public good

Two prolific writers of letters to the newspapers are, or have been, "Disgusted" of Tunbridge Wells, and "Pro Bono Publico". The latter always writes quite disinterestedly, merely putting into words the thoughts of less-articulate fellow members of the public, their implicit support making firm his own *locus standi* (*q.v.*).

> *Pro bono* can also mean "free of charge". "The Tax Advice for Older People project provides pro-bono advice from chartered taxation advisers for low-income earning older people."
>
> The Guardian.

This is another of the useful Latin phrases which lawyers are now discouraged from using. I understand that the search for a suitable, succinct and clear English substitute is ongoing and promises to be so for some years ahead. (*Cf.* **"in camera"** *supra*.)

Pro bono omnium—"For the good of all" is the motto of Guinness Mahon Holdings, Ltd., linked possibly to the slogan "My goodness, my Guinness"? *Omnia pro bono*—"All things for good"—is the motto of the Murdoch family and of the Manchester Port Health Authority.

Procul, O procul este, profani
—Virgil, *Aeneid*, vi. 258
Begone, begone, O ye profane ones.

These words were spoken by the Cumaean Sybil as Aeneas prepared to enter the Underworld. Here is an extract from John Dryden's translation of the relevant passage:

> Then earth began to bellow, trees to dance,
> And howling dogs in glimm'ring light advance,
> Ere Hecate came. "Far hence be souls profane!"
> The Sibyl cried, "and from the grove abstain!
> Now, Trojan, take the way thy fates afford;
> Assume thy courage, and unsheathe thy sword."

The profane souls in question are those who have not been initiated into the rites of whatever ceremony is in progress. *Procul, O procul este, profani* is inscribed over the doorway to Henry Hoare's Temple of Flora at Stourhead, perhaps as a rune to repel visitors who are not prepared in spirit for enjoying the beauties of the place.

Henry Fielding in *Tom Jones* quotes this line when describing Tom's reaction to Dr Thwackum's approach to the cosy bower where Tom and his paramour Molly had been enjoying Venus' sports.

"*Procul, O procul este, profani! Bahlasti! Ompehda!*" is the first line of Khoury's "Crone Ritual", written for the Sybilline Order of Texas.

Pro forma
As a matter of form

In government circles certain problems have always cropped up frequently, and traditional ways have been devised of dealing with them. Often a standard letter will suffice, *mutatis mutandis*, to deal with any such problem, the reply being in a standard form, in short, a reply *pro forma*.

David Mitchell in *Cloud Atlas* reports that newspapers across the continent had written to request interviews. "I have the pleasure of despatching a polite but firm *pro forma* rejection to each."

In the late 1940's I worked for a disastrous fortnight in an R.A.F. squadron office. The Flight Sergeant in charge was always asking me to send out "pro formas" to be filled in. Now my successor will simply be sending out "forms" to be filled in (or more probably—*O tempora!*—to be filled "out").

Propaganda (fide)

For spreading (the faith)

According to Chambers' dictionary, a congregation of the Roman Catholic Church was formed by Pope Gregory XV in 1622 charged with spreading the Catholic faith. The phrase used—*de propaganda fide*—"concerning the faith to be propagated"—has given us the word "propaganda". This word has by now acquired a thoroughly pejorative flavour, so that "propaganda" is seen to be composed, if not of blatant lies, then of statements which are to be taken *cum grano salis*.

> "The present successors of the apostles, the disciples of Dr Pusey and tools of the Propaganda, were at that time being hatched under cradle-blankets, or undergoing regeneration by nursery-baptism in wash-hand-basins."
>
> Charlotte Brontë, *Shirley*.

Pro patria

For (one's) country

> "Then, during the war, the clouds had lifted. One could be kind to wounded soldiers—be kind *pro patria* and with a blameless conscience."
>
> Aldous Huxley, *Eyeless in Gaza*.

This phrase is inscribed on many war memorials, including the memorial erected on the Battery Rocks in Penzance. It is also the motto of the Royal Canadian Regiment and of many families, including those of Earl Wavell and of Newton of that Ilk.

(*Vide* "**Dulce et decorum est**" *supra*.)

Pro rata

In proportion

"The cost of hiring a boat is £12 per hour, with parts of an hour being charged *pro rata*." From this we can calculate that the charge for 1½ hours will be £18 while that for ¾ hour will be £9.

Pro rege et lege

For the king and the law

This is the motto of Leeds United Football Club, shared with the city of Leeds itself. The *Pro Rege et Lege* panel, displaying the Leeds coat of arms, was the first panel of the Leeds tapestry to be completed (in 2002). The sixteen panels of the tapestry are displayed in the Leeds Central Library.

Pro re nata

(Created) for a special occasion

On medical prescriptions this is abbreviated to "prn" and means "(take) when needed." The phrase is a shade more elegant that its modern cognate, "one-off".

The Free Church of Scotland constitution makes provision for *pro re nata* meetings designed to deal with unforeseen situations which require urgent action.

> "He invented rule and reference *pro re nata*…"
>
> Rudyard Kipling, "The Pit That They Digged".

W. S. Gilbert's Mikado planned to "make the punishment fit the crime", devising ordeals *pro re nata*, such as that of the billiard sharp, made to play "on a cloth untrue, with a twisted cue and elliptical billiard balls". (It would be pedantic in the extreme to suggest that such balls would be something like oblate spheroids rather than elliptical.)

In "The Handbook of Hymen", O. Henry uses the phrase as a malapropism for *persona grata*. "We was soon *pro re nata* with the best society in Rosa."

*Cf. "**Ad hoc**" supra.*

Pros and cons

Pros and contras, arguments for and against

> "After discussing the pros and cons of the matter, including the fact that we were already late for class, we decided to leave the headmaster's body lying where it was."
>
> P. J. Dorricot, *The Nursery Slopes*.

Prosit tibi

May it go well with thee

"Prosit" is still used as a toast especially in Germany, pronounced as if the "i" were absent, but in Britain it has yet to replace "Cheers", "Bottoms up", &c.

"Suddenly the dance finished, Loerke and the students rushed out to bring in drinks. There was an excited clamour of voices, a chinking of mug-lids, a great crying of 'Prosit—Prosit!'"

D. H. Lawrence, *Women in Love*.

Pro tanto

For so much, to that extent

"Every change is a shock; every shock is a *pro tanto* death."

Samuel Butler, *The Way of All Flesh*.

"Subtract any one [mind-]centre from the intimate physiological co-operation, the self is *pro tanto* weakened or mutilated."

Henry Maudsley, "Body and Will".

Pro tempore (pro tem)

For the time being

"The services of Mr William Terence Keogh as acting consul, *pro tem.*, were suggested and accepted."

O. Henry, *Cabbages and Kings*.

The Free Church of Scotland constitution mentions that "in the absence of the Clerk, some one is appointed... to act as Clerk *pro tempore*."

A young lady who came in once a week during the 1939-45 war to help my mother keep our house clean used to explain that she was only working in this way "pro tem" until such time as her husband returned from the war.

Proviso

A (legal) condition

The full Latin term is *proviso quod*, "it being provided that".

"Very well, darling, I shall stop divorce proceedings, and be your ever-loving husband once more till death us do part, with one *proviso*—that you never again ask me to eat lettuce." (Any husband to any wife.)

Prox.

Proximo (mense), during the next month following

In a letter written on, say, 4th May, a mention of "16th *prox*." would refer to 16th June coming. The 16th May would be referred to as "16th *inst*." This practice was once widespread but apparently has now been discontinued.

*Vide "**inst.**" supra.*

Proxime accessit

Came (close) second

Used in the ancient universities to indicate on lists of prizewinners those who didn't quite come first, although some as a consolation award a "Proxime Accessit" prize. Carmel College in Aukland, New Zealand, awards both a "Dux" Cup and a "Proxime Accessit ad Ducem" ("second to the Dux") Cup each year.

Pudenda

(Bodily parts) to be ashamed of

These are the bits below the waist about which Adam and Eve became self-conscious following the unfortunate incident of the apple, and to hide which "they sewed fig-leaves together and made themselves aprons." In these more enlightened days, we are perhaps less ashamed of them and indeed display some of them more or less proudly, according to the extent of our natural endowments, when on a nudist beach. Nevertheless we do tend to keep them modestly covered up in Waitrose or in Westminster Abbey, unless we happen to be very young and very feminine.

The pudenda include A. P. Herbert's "portions of a woman that appeal to man's depravity", which "are constructed with considerable care", and to which doctors have given "delightful Latin names". Most of these names started off life as euphemisms. The *vagina*, for instance, is a sheath: every good blade should have one; while *clitoris* was borrowed coyly from the Greek *kleitoris*.

Men also possess (perhaps less delightful) pudenda. "The features were swollen. The body, white and flabby, without hair, seemed a woman's except for the obscene spectacle of the flaccid *pudenda*." Umberto Eco, *The Name of the Rose*.

Pulveris exigui iactu

—Virgil, *Georgics*, iv. 86

The scattering of a little dust

The full quotation runs: *Hi motus animorum atque hæc certamina tanta / Pulveris exigui iactu compressa quiescent*—"All this turbulence of mind and all this savagery of conflict can be quelled and laid to rest by the scattering of a little dust." Practical advice to farmers on how to subdue a swarm of warring bees!

Horace uses similar words in *Odes* I, xxviii when he reflects on the fate of Archytas, a man of genius, now in his simple grave, the recipient of *Pulveris exigui prope litus parva Matinum munera,...*—"the paltry gifts of a little dust

beside the Matine shore". (Three handfuls of dust were thrown on Roman soldiers killed in battle.)

"Queen Charlotte... has left a legacy of snuff to certain poor-houses; and in her watchful nights this poor woman takes a pinch of Queen Charlotte's snuff, 'and it do comfort me, sir, that it do!' *Pulveris exigui munus.*" (The gift of a little dust.)

W. M. Thackeray, *The Roundabout Papers.*

"Lord John Drummond's hopeful scheme for seizing Edinburgh Castle was quieted *pulveris exigui jactu*, 'the gentlemen were powdering their hair' drinking at a tavern, and bungled the business."

Andrew Lang, *A Short History of Scotland.*

Q

Qua

As, simply as

"A chimney-sweeper, *qua* chimney-sweeper, is not very senti-mental;…"

W. Bagehot, "John Milton".

"His verdict was that the spots *qua* spots didn't amount to a row of beans and could be disregarded."

P. G. Wodehouse: *Aunts Aren't Gentlemen.*

"And now the story can be defined…. *Qua* story, it can only have one merit: that of making the audience want to know what happens next."

E. M. Forster, *Aspects of the Novel.*

Qua cursum ventus

—Virgil, *Aeneid*, iii, 269

Where the wind blows

This is part of a longer extract: *Qua cursum ventusque gubernatorque vocabat—* "Where the wind and the steersman (guv'nor) determine the course".

In *The Oxford Book of English Verse* and also in Palgrave's *Golden Treasury*, the heading *Qua cursum ventus* is given to A. H. Clough's poem "As ships becalmed at eve…", written in regret at the estrangement of former friends.

Quaero

I search for

This is the motto of 544 Squadron of the R.A.F, and is also the name chosen for the European internet search engine sponsored by France and Germany. Another instance of Latin being chosen as a *lingua franca*?

Quaestio
I ask

Not used in English writing very much, if at all, but interesting because, like *"Io"* (*q.v.*), this word gave us a punctuation mark, *viz* the question mark "?", formed originally from the first and last letters of "quaestio" set one upon the other.

Quam celerrime
As quickly as possible

A horse called *Quam Celerrime* (by Xaar out of Divine Secret) may well be running today at Haydock Park.

> "'Get the same car, Kershaw—nice, comfy seats—and pick me up from home *quam celerrime*.' 'Pardon?' 'Smartish!'"
>
> Colin Dexter, The *Remorseful Day*.

Quarto
Fourth

The size of page obtained when a sheet of paper has been folded so as to make four leaves of a book; written 4to for short. The name is applied also to a book composed of sheets folded in this way. *Cf. "octavo", supra.*

Quasi
As if, like

A "quango" is a Quasi-Autonomous Non-Governmental Organization. A quasi-historical novel is based only loosely on such historical facts as are known for (more or less) certain.

> "Lewis stood above the mother and child, smiling quasi-paternally and drawing the back of his right index-finger lightly across the cherubic cheek."
>
> Colin Dexter, *The Remorseful Day*.

Quasi cursores vitai lampada tradunt
—Lucretius, *De Rerum Natura*, ii. 1
Like runners who pass on the torch of life

That is, who pass on the torch of life and having done so, die. The preceding line runs: *Inque brevi spatio mutantur sæcla animantum*—"And in a brief space of time generations of living creatures succeed one another". (N.B., *"vitai"* is used apparently only by Lucretius in place of the normal genitive singular of *vita* which is *vitae*.)

189

The idea is captured in Rupert Brooke's, "The Hill".

> "'And when we die
> All's over that is ours; and life burns on
> Through other lovers, other lips,' said I,…"

and less comfortably in Walt Whitman:

> "Those corpses of young men,
> Those martyrs that hang from the gibbets,…
> … live elsewhere with unslaughtered vitality.
> They live in other young men, O Kings!
> They live in brothers, ready to defy you!"

Sir Henry Newbolt wrote a poem with the title *Vitaï Lampada*—"There's a breathless hush in the close tonight…"

"Lampada" derives from the Greek "lampas", meaning a torch or lamp, the old lamp burning oil and with a wick, so old in fact that the word has travelled with the artefact all over Europe and into neighbouring regions. The Portuguese for "lamp" is "lampada"; the word "lamp" or a variant of it (lampa, lampe, etc.) still exists in most European languages today, from Russian, Hungarian, Serbo-Croat, through all the Scandinavian languages to Irish and Welsh, as well as in Turkish and Armenian.

Quasi Cursores is the motto of Oakham School, Rutland.

Lampada ferens, "bearing torches", is the motto of Hull University. *Cf.* **"timeo Danaos"** *infra.*

Quem Juppiter vult perdere, dementat prius
—James Duport
Whom Jupiter wishes to destroy, he first sends mad
Several versions of this cheerful thought exist, and they tend to intermingle. *Vide* **"quos deus…"** *infra.*

Quia amore langueo
—Song of Solomon, ii. 5
Since I languish for love
The full Vulgate version of the verse is *Fulcite me floribus, stipate me malis, quia amore langueo.* The Authorized Version renders this as "Stay me with flagons, comfort me with apples: for I am sick of love". (*Floribus* is "with flowers" rather than "with flagons", and more modern versions have "with raisins". The original Hebrew has "grape-cakes".)

The Authorized Version is slightly misleading in its use of the phrase "sick of love", which is analogous with "sick of the palsy", and which means "love-sick" rather than *fatigatus et ægrotatus*.

In *The Oxford Book of English Verse*, the heading *Quia Amore Langueo* is given to an anonymous 14th century poem "In a valley of this restles (*sic*) mind", in which each of the fifteen stanzas ends with *Quia amore langueo*. In this allegorical poem Christ is wooing mankind, and yearns for His love to be returned. Part of this poem was set to music for an *a capella* chorus by Francis Pitt in 1989, with the title *Amore Langueo*.

Qui desiderat pacem, praeparet bellum

—Flavius Vegetius Renatus, *De Rei Militari c.* 390 B.C.
Whoever seeks for peace, let him prepare for war
Cf. "si vis pacem, para bellum" infra.

Quidnunc

What now?

A gossip, always asking after the latest scandal. (In Latin the two words are separate: "Quid nunc?")

The members of the "Quidnuncs" cricket team have all played cricket for Cambridge University, usually in the 'Varsity match against Oxford. Patrick Campbell (the 3rd Baron Glenavy) wrote for *The Irish Times* under the pseudonym "Quidnunc".

> "It so happening that some considerable amount of youthful energy and quidnunc ability were required to set litigation afloat at Hong-Kong, Mr Romer was sent thither as the fittest man for such work."
>
> Anthony Trollope, *Doctor Thorne*.

> Mrs Dangle: "I have no patience with you!—haven't you made yourself the jest of all your acquaintance by interference in matters where you have no business? Are you not called a theatrical Quidnunc...?"
>
> R. B. Sheridan, *The Critic*, I, 1.

Quid pro quo

Something equivalent in return

F. P. Smoler, writing in *The Observer*, mentions "the gangster Frank Costello, with whom [J. Edgar] Hoover had a notorious *quid pro quo*", a mutual understanding of give and take.

"At the time, though, he was not aware... of the extraordinary service he would have to render as the *quid pro quo* of the agreement."

Colin Dexter, The Jewel that was Ours.

When the secretary of a village football club wrote asking a town club of somewhat higher standing for a friendly match, the secretary of the other club wrote suggesting a date for the game "providing you will be willing to give us a *quid pro quo*", i.e., a return game. The first secretary replied saying: "My committee has asked me to send the pound for the professional you mentioned, although they are surprised at such a request from a club of your standing".

The technically correct plural of *quid pro quo* is either *qua pro quo* or *quæ pro quo*, but it seems sensible to follow the example of such writers as Ivor Brown who, in *Chosen Words*, mentioned *quids pro quo*. This is preferable to the frequently seen *quid pro quos*.

Quietus (est)
He is quit

A legal term indicating that someone has discharged all his debts and is free to go. In "The Duchess of Malfi" the Duchess tells her newly-acquired husband, Antonio, her former steward:

> I thank you, gentle love:
> And 'cause you shall not come to me in debt,
> Being now my steward, here upon your lips
> I sign your *Quietus est*.

For others one's *quietus* is one's end.

> "For who would bear the whips and scorns of time,...
> When he himself might his quietus make
> With a bare bodkin?"

Shakespeare, Hamlet, III, i.

"Then I turned to see how Good had fared with the big bull, which I had heard screaming with rage and pain as I gave mine his quietus."

H. Rider Haggard, King Solomon's Mines.

Qui nullum fere scribendi genus non tetigit, Nullum quod tetigit non ornavit

Who left scarcely any style of writing untouched, and touched nothing that he did not adorn

This forms part of the epitaph which Samuel Johnson composed for Oliver Goldsmith (1728-64), and which can be found in Westminster Abbey. When somebody suggested it should have been in English, Johnson retorted that he would never consent to disgrace the walls of Westminster Abbey with an English inscription. "The language of the country of which a learned man was a native is not the language fit for his epitaph, which should be in ancient and permanent language. Consider, Sir, how you should feel, were you to find at Rotterdam an epitaph upon Erasmus *in Dutch!*"

Quis custodiet ipsos custodes?

*Vide "**pone seram,...**" supra.*

Quis desiderio sit pudor aut modus Tam cari capitis

—Horace, *Odes*, I, xxiv. 1,2
What shame should there be or what limit in grief for one so dear?

This poignant thought appears frequently in Latin inscriptions on tombstones and memorials in churches. *Quis desiderio sit pudor* is the name of a cantata composed by Karl Graun (1704-59) on the death of King Frederick William I of Prussia.

Quod erat demonstrandum (Q.E.D.)

—Euclid
Which was to be demonstrated

On a note of triumph the initials Q.E.D. appeared at the conclusion of each proof in the geometry book I used at school, ignoring the fact that for myself and for my classmates the logic of the steps leading to the proof was usually completely incomprehensible. *Vide "**pons asinorum**" supra.*

> "So, the matter was clear: one, the shoes in the cabin belonged to Joanna Franks; two, the shoes had been worn by the drowned woman; therefore, three, the drowned woman was Joanna Franks—QED."
>
> Colin Dexter, *The Wench is Dead.*

Q.E.D. is the name for a website for computer graphics.

Quod vide (q.v.)
Which see
This is an invitation to look at something. If there is more than one thing the writer would like you to see, he will use *qq.v.* standing for *qua vide*—"Which (plural) see".

Quondam
Formerly
> "Here, waiting to be reborn, were the tribal memories of Arthur, *quondam Rex que futurus*, the once and future king."
> Frank Morley, *The Great North Road.*

More often used as an adjective to mean "former". "When... Robert Adley, M.P., spoke out against his quondam guru [Viscountess Thatcher] and called her ladyship 'a former Finchley fishwife'..." Pendennis, *The Guardian.*

Quorum
Of whom
Used originally in connection with the number of justices of the peace who had to be present in court before business could begin; and thence as a term for the magistracy itself.

> "I must not omit that Sir Roger [de Coverley] is a Justice of the *Quorum*; that he fills the chair at a Quarter-Session with great Abilities, and three months ago gain'd universal Applause by explaining a Passage in the Game-Act."
> Richard Steele, "The Spectator Club".

Now used to indicate the minimum number of members of any committee or suchlike body who must be present before business may commence.

In the opening lines of *The Merry Wives of Windsor*, Slender manages to mangle the word, referring to Justice Shallow as "In the county of Gloucester, justice of peace and 'Coram'."

Quos deus vult perdere, prius dementat
—Boswell's Johnson
Whom God wishes to destroy, he first sends mad
D. H. Lawrence quotes this thought in his poem "It is strange to think..."

"Will the Proustian lot go next?
And then our English imitation intelligensia?
Is it the *Quem vult perdere Deus* business?"

In this quotation, as in that which follows, the singular *quem* replaces the plural *quos*.

"They cut down repairs;… and… they hid their defeeciences (*sic*) wi' paint an' cheap gildin'. *Quem Deus vult perrdere prrius dementat*, ye remember."—Rudyard Kipling, "Bread upon the Waters". In Kipling's day Chief Engineers in the merchant fleet could use Latin when the occasion called for it. *O tempora…*

*Vide "**quem Juppiter vult perdere…**" supra.*

Quota
A share

A useful term based on the Latin *quot?*—"how many?" and familiar from its use in deciding how much fish, milk, etc, a particular person or organization may catch, produce, market, import or export.

"Richard was careful to put in his daily quota of press-ups—twenty before breakfast, twenty after lunch, and twenty coming home on the train."

Quot homines, tot sententiae
—Terence, *Phormio*, 454

However many men, so many opinions

On 8th June 2005 Hansard reports that Sir Menzies Campbell commented in the House of Commons on the apparent multiplicity of opinions on the Opposition benches: "I know that it is advised that Latin be used sparingly in the House, but I cannot help saying, '*Quot homines, tot sententiæ*'."

Quo vadis?
—John xvi. 5

Whither goest thou?

Jesus tells his disciples: "But now I go my way to him that sent me; and none of you asketh me, Whither goest thou?"

At a later date, so the legend has it, St. Peter was fleeing from certain death in Rome when he met Jesus, and asked Him this question. Jesus replied that He was going to Rome to be crucified again. Suitably shamed, Peter returned to Rome to meet his own fate.

As well as being the name of a restaurant in London, *Quo Vadis* is the name of a book written by Henryk Sienkiewicz in 1896, and subsequently made into a film in 1902. Other films followed, the best-known being made in 1951 and starring Robert Taylor and Deborah Kerr.

Quo vadis sequimur—"Whither thou goest we follow"—is the motto of Didsbury College, Bristol.

R

R (Rex, Regina, or Recipe)
King, Queen, or recipe

Radix malorum est cupiditas
The love of money is the root of (all) evil

This is a shortened form of the verse in 1 Timothy vi. 10: *"Radix enim omnium malorum est cupiditas"*. Chaucer quotes it in the Prologue to the Pardoner's Tale:

> "My theme is alwey oon, and evere was –
> *Radix malorum est Cupiditas"*.

Rara avis in terris, nigroque simillima cycno
—Juvenal, *Satires*, vi. 165
A rare bird on earth, like a black swan

Juvenal knew nothing of the black swans of Australia: his simile carried weight. The reference was to a chaste and faithful wife. To be fair, he said that a good man is a rare animal too: *Vir bonum est animal rarum.*

Jeremy Sams, writing in *The Independent*, said of Lorenzo the Magnificent that "he was after all, that *rara avis*, a Jewish Catholic priest with a wife and children".

Rara Avis is the name of a rainforest reserve in Costa Rica, and also of an Alternative band from Bratislava.

Re
Concerning

"*Re* your complaint about the curious behaviour of our representative, we have now fully investigated the circumstances, and confirm that she…"
Two letters in place of ten seems admirable economy. *Cf. "in re" supra.*

Recipe (℞)
Take

The tri-syllabic pronunciation of "re-ci-pe" betrays its Latin origins as the imperative of *recipere*, "to take". The stroke (sometimes a curlicue) on the tail of the R is a mark of abbreviation.

Reductio ad absurdum
Reduction to the absurd

A method of proof which begins by making assumptions and which follows the logical implications of those assumptions until a conclusion is reached "which is absurd", thereby showing that one or more of the original assumptions must be false.

> "If there be two boarders on the same flat,… and the wrangle between one boarder and the landlady be equal to the wrangle between the landlady and the other, then shall the weekly bills of the two boarders be equal also,…
>
> For if not, let one bill be the greater.
>
> Then the other bill is less than it might have been—which is absurd."

> Stephen Leacock, *Literary Lapses*,
> "Boarding-house Geometry".

[Although the following passage is completely outside the remit of this book, it seems a great shame to deprive the reader of another piece of "Boarding-house Geometry": "The landlady of a boarding-house is a parallelogram—that is, an oblong angular figure, which cannot be described, but which is equal to anything."]

In *Cloud Atlas*, David Mitchell argued that "The *reductio ad absurdum* of M.D.'s view [that only professional diplomats, inveterate idiots and women view diplomacy as a long-term substitute for war],… was that science devises ever bloodier means of war…"

Nowadays the phrase is used to highlight any absurdity. In an *Observer* article on the question of abortion in Ireland, Emily Bell quoted the *Irish Times* as describing the sequence of events as "just the latest *reductio ad absurdum* in the theatre of the absurd of Irish public life".

Referendum
To be referred to

A referendum is a call to the people to give their opinion on a particular question. The plural of referendum is *referenda*, but this would suggest that more than one question is asked, rather than that more than one referendum is to be issued. In the latter case, we have to accept the plural "referendums".

Regalia
Symbols of royalty

Originally these could also be the powers attached to the throne, but now the term applies only to visible symbols of majesty—the crown, the sceptre, the orb, the sword of state, &c. Other organizations, particularly the Masonic orders, also have their regalia.

The present royal regalia were made for the coronation of Charles II after the Restoration of 1660, the mediaeval regalia having been destroyed at the behest of Parliament in 1643.

Regina
The Queen

Criminal cases are brought to court by the Director of Public Prosecutions. The Crown Prosecution Service acts in the name of the Queen, and so each such case is referred to as *Regina versus* the accused. At times when the monarch happens to be a king, then the case is *Rex versus* the accused.

Regina Coeli
Queen of Heaven

This is the title of an antiphon or prayer to the Blessed Virgin Mary at Easter, dating from the twelfth century. The prayer begins: *Regina Coeli, laetare...*—"Queen of Heaven, rejoice..." *Coeli* is pronounced as the Italians would pronounce "celi", showing the influence of the Roman Catholic Church, to whom after all *Regina Coeli* is special. The pronunciation of Ecclesiastical Latin recommended by Pope Pius X was made clear in the *Liber Usalis*, a former chant book for Mass. (*Vide* also "***ora pro nobis***" *supra*.)

Coeli is the genitive singular of *coelum*, a neuter noun. (Incidentally the spelling *coelum* for the classical Latin *caelum* is said to be an error perpetrated in the Middle Ages and perpetuated ever since, although the standard dictionaries of Latin now use *caelum* in preference to *coelum*.) However *caelum/coelum* in the singular means "the heavens", so that *Regina Coeli* strictly means "Queen of the heavens". From this it follows that the plural of *coelum* should not mean very much, but if *coelum* has a plural, then as a neuter noun it should have the plural *caela/coela*. However in *pleni sunt coeli et terra gloria tua*, "the heavens and the earth are full of thy glory", we appear to have the

199

plural *coeli*, which suggests that the Church at some time reclassified *coelum* as masculine. Some fields of Latin grammar are fluid.

From time to time, we find the Virgin allotted an extended territory for her realm, as when she is addressed as *Regina Caelorum*, specifically as "Queen of the Heavens".

Rem acu tetigisti
—Plautus, *Rudens*, V, ii. 19
You have touched the thing with a needle
It seems the Romans had a more delicate touch than the barbarians who displaced them, who were disposed to hitting the nail on the head.

> "Extremely gratifying, sir," he said, and I agreed with him that he had *tetigisti*-ed the *rem acu*.
> P. G. Wodehouse: *Aunts Aren't Gentlemen.*

> "'*Rem acu* once again,' said Sir Piercie, 'and not without good cause, since my neck, if I remained, might have been brought within the circumstance of a halter.'"
> Sir Walter Scott, *The Monastery.*

Requiem
Rest
The first word of the Requiem Mass, the Mass for the Dead.

Requiem aeternam dona eis, Domine, et lux perpetua luceat eis
–From the Requiem Mass
Grant them, O Lord, eternal rest, and may light perpetual shine upon them
If this request is put into the singular, it becomes *Requiem aeternam dona ei, Domine, et lux perpetua luceat ei*—"Grant him/her…", the dative of *is* being *ei* in both the masculine and the feminine.

Requiescat in pace (R.I.P.)
May he/she rest in peace
R.I.P. is a familiar inscription on tombstones and memorial tablets.
> "Lady Mary did not live long after her return to England…. *Requiescat in pace*; for she quarrelled all her life."
> W. Bagehot, *Literary Essays*, "Lady Mary Wortley Montague".
> "After running up the house [the mine-owner] finds he only had $2.80 left to furnish it with, so he invests that in whisky and jumps

off the roof on a spot where he now requiescats in pieces."

O. Henry, "Philanthromathematics".

In *The Oxford Book of English Verse*, the heading *Requiescat* is given to Matthew Arnold's poem, "Strew on her roses, roses, And never a spray of yew. In quiet she reposes:…"

Rerum cognoscere causas
To know the causes of things

The motto of *inter alia* the London School of Economics. *Vide "**felix qui potuit rerum cognoscere causas**" supra.*

Res ipsa loquitur
The thing speaks for itself

Or "The facts speak for themselves". On the surface it suggests the argument to end all argument, but for a description of its full legal implications, see, for example, John Gray's *Lawyers' Latin* (Hale).

Res on its own is a versatile word with a very wide variety of meanings and could mean literally "any thing". One meaning could be "the matter in hand".

> "I rapped [my aunt] sharply on the top-knot with a paper-knife of Oriental design…
>
> 'Don't wander from the *res*….'"
>
> P. G. Wodehouse, *Much Obliged, Jeeves*.

Respice finem
Look to the end

The anonymous writer of *Gesta Romanorum* wrote: *Quicquid agas, prudenter agas, et respice finem*—"Whatever you do, do it circumspectly, and keep the end in view".

In *The Oxford Book of English Verse*, the heading *Respice Finem* is given to Francis Quarles' epigram, "My soul, sit thou a patient looker-on; Judge not the play before the play is done:… the last act crowns the play."

Respice finem is the name of a Czech documentary film of 1967 by Jan Spáta about the loneliness, wisdom and humility of old women. It is also the motto of, *inter alia*, the family of Dickson of Corstorphine; of Homerton College, Cambridge; of Newmarket, and of 285 Squadron of the R.A.F.

Resurgam

I shall rise again

This terse epitaph inscribed on a gravestone was popular in the sixteenth and seventeenth centuries, but became less popular later.

"[Helen's] grave is in Brocklebridge Churchyard: for fifteen years after her death it was only covered by a grassy mound; but now a gray marble tablet marks the spot, inscribed with her name, and the word '*Resurgam*'."

Charlotte Brontë, *Jane Eyre*.

Resurgam is said to have been found engraved on a lump of stone excavated from the ruins of Old St. Paul's, destroyed in the Great Fire of London, 1666, carrying promise of the successful rebuilding of the cathedral. It is the motto of the families of Blake of Tillmouth and of Stewart of New Hall, and of the city of Portland, Maine, the motto referring to Portland's recoveries from four devastating fires.

"Resurgam" was the name of the first mechanically-powered (steam-driven) British submarine, designed and built by Rev. George Garrett in 1879. The name reflected her builder's confidence in her ability to resurface, and her trials proved successful, although she was lost at sea when under tow in 1880.

R.I. (Rex Imperator, Regina Imperatrix)

King Emperor, Queen Empress

*Vide "**Ind. Imp.**" supra.*

Rigor mortis

A stiffening of the body in death

Apparently not only in death but occasionally in life also, since "Rigor Mortis" was the nickname given to a particularly unbending nurse in Richard Gordon's *Doctor in the House*.

Ian Buruma, writing in *The Guardian*, suggests that making a utensil as a pure work of art "can lead to decadence, when the stylised performance hardens into a kind of aesthetic *rigor mortis*".

Rigor Mortis is the name of a Thrash Metal band founded in Texas.

Rostrum

A beak, a prow

A pulpit or platform, such as that in the Forum in Rome from which orators addressed the public, and which was decorated with the prows of ships.

Ruat coelum, fiat justitia

Though the heavens fall, let justice be done
   *Vide "**fiat justitia,…**" supra.*

Rus in urbe

Countryside in the town

Martial uses this phrase in his *Epigrams*, xii, 57, 21 (A.D. 103).

> "Bloomsbury is the very height of the mode… 'Tis *rus in urbe*. You have gardens all the way to Hampstead."
>
> W. M. Thackeray, *Henry Esmond*.

Per contra the County Borough of Solihull in Warwickshire has adopted the reverse of this concept as its motto; *Urbs in Rure*, "Town in the Countryside".

Custodes Ruris in Urbe—"Guardians of the Countryside in the City"—is the motto of the Wimbledon and Putney Common Conservators.

S

Sal
Salt

Sal volatile, or smelling salts containing ammonium carbonate, could be found in any lady's reticule in the days when ladies were prone to fainting at the drop of a hat or a handkerchief. Sal ammoniac or ammonium chloride was one of the four "spirits" of the alchemists.

> "The firste spirit quyksilver called is,
> The second orpyment, the thridde, iwis,
> Sal armonyak, and the ferthe brymstoon."
> > Chaucer, The Canon's Yeoman's Tale.

> "Only the swift deployment of the *sal volatile* bottle restored Aunt Laetitia to a state of automobility and saved us the effort of carrying her nineteen stone upstairs to her bedroom."
> > P. J. Dorricot, *Escape from the Nursery*.

Salve
(God) save you!

Used as a greeting or as a farewell (God speed!), or as a benediction following a sneeze. "**SALVE**" is incised as a welcome on the granite threshold of Pencarrow House in Cornwall.

In *The Oxford Book of English Verse*, the heading *Salve!* is given to a poem by T. E. Brown which includes the line "Then bid the man God-speed!"

Sanctum sanctorum
Holy of holies

According to Brewer's Dictionary, the *Sanctum sanctorum* was the "Holy of Holies in the Jewish Temple, a small chamber into which none but the high priest might enter..." It is applied to any place, physical or metaphorical, where a man or woman may be safe from intrusion.

"Mdlle. Reuter turned her eye laterally upon me, to ascertain, probably, whether I was collected enough to be ushered into her *sanctum sanctorum.*"

Charlotte Brontë, *The Professor.*

"I also got to see the small room in which he works, which... is like a *santum (sic) sanctorum.*"

Report in *The Guardian.*

Jonathan Keates, writing in *The Observer*, cited a writer's "essay on football, that *sanctum sanctorum* of British maleness..."

This style of phrase was used to express the superlative in Hebrew, and the Holy of Holies is therefore the holiest place. Similarly the phrase *vanitas vanitatum (q.v. infra)*, "Vanity of vanities", to be found in Ecclesiastes, denoted the utmost, the final vanity.

Sanctus, sanctus, sanctus,
Dominus Deus Sabaoth,
pleni sunt coeli et terra gloria tua.
Hosanna in excelsis

—The Mass

Holy, holy, holy, Lord God of hosts, heaven and earth are full of thy glory. Hosanna in the highest.

Known understandably as "The Sanctus", this is part of the Communion service in the Book of Common Prayer.

Sapere aude

—Horace, Epistola I, 2, 40

Dare to be wise

The motto of Manchester Grammar School, of Oldham, and of Oxfordshire County Council; and the name also of an Australian Heavy Metal band.

Sartor Resartus

The tailor patched up

Literally "The tailor re-tailored". The title of a book by Thomas Carlyle (1833), in which Carlyle examines and comments on the distinction between down-to-earth empiricism ("patching together") and high-minded romanticism. It is the biography of a fictional Diogenes Teufelsdröckh whose *magnum opus* was *Clothes, Their Origin and Influence*, and in the book Carlyle seeks to study Teufelsdröckh and his origin and influence.

Scilicet (sc.)
Namely, to wit

This is one of a number of expressions (*cf. "i.e.", "viz"*) used to specify who or what we are talking about. *Scilicet* tends to refer to someone we have already mentioned but whose identity is not clear from the context.

> "He (*sc.* Dr Johnson) disapproved of introducing scripture phrases into secular discourses. This seemed to me a question of some difficulty. A scripture expression may be used like a highly classical phrase to produce an instantaneous strong impression."
> James Boswell, *The Life of Samuel Johnson, LL.D.*

Sculpsit
Sculpted
Cf. fecit, pinxit.

Semper eadem
Always the same

The motto of Queen Elizabeth I and of later English queens, and only of queens, since *eadem* is feminine. However, families, cities and schools are also feminine and it is the motto of the families of Cullimore, Ovey and Panton, of the City of Leicester, and of Elizabeth College, Guernsey, and of Ipswich school.

One of the poems in Baudelaire's *Les Fleurs du Mal* bears the title *Semper Eadem.*

Semper fidelis
Ever faithful

This is the motto of many prominent families, including those of Firth of the Flush and Thompson of Old Nunthorpe, and also of the East Devon Militia, the City of Exeter, the Plymouth Argyle Football Club, the U.S. Marine Corps, and the Reliance Mutual Life Assurance Society.

Semper paratus
Always prepared

I was a keen Boy Scout in my youth and young manhood, and our motto was "Be Prepared". Had I been a French "Éclaireur", I should have been "Toujours Prêt", and had I been a Roman *Puer Explorator*, I should no doubt have been *Semper Paratus*.

Tom Lehrer wrote a song about the Boy Scouts of America, which included the advice to any scout with amorous feelings who met a Girl Scout who was similarly inclined: "Don't be scared, be prepared".

This is also the motto of several prominent families, including those of Clifford, Elphinstone of Sowerby, Usticke, and Upton of Ingmire, and also of the U.S. Coastguard.

Seriatim
One after another, in regular order
> "Ye're under sealed orders," said he, tee-heein' an' scratchin' himself. "Yon's they—to be opened *seriatim*."
>> Rudyard Kipling, "Bread upon the Waters".

> "Morse was visited by one of the ten-a-penny dieticians in the place... who took him *seriatim* through a host of low-calorie vegetables on which he could 'fill up' *ad libitum*: asparagus; bamboo-shoots; beans (broad);..."
>> Colin Dexter, *The Wench is Dead*.

Sic
In this way, in this manner
Used to make it clear that whatever is printed is of someone else's devising; or that, believe it or not, this is the truth.

"In his letter he wrote: 'The new regulations have not superceded (*sic*) the old regulations but have clarified them'." *Sic* here means: "Have no fear; I know how to spell 'superseded' if he doesn't."

> "He claimed to have slept with 3000 (*sic*) women during the three weeks that he spent in Paris."
>> Q. Q. Enwright, *Mistress and Maid*.

Sic itur ad astra
Such is the way to the stars
> Vide "***macte nova virtute***" *supra*.

Sic transit gloria mundi
—Thomas à Kempis, *De Imitatione Christi* (Of the Imitation of Christ)
Thus passes the glory of the world
À Kempis in fact wrote: *O quam cito transit gloria mundi*—"O how swiftly passes..." The phrase *Sic transit...* derives from this and is used at the enthronement of a new pope. Three times a monk interrupts the ceremony,

holding a piece of burning flax on a pole and saying *Sic transit gloria mundi* as the flax burns away. *Cf. "**memento hominem**" supra.*

> "... as I reached the spot, there was nothing left but the sweep of a white muslin curtain, and a balsam plant in a flower-pot, covered with a flush of bloom—'sic transit,' et cetera."
>
> Charlotte Brontë, *Shirley*.

At some time in the future, if it has not already happened, an Asian-owned transport firm will find a receptionist who can legitimately answer the telephone with the phrase: "Sikh Transit, Gloria Munday."

The phrase can be adapted to lament the passing of the glory of places of lesser extent, such as a town.

> "Outside the railings, the hollow square of crumbling houses, shells of a bygone gentry, leaned as if in ghostly gossip over the forgotten doings of the vanished quality. *Sic transit gloria urbis.*"
>
> O. Henry, "Proof of the Pudding".

Sic volo sic iubeo
Such is my will, such is my command

In his *Satires*, vi. 223, Juvenal presents the picture of a vindictive wife demanding of a hen-pecked husband that a slave be crucified for an imaginary misdemeanour: *Hoc volo, sic iubeo, sit pro ratione voluntas*—"This I wish, thus I command, let my will be reason (enough)." From this derives the (fairly) commonly-used phrase, *sic volo, sic iubeo*.

> "When Lady Kew said *Sic volo, sic jubeo*, I promise you few persons of her ladyship's belongings stopped, before they did her biddings, to ask her reasons."
>
> W. M. Thackeray, *The Newcomes*.

A review of Georges Duby's *France in the Middle Ages* recognises that "It is a major tribute... that he has been able to deal with publishers in his *sic volo sic iubeo* style."

"Surely you're not mowing the lawn at this time of the year? It's mid-winter!" "I'm doing it to please my wife. She wanted it done." "Why?" "*Sic volo, sic iubeo*. Who can fathom the workings of a woman's mind?"

LIVING LATIN

Si monumentum requiris, circumspice
If you want a monument, look around you

This appears on Sir Christopher Wren's memorial stone in St. Paul's Cathedral, set there by his son, Christopher. The old pronunciation can be inferred from the story of the old verger who believed that the last word translated as "Sir, come, spy, see".

Si Monumentum Requiris is the title of a poem by the Australian poet Bruce Dawe, dedicated to the orthopaedic surgeon Dr Wai-ki Pun who gave him two new hips.

In *Eyeless in Gaza*, Aldous Huxley conflates two quotations, this one and Horace's *Parturient montes, nascetur ridiculus mus (q.v.):*

"Millions of books.... Mountains of the spirit in interminable birth-pangs; and the result was—what? Well, *si ridiculum murem requiris, circumspice.*" (If you want to see a laughable little mouse, just look around you.)

The State of Michigan has adapted this phrase for its motto:—*Si quaeris peninsulam amoenam, circumspice* "If you seek a pleasant peninsula, look around you".

Simplex munditiis
Simple in (her/his/their) elegance

Horace, in his *Odes* I, v, so addresses his *quondam* girl-friend: "Pyrrha,... simple in thy elegance".

> "I should be glad to see you the instrument of introducing into our style that simplicity which is the best and truest ornament of most things in life, which the politer age always aimed at in their building and dress, *simplex munditiis*, as well as in their productions of wit."
>
> Jonathan Swift, "On Style".

In *The Oxford Book of English Verse*, the heading *Simplex Munditiis* is given to Ben Jonson's poem, "Still to be neat, still to be drest / As you were going to a feast;..." admonishing a girl who was always and unfailingly dressed up to the nines.

Simplex Munditiis is the motto of Viscount Simonds, and of the families of Philips and of Symonds of Pilsdon.

Sine die
Without a day (being fixed)

When a law sitting or other gathering is adjourned *sine die*, it means that it has finished its business and almost certainly will never be reconvened.

"Stuart continued to maintain that theirs was best, being representative of the middle course.

"The MEETING adjourned sine die."

Julian Barnes, *Talking It Over*.

Sine metu
Without fear

This is the motto of the branch of the Jameson family which invented Jameson's Irish whiskey, (*cf.* "***acta non verba***" *supra*) and it appears on all their bottles. It is also the name of an Irish reel, whose connection with whiskey is open to conjecture.

Sine qua non
Without which nothing (happens)

Short for *causa* (or *conditio*) *sine qua non*. It is the motto of 540 Squadron of the R.A.F.

"Mr Wilson held, secondly, that the *sine qua non*, the great prerequisite to a good paper currency, was the maintenance of an adequate reserve by the issuer."

W. Bagehot, "The Right Hon. James Wilson".

"And we have the Unity of Action, or should have, because this condition is surely a *sine qua non* of all good writing…"

Philip Larkin, "What Are We Writing For?"

"It is a *sine qua non* of the Coarse costume that it is impossible to move in it."

Michael Green, *The Art of Coarse Acting*.

In Nichola Thorne's *Never Such Innocence*, Constance had been taught that "respect for her elders was a *sine qua non* of existence".

A government farming expert, speaking on the radio about grassland, once famously remarked that a *sine qua non* of a good ley was a firm bottom.

Si non oscillas, noli tintinnare
If you don't swing, don't ring

Hugh Hefner's Playboy Mansion in Chicago boasted a brass plate on the door with this Latin inscription.

Siste, viator

Pause, traveller

An invitation to passers-by to pause long enough to read an inscription on a tomb or memorial.

Sit venia verbo

May the word be allowed

Literally "may there be permission to the word" or "forgive the expression" or even "Pardon my French". A useful phrase, used mostly by German writers following Nietzsche, but there is no reason why English writers should not adopt it. In *The Guardian*, in an extract from *On Love and Death*, translated from the German by Anthea Bell, Patrick Süskind says "... the entire act... has something terribly well-constructed about it, and indeed—*sit venia verbo*—can be described as Kleist's *magnum opus*."

Sit venia verbo is the title of a book by Michel Deutsch and Philippe Lacoue-Labarthe.

Si vis pacem, para bellum

If you want peace, prepare for war

This is an adaptation of a suggestion urged by Vegetius *c*. 390 B.C. in his *De Rei Militari*—"On War". It is the motto of 604 Squadron (County of Middlesex) of the Auxiliary Air Force.

NATO in its peace-keeping role adopted the 9 mm Luger Parabellum cartridge for use in pistols and sub-machine-guns.

Cf. "**qui desiderat pacem...**" *supra.*

Soles occidere et redire possunt:
Nobis cum semel occidit brevis lux
Nox est perpetua una dormienda

—Catullus, *Carmina* v

Suns of heaven may set and rise again,
For us, when once our own brief light is out,
Our night is one eternal sleep

This somewhat gloomy thought is of one mind with *Carpe Diem* (*q.v. supra*), and is addressed with high optimism to a modest young lady, Lesbia. *Vivamus, mea Lesbia, atque amemus*—"Let us live, my Lesbia, and let us love" (*q.v. infra*.)

Andrew Marvell had the same trouble with his coy mistress:

> "The grave's a fine and private place,
> But none I think do there embrace."

Catullus was confident that this line of argument could not fail to bear fruit. The next line is *Da mi basia mille*—"Give me a thousand kisses", and then a thousand more, practically *ad infinitum*. For a pretty faithful translation into English of the whole poem, *vide* S. T. Coleridge, "My Lesbia, let us love and live".

Nox dormienda is the title of a novel by Kelli Stanley, and the phrase occurs frequently thoughout the text of Anthony Burgess's novel, *The Kingdom of the Wicked*.

Solidus (s.)
Shilling

The solidus was a Roman coin which gave its name in the Middle Ages to the British shilling; British "pounds, shillings and pence" were indicated by the letters "£ s d" which stood for "libræ, solidi, denarii". So 20s. = £1 meant either "twenty shillings make a pound" or "twenty solidi make one libra". The "s." of "solidi" became lengthened, as some letter s's still are in German, and as many English s's used to be, giving rise incidentally to the erroneous view that e.g. "Miſs Marple" was inexplicably the same as "Miſs Marple". (This way of writing "Miss" with the long s (ſ, italic ſ, distinct from f and ſ) persisted well into the second half of the nineteenth century in Britain.) So 20s. was written for much of the time as 20/-, and 2s. 6d. was written as 2/6. Furthermore the use of the long "s" was extended by analogy so that £3 15s. 6d. was written as £3/15/6.

The "long s" is still in use today as a "forward slash" or a fraction bar—we write 3/7 for "three sevenths"—and the technical term for this symbol "/" is still "solidus".

Vestiges of the "solidus" persisted in Italy until not so long ago when 20 soldi were worth one lira: in France the 5 centime coin was (still is?) known as a "sou". "Solidi" were used to pay fighting men in an army, who are consequently still known as "soldiers".

Solitudinem faciunt, pacem appellant
—Tacitus, *Agricola* 30
They make a wilderness and call it peace

Calgacus, the British leader, had no illusions about the *Pax Romana*. It seems that a scorched-earth policy is nothing new.

William Keegan, writing in *The Observer*, observed that "Tacitus summed up the situation in Iraq nearly 2,000 years ago, when writing about a country closer to home: 'Ubi solitudinem faciunt, pacem appellant'". ("Where they create a wilderness, they call it peace.")

In Iris Murdoch's *The Time of the Angels*, Marcus Fisher alters the tense from present to perfect: "They have made". He notes that a large area around the old Rectory and church tower has been cleared, and is told that planning permission to develop it had been withdrawn at the last moment. He comments: "*Solitudinem fecerunt* all right".

Solus
Alone

"Enter WITGOOD, a gentleman, *solus*." A stage direction from Act I of Thomas Middleton's "*A Trick to Catch the Old One*".

> "I know I did not reason, I did not plan or intend; yet, whereas one moment I was sitting solus on the chair near the table, the next I held Frances on my knee, placed there with sharpness and decision, and retained with exceeding tenacity."
>
> Charlotte Brontë, *The Professor*.

Solus has largely lost its place in English writing to its Italian derivative "solo", so that in 1933 Wiley Post became the first man to fly round the world *solo* rather than *solus*.

Cf. "**Nunquam se minus otiosum...**" *supra*.

Solvitur ambulando
It is solved by walking

That is, by observation and by poking one's nose into things, rather than by sitting and cogitating on the details of the crime supplied by someone else. Colin Dexter heads chapter 13 of *The Jewel that was Ours* with this phrase. It is also for some reason the motto of the family of Lord Pearson.

In "What the Tortoise said to Achilles", Lewis Carroll looks at Zeno's paradox in which Achilles is chasing a tortoise. Achilles starts at point A, the tortoise at point B. When Achilles arrives at B, the tortoise has moved on to point C. When Achilles arrives at C, the tortoise has moved on to D, and so *ad infinitum*. So by this argument Achilles can never catch up with the tortoise. However, in a trial run set up by Carroll, Achilles does not even have to break into a trot to overtake the tortoise. "'It can be done,' said Achilles. 'It has been done! *Solvitur ambulando*'."

By his own admission, the travel writer Patrick Leigh Fermor was a "rather rackety" figure before he cured his ills by walking. When, relatively late in life, he became a mentor to Bruce Chatwin, the younger writer adopted Leigh Fermor's motto, *solvitur ambulando*—"it is solved by walking".

Somnia vana

—Ovid, *Metamorphoses* ii. 614

Empty dreams

*Vide "**aegri somnia**" supra.*

Species

Species

This is the singular form in Latin, so we must talk about a species and not about a specie. The word "specie", from the Latin *in specie*, refers now only to (coined) money.

*Vide "**genus**" supra.*

Splendide mendax

—Horace, *Odes* III, xi. 35

Splendidly false, or Nobly untruthful

The poet was in love with Lyde, a timid girl, and as part of his courting technique, placed before her examples of feminine courage. Here he is heaping praise on Hypermnestra, one of the fifty daughters of Danaus. Danaus had instructed each of his daughters to kill her husband on their wedding night, but Hypermnestra refused, breaking her promise to her father and warning her husband to fly for his life, having presumably decided that he was worth saving. The phrase *splendide mendax* has appealed to writers ever since, and it is used particularly to applaud the use of feminine wiles, however deceptive, when these are employed for humanitarian ends.

The charge was levelled not only at women. The frontispiece to an early edition of *Gulliver's Travels* shows Gulliver's picture with below it the comment "*Splendide mendax*", a hint that Gulliver's tales were to be taken *cum grano salis*.

Splendide mendax is the *locus classicus* of an oxymoron.

S.P.Q.R. Senatus Populusque Romanus

The Senate and People of Rome

This was the motto of the city of Rome, and was displayed on its coinage and on banners, etc., and can be seen today on its drain covers. For some reason the letters S.P.Q.R. also surfaced in the coat-of-arms of Queen Elizabeth I of England.

Stabat mater dolorosa, iuxta Crucem lacrimosa

—Jacopone da Todi (*alias* Jacobus de Benedictis)

The sorrowing mother was standing weeping by the Cross

The words of this mediaeval Latin hymn have been set to music by many of the great composers of the past, notably Palestrina, Schubert, Rossini, and Dvorak.

Vide also "***mater dolorosa…***" *supra.*

Status quo (ante)

Previous state, situation

> "The exact mind which of all others dislikes the stupid adherence to the *status quo*, is the keen, quiet, improving Whig mind;…"
>
> W. Bagehot, "The First Edinburgh Reviewers."

> "Nature, and Nature's laws, lay hid in night,
> God said, *Let Newton be!* and all was light."
>
> Alexander Pope.

> "It did not last: the Devil howling *Ho*,
> *Let Einstein be*, restored the status quo."
>
> Sir John Squire.

"Status Quo" for no apparent reason is the name of a popular music group.

Cf. "***in statu quo***" *supra.*

Stella maris

Star of the sea

This title is often given to the Blessed Virgin Mary. It is the motto of Broadstairs Urban District Council in Kent.

Stet

Let it stand

Used by a printer's reader when he has second thoughts about altering a section of copy, reversing his original decision to change or delete it.

Diana Athill wrote a book about her life as a publisher and called it *Stet*.

Stipendium peccati mors est
—Romans vi. 23
The wages of sin is death
Faustus in Marlowe's play *Doctor Faustus* reads this verse aloud: "For the wages of sin is death; but the gift of God is eternal life through Jesus Christ our Lord." The Vulgate reads: "*Stipendium enim peccati, mors*".

William Albright wrote a piece for organ, piano and percussion called *Stipendium peccati*.

Suaviter in modo
Gently in manner
*Vide "**fortiter in re**" supra.*

Sub judice
Under consideration by the courts
Severe restrictions exist on the reporting or discussion in print of any matter which is *sub judice*, for fear of a jury being influenced by anything except the evidence properly presented to them in court.

Sub poena
Under penalty (if you do not turn up)
This is the origin of the verb "to subpoena" and of the phrase "to issue a subpoena", whereby a witness is required to appear in court at a particular time, and stands liable to some penalty if he fails to turn up.

As part of the attempt to remove Latin from the proceedings in English and Welsh civil courts, the phrase "witness summons" has recently replaced the noun "subpoena".

Sub rosa
Under the rose
That is, confidentially, or secretly. Charles Lamb uses the English version in "Mrs Battle's Opinions on Whist": "… I have heard her declare, under the rose, that Hearts was her favourite suit." Richard Condon, two hundred years on from Lamb, in *The Final Addiction*, uses the Latin: "Intending to devote the rest of his life to public service,… [Osgood Noon] climbed the ladder slowly,… starting as Deputy Director of the Kansas Bureau of Fisheries, a *sub-rosa* CIA post,…"

"On her next *sub rosa* visit, the Blums' door had been answered by an elderly stranger."
Jacqueline Briskin, *The Naked Heart.*

"Sub Rosa" is the title of a play by David Leddy.

Thomas Browne tells us that the rose was the flower of Venus (*Rosa Flos Veneris*) and was dedicated to Harpocrates, the god of Silence, as a bribe to persuade the latter not to reveal details of Venus' love life. (We are not sure whether or not the bribe was effective—probably not.) The phrase *sub rosa* is said to arise from the custom of a host at dinner hanging a rose above the table as an assurance that anything said at the table would (with luck) be treated by all present as a matter of the strictest confidence.

Sub specie aeternitatis
—Spinoza, *Ethics*.
Taking a long-term view, in the eye of time
Literally, "beneath the gaze of eternity".

> "That's to say, you've got to slaughter half the existing number of men and women. Which might, *sub specie aeternitatis...* , be an excellent thing."
>
> Aldous Huxley, *Point Counter Point*.

Writing of new pictures in *Still More Prejudice*, Arthur Bingham Walkley says: "The truth is, brand-new pictures intimidate me.... It seems absurd to regard things with the paint hardly dry on them *sub specie aeternitatis*."

Writing in *The Guardian* about the film *Gravity*, Giles Fraser says, "Looking down on the world, *sub specie aeternitatis*, [Sandra] Bullock's isolation is complete and terrifying,... "

Suggestio falsi
The implication of falsehood
*Vide s.v. "**suppressio veri**" infra.*

Sui generis
Of its own kind, "one of a kind"
Writing in *The Observer* Anthony Burgess said: "The genre [of Angus Wilson's *The Old Men at the Zoo*] was unclear... but is now perhaps seen as *sui generis*;..."

MrBurgess here mixes in a very pleasing way three languages, the import of his judgement being that the genre is a genre of its own, and can be subsumed into no other *genus, q.v.*

> "It was odd, that drive back to London. Odd? Rather, spectacularly *sui generis*."
>
> Julian Barnes, *Talking It Over*.

"Jacqueline was a very remarkable person, a rare spirit, a woman in all respects *sui generis.*"

Q. Q. Enwright, *Mistress and Maid.*

Sometimes used in the sense of "one-off". "Peppone wrinkled his forehead. 'Monsignore,' he explained solemnly, 'it was a question of a *casus belli*, an affair *sui generis*, as they say.'" Giovanni Guareschi, *The Little World of Don Camillo.*

Summa cum laude
With highest praise
Used particularly to denote the award in the U.S.A. of a university degree of the highest class, more or less equivalent to a British first class degree. Below this class is *magna cum laude*, "with great praise", and below this is plain *cum laude*.

Nearer home, a friend who is a dentist obtained her degree of Bachelor of Dental Science in the University of Wales (*Universitas Cambrensis*) in 1978 and her certificate is written in Latin. It records that she passed with distinction—*summa cum laude*.

Summum bonum
The highest good
Lucretius, in *De Rerum Naturae*, v. 958, mentions optimistically: *Bonum summum quo tendium omnes*—"The highest good at which we all aim".

Summum Bonum by David Dunson was offered on eBay as a "Mega Rare CD".

Sunt lacrimae rerum et mentem mortalia tangunt
—Virgil, *Aeneid*, i. 462
Tears abound in all things and human suffering touches the heart
This was Aeneas' anguished cry when he saw scenes of the battles of Troy depicted in carvings on the walls of the temple in Carthage, his grief brought on particularly by the image of King Priam.

"Mackail, who had married Burne-Jones' daughter, gave to his Virgil an eightyish air, the *lacrimae rerum* spilled over… with a morbid distress."

Cyril Connolly, *Enemies of Promise.*

In David Mitchell's *Cloud Atlas*, Robert Frobisher's suicide note concludes with the words *Sunt lacrimæ rerum*, while the whole quotation furnishes a heading to chapter 34 in Colin Dexter's *The Remorseful Day*.

Carl Orff wrote an *a capella* piece for six male voices called *Sunt lacrimæ rerum*.

Supera moras
Overcome delays

Or "Remove your finger". This is the motto of Bolton Wanderers Football Club.

Superbia in proelio
Pride in battle

This is the motto of Manchester City Football Club.

Suppressio veri suggestio falsi (est)
Suppression of the truth (is tantamount to) the implication of a falsehood

There seems to have been little need to coin the phrase "economical with the truth". This maxim has the force of law behind it. Insurance companies in particular require their policy-holders to reveal all relevant facts when applying for cover.

> "It seems—and who so astonished as they?—that they had held back material facts; that they were guilty both of *suppressio veri* and *suggestio falsi* (well-known gods against whom they often offended);…"
>
> Rudyard Kipling, *Stalky and Co.*

In *The Bell*, Iris Murdoch says: "Michael did not share James' view that *suppressio veri* was equivalent to *suggestio falsi*", that withholding the truth was tantamount to promoting a lie.

Supra
Above

Vide supra is an invitation to look for a reference in earlier pages of a book or article.

Sursum corda
—The Mass
Lift up your hearts
> "[The dance] was also a bit of acting; love, sweet innocence, tears, a *sursum corda* expressed in music and movement."
> Isak Dinesen, "The Poet" in *Seven Gothic Tales*.

> "A telegram from Sir Oliver Lodge is read out. 'Our great-hearted champion will still be continuing his campaign on the Other Side, with added wisdom and knowledge. *Sursum Corda*.'"
> Julian Barnes, *Arthur and George*.

Sursum Corda is the title of a poem by Ralph Waldo Emerson. It is also the motto of the families of Howison, Langton and McGillycuddy. It has been suggested that Heart of Midlothian Football Club, which does not appear to have a club motto, might well adopt as its motto *Sursum Corda*, translatable as "Up the Hearts!"

Suum cuique bene olet
—Erasmus, *Adagia*
What is one's own smells sweet
Erasmus, in his *Adagia*, left his readers to supply for themselves the answer to "one's own what?"

> "Does not Freud underrate the extent to which nothing, in private, is really shocking as long as it belongs to ourselves? *Suum cuique bene olet*."
> C. S. Lewis, "Psycho-analysis and Literary Criticism".

Suum Cuique is the title of a poem by Ralph Waldo Emerson, "The rain has spoiled the farmer's day... I will attend my proper cares".

S.v. (Sub verbo, sub voce)
Under the word
An invitation to look in a dictionary or an index for an entry under a particular word.

T

Tabula rasa

A clean slate

Often used to refer to the human brain before it becomes cluttered with information. Peter Conrad in a book review in *The Observer* says: "Locke remarked, thinking of the *tabula rasa* of the infantile mind, that in the beginning all the world was America".

> "I want to lay my life before her, don't you see? I'm starting over, I'm clean, I'm *tabula rasa*,..."
>
> Julian Barnes, *Talking It Over*.

It might have been better if the journalist who talked about theories that "children are not 'tabula rasa'", had opted to use the plural form, which is *tabulae rasae*.

The Laurel and Hardy fan club, "The Sons of the Desert", has the motto *Duae tabulae rasae in quibus nihil scriptum est*—"two clean slates on which nothing has been written" or "two minds without a single thought".

Taedium vitae

Boredom, the tedium of living

> "The notion of liberty amuses the people of England, and helps to keep off the *tædium vitæ*."
>
> James Boswell, *The Life of Samuel Johnson, LL.D.*

In his "Notes on Shakespeare", Coleridge quotes Hamlet's first soliloquy, "O that this too, too solid flesh would melt", and comments: "This *tædium vitæ* is a common oppression on minds cast in the Hamlet mould, and is caused by disproportionate mental exertion, which necessitates exhaustion of bodily feeling".

In *The Picture of Dorian Gray*, Oscar Wilde describes the hero of a novel as being "sick with that *ennui*, that terrible *tædium vitæ*, that comes on those to whom life denies nothing". Wilde wrote a poem with the title *Tædium Vitæ*— "To stab my youth with desperate knives..."

Tandem
At length
The English use of this word is a pun upon the Latin. The OED gives a late eighteenth century example of its use, from Grose's Dictionary of the Vulgar Tongue: "Tandem—a two-wheeled chaise, buggy or noddy, drawn by two horses, one before the other, that is *at length*". If three horses were under harness in this way, the arrangement was known as random-tandem. The tandem bicycle came on the scene *circa* 1884.

Writing in *The Guardian*, Sue Arnold suggests; "You should probably listen to this collection [of Shakespeare extracts] in tandem with the same plays broadcast on Radio 3 over the past five years…" If she means, "first one version, then the other", then "tandem" is appropriate. However "in tandem with" is occasionally used, it seems, to mean "alongside" or "in conjunction with" or "parallel with", and this is a wrong use of the phrase.

Te Deum laudamus
We praise thee, O God
The canticle sung at Mattins, which, tradition says, was composed by St. Ambrose while baptizing St. Augustine *c*. A.D. 386. However it is now thought to have been written by Nicera, Bishop of Remesiana (*ob. ca.* A.D. 414).

> "Very nice! When savage wild dogs bark in Wragby, and savage wild pit-ponies stamp on Tevershall pit-bank! *te deum laudamus!*"
> D. H. Lawrence, *Lady Chatterley's Lover*.

Tempora mutantur nos et mutamur in illis
—Raphael Holinshed
Times change, and we too change along with them
This phrase first appeared in *Proverbalia Dicteria* published by A. Gartneus in 1566, but is credited earlier to Lothair I, who was Holy Roman Emperor *c*. 850.

> "'Times change, yes. *Tempora mutantur et nos mutamur in illis.*' 'I think,' said the priest, 'that the line should read *Tempora mutantur nos et mutamur in illis*. Otherwise the hexameter won't scan, will it?'"
> Colin Dexter, *Death is now my Neighbour*.

> "Poor James… such curly hair he had then… *nos et mutamur.*"
> Aldous Huxley, *Eyeless in Gaza*.

"In Queen Victoria's day a girl would never have dreamed of mentioning livers in mixed company." "Very true, sir. *Tempora mutantur, nos et mutamur in illis.*" P. G. Wodehouse, *Aunts Aren't Gentlemen.*

Tempora Mutantur is the nickname of Haydn's symphony no. 64: one of W. S. Gilbert's *Bab Ballads* was entitled *Tempora Mutantur.*

Tempus edax rerum

—Ovid, *Metamorphoses*, xv. 234
Time the devourer of things

> "'Mr Western a daughter grown up!' cries the barber. 'I remember the father a boy; well, *tempus edax rerum!*'"
>
> Henry Fielding, *Tom Jones.*

But we must be fair, for Time is also a healer, and the same speaker acknowledged this later.

"'Time, however, the best physician of the mind, at length brought me relief.' 'Ay, ay; *tempus edax rerum,*' said Partridge." Henry Fielding, *Tom Jones.*

Tempus edax rerum is the name of a Doom Black Metal group in Brazil.

Tempus edax rerum appears on a sundial which was fixed to the wall of Gulval Church, near Penzance, until contemptible thieves stole it in 1998. It is tempting, albeit unchristian, to hope something devours them, even if it is only remorse.

Tempus fugit

Time flies (or flees)
This distils the essence from "*Sed fugit interea, fugit inreparabile tempus*"— "Time is fleeing, fleeing beyond recall." Virgil, *Georgics*, iii. 284.

> "Yet, in asking that question [about the future of GMTV], there is also an inevitable feeling of *tempus fugit.*"
>
> Report in *The Guardian.*

I was told the following story by an elderly and rather prim lady I met in Eastbourne many years ago.

Two old folk were sitting on a sea-front bench contemplating the evening scene. One said, "Well, *tempus fugit* be creeping on." The other replied, "Yes, they be creeping on me too."

Terminus ad quem
The inevitable result

The culmination, the "limit to which". Michael Hofmann, writing in *The Guardian*, said: "It (*sc.* the history of Germany) comes inevitably down to Hitler, the *terminus ad quem*". Conversely *terminus a quo* is a "starting point".

These two terms are also used in a slightly different context, together with the related (and preferred) pair *terminus ante quem*—"the limit before which", and *terminus post quem*—"the limit after which", to mark the limits of the time at which an event could have taken place. For example, the *terminus ante quem* for a borough charter for Looe, Cornwall, *circa* 1212, is taken to be the date at which one witness inherited his estate and title, while the *terminus post quem* is the date at which another witness is known to have died.

Terra firma
Firm ground

> "It is alleged that [Hartley Coleridge] hardly knew that Ejuxrea, which is the name of his kingdom, was not as solid a *terra firma* as Keswick or Ambleside."
>
> W. Bagehot, "Hartley Coleridge".

> (An air hostess *loquitur*.) "'A Mr Tull? A Mr Tull at all.' This… was airspeak; no one on *terra firma* would ever talk like that."
>
> Martin Amis, *The Information*.

The (racist?) story is told of the old Negro (sorry, Afro-American) who was given his first flight in a light and rather aerobatic aircraft. When asked whether it was a relief to be back on *terra firma*, he replied, "Shuah, and the more firma, the less terra."

Not to be confused with *terra cotta* which is "cooked" rather than "firm", and is moreover Italian.

Terra Incognita
The Unknown Land

A name given most commonly to Antarctica, the last of the unexplored regions of the earth, apart from a small area of Norfolk. The name is still in popular use and Google presents 1,260,000 choices to the searcher.

> "All my life, sophisticated, idiotic women have taken it upon themselves to *understand* me, to *cure* me, but Eva knows I'm *terra incognita*, and explores me unhurriedly,…"
>
> David Mitchell, *Cloud Atlas*.

"So. So there I am in some *terra incognita* by the name of Stoke Newington..."

Julian Barnes, *Talking It Over*.

S. T. Coleridge, in his notes on Shakespeare's *Richard II*, uses the term in its plural form and in a non-geographical sense. "... mark in this scene (ii.2) Shakespeare's gentleness in touching the tender superstitions, the *terræ incognitæ* of presentiments, in the human mind;..."

Terra Nullius
Nobody's land

Most of the earth's land surface is claimed by some government as part of its domain (some bits by more than one government), but one or two patches have slipped through the net, and are regarded as *terra nullius*, land belonging to nobody. One such patch is Bir Tawil on the border between Egypt and Sudan. In June 2014, Jeremiah Heaton planted a flag here to claim the region, which is about the size of Warwickshire, as a new sovereign state, the Kingdom of North Sudan, but since the area has no settled population, the rest of the world failed to take him seriously. Other such patches of *terra nullius* exist along the Danube River and along the Croatia–Slovenia border.

The occupation of Australia by Europeans has been justified by some in the past who regarded the land as *terra nullius*, the aboriginal peoples not fitting the new occupants' concept of what constituted a "government".

Tertium quid
A third something

In alchemy, a mixture of two things which differs noticeably from both.

In "The Chemist to his Love", the chemist laments that his love cannot be potassium and he *aqua fortis*, in which case they would together become nitrate of potash, and live happily "until death should decompose the fleshly tertium quid".

Tertium quid was used in the Christological debates of the fourth century with reference to the followers of Apollinaris who spoke of Christ as something neither human nor divine, but a mixture of the two, and therefore a "third thing".

More recently *tertium quid* has been used for the uncertain or missing element in a trio of things or persons, when two of the trio are already known. In Erskine Childers' *The Riddle of the Sands*, the narrator so refers to an unknown member of the opposing camp: "Her skipper's safe anyway; so's Böhme, so's the Tertium Quid,..."

Rudyard Kipling in *Wee Willie Winkie*; "At the Pit's Mouth", states: "Once upon a time there was a Man and his Wife and a Tertium Quid". Robert Browning gave the title *Tertium Quid* to his fourth book of "The Ring and the Book". Had Carol Reed's film "The Third Man" been made in Ancient Rome, it might well have been entitled *Tertium Quid*.

Thesaurus

Treasure

Roget's *Thesaurus of English Words and Phrases* contains the language's verbal treasure. The word originally was Greek, but was assimilated into Latin, and from thence gave us in time our own word "treasure". The maxim *Ubi thesaurus, ibi cor* is a paraphrase of the Vulgate rendering of Matthew vi. 21: "For where your treasure is, there will your heart be also."

Robert Hall's memorial in Exeter Cathedral contains the lines:

> *Vivus thesaurarius,*
> *Mortuus thesaurus,*
> *Vivus, mortuus, residentiarius*
> In life (our) treasurer,
> In death a treasure,
> In life, in death, a resident.

Thesauros in Agro—"Treasures in the Field"—was the motto of Wisbech Rural District Council.

Timeo Danaos et dona ferentes

—Virgil, *Aeneid*, ii. 48

I fear the Greeks, even when they come bearing gifts

The gift in question was the wooden horse (Sinon) left outside the gates of Troy, and the speaker is Laocoon, voicing his misgivings at the sight of it.

> "… on the principle of '*timeo Danaos*' etc., I instantly smelt a ruse…"
> Erskine Childers, *The Riddle of the Sands.*

> "Tell Mrs Boswell that I shall taste her marmalade cautiously at first. *Timeo Danaos et dona ferentes.* Beware… of a reconciled enemy."
> James Boswell, *The Life of Samuel Johnson, LL.D.*

Et dona ferentes is the title of Kipling's poem "In extended observation of the ways and works of man".

The 216 (Bomber Transport) squadron of the R.A.F. has the motto *CCXVI dona ferens*—"216 bringing gifts".

Timeant Danaeios, "Let them fear those belonging to Danae", is the motto of H.M.S. Danae.

Timor mortis conturbat me
—The Office of the Dead.
The fear of death disturbs me
This refrain from the Roman Catholic Office of the Dead is used by William Dunbar in his poem "Lament for the Makaris" (makers, *sc*. poets). In the poem he rehearses the names of twenty-four poets who have died recently and of another who is *in extremis*: surely Dunbar himself must be next in line.

> I that in heill was and gladness
> Am trublit now with great sickness
> And feblit with infirmitie: -
> *Timor mortis conturbat me.*

> "'Oh,' he said, 'I don't want to die, why should I?... But... it doesn't interest me, you know.'
> ""'Timor mortis conturbat me",' quoted Birkin, adding—'No, death doesn't really seem the point any more.'"
> D. H. Lawrence, Women in Love.

Totis viribus
With all (my) strength
> "I have passed over all the Doctor's other reproaches upon Scotland but the sheep's head I will defend *totis viribus*."
> James Boswell. The Life of Samuel Johnson, LL.D.

Totis Viribus was the motto of Goode, Durrant & Murray (Consolidated) Ltd., an Australian firm which dealt in Wheatstone Anglo concertinas until it was taken over by another firm in 1985. It is also the motto of 414 (Black Knight) Squadron of the Royal Canadian Air Force, and of Epsom Normal Primary School, New Zealand.

Trivia
Trifles
A short while ago the *Radio Times* contained a regular column entitled "Film Trivia", a collection of unimportant though not uninteresting stories connected with the making of well-known films.

Tu quoque
And you too: "You're another!"

A deadly insult, and a phrase used by Ovid in his *Tristia*, ii. 39. Kipling used Latin judiciously in his writing, but sadly failed to do so in the following passage from "The Man who would be King": "And all the time… Kings are being killed on the Continent, and Empires are saying, 'You're another,…'"

An *argumentum tu quoque* is a defence of one's actions based on the claim that the accuser is or has been the perpetrator of similar actions.

Tityre, tu patulae recubans sub tegmine fagi
—Virgil, *Eclogue*, I, 1
Tityrus, thou liest canopied beneath thy spreading beech

Tityrus was clearly one of the leisured classes, and the name "Tityre-tu" attached itself in the 17th century to a group of aristocratic hooligans who, having become bored with lying canopied under their spreading beech trees, had nothing better to do than run riot and cause trouble in the streets. *Tityre-tu* was earlier the name given to a 1620's crypto-Catholic group.

Longfellow translated the whole poem: "Tityrus, thou in the shade of a spreading beech-tree reclining,…"

> "Nosey senior… was reposing *sub tegmine fagi*… , in a sort of tea-garden arbour, overlooking a dung-heap."
>
> R. S. Surtees, *Jorrocks' Jaunts and Jollities.*

Sub Tegmine Fagi is the subtle motto of the family of Beech of Brandon Hall, Coventry.

U

Ubique
Everywhere

This is the motto of the family of O'Brien-Twohig, and of the Corps of Royal Engineers and of the Royal Regiment of Artillery. Rudyard Kipling wrote a panegyric to the motto of the "Royal Artillery" entitled *Ubique* and offering nineteen meanings to the word, such as "that 'orse's scream that turns your innards cold!", but concluding that "There's nothin' this side 'Eaven or 'Ell Ubique doesn't mean!"

In *The Oxford Book of English Verse*, the heading *Ubique* is given to a poem by Joshua Sylvester whose last two lines are: "Whereso'er I am,—below, or else above you—Whereso'er you are, my heart shall truly love you,…"

Ultimo mense (ult).
In the last month

In a letter written on any day in, say, May, a mention of "*ult.*" would refer to any day in the previous month, *viz* April.

"The Association acknowledged receipt of his favour of 24th ult. with enclosure as stated." O. Henry, "A Night in New Arabia".

This practice was once widespread but has now more or less been discontinued. *Cf.* **"inst."** *supra.*

Ultima ratio
The final reason or argument

War has been described as *ultima ratio regum*—"the final argument of kings."

Patrick O'Brian, in *Ionian Mission*, suggests that the truth would remain unaltered if "Captain Aubrey were to turn his cannon—the *ultima ratio regum* and other bullies—on Professor Graham".

Louis IV of France had *Ultima ratio regum* embossed on each of his cannons; and *Ultima ratio regum* is the name of a track on the album *Domus Mundi* by the Austrian symphonic black metal band Hollenthon.

The phrase crops up sometimes in dispatches from the battle of the sexes. "Having twice sallied out and been beaten back, she now, as I expected, tried the *ultima ratio* of women, and had recourse to tears." W. M. Thackeray, *Henry Esmond*.

Ultima Thule
Farthest Thule
Virgil in his *Georgics*, I, 30, mentions *Ultima Thule*, the island which is the northernmost part of Earth's dry land. Longfellow wrote a clutch of poems under the general title *Ultima Thule*, of which one contains the line "Ultima Thule! Utmost Isle!"

In "The Pit and the Pendulum", Edgar Allan Poe uses the phrase in a non-geographical sense. "… *the pit*, typical of hell and regarded by rumour as the Ultima Thule of all [the Inquisition's] punishments".

Nowadays "Thule" is the name given to one of the northernmost settlements in Greenland. A small rock in the South Atlantic is called "South Thule".

Ultimatum
A final warning
One of the best known of these is the ultimatum given by Britain to Germany to withdraw from Poland in 1939, her refusal to do so leading to the Second World War.

Ultra
Beyond
Outside the visible spectrum of light lie on one hand the infra-red (*q.v.*) rays and on the other the ultra-violet. There is neither up nor down to the spectrum, except that red is on the top of the rainbow and violet on the bottom, so both sets of invisible rays could legitimately claim the prefix "ultra". "Ultra-sound" is sound beyond the normal range of human hearing.

Used also to mean "excessively". "My husband isn't ultra-bright at this time in the morning."

Vide also "***ne plus ultra***" *supra*.

Ultra vires
Beyond one's powers
Most organizations, committees and courts of law have a constitution, written or otherwise, which defines their duties and the power they have to see that their decisions are acted on. If they attempt to do anything which

is beyond this agreed power, they are acting *ultra vires* and can be called to account for their excess enthusiasm.

Urbi et orbi
To the city and to the world

This motto is affixed to the gates of the Vatican. Formerly it was the standard opening phrase of Roman proclamations and it is now the formula accompanying papal rescripts. The Pope addresses Rome and the world in his Easter message *Urbi et Orbi*, and *Urbi et Orbi* is the name of the blessing given by the Pope in St. Peter's Square at Easter and Christmas.

Ursa major
The Great Bear

This is the constellation known otherwise as "Charle's Wain" or "The Plough". The Little Bear is correspondingly "Ursa Minor". The pointers of the Great Bear indicate the Northern Star, "Polaris", and since the Greek for "bear" is "arktos", the northern latitudes are the Arctic, while the southern latitudes are the Antarctic.

> "My father's opinion of Dr Johnson may be conjectured from the name he afterwards gave him, which was URSA MAJOR."
> James Boswell, *The Life of Samuel Johnson, LL.D.*

Usque ad finem
To the very end

> "That was the way. To follow the dream and again to follow the dream—and so –…—*usque ad finem*…."
> Joseph Conrad, *Lord Jim*.

Usque ad finem is the motto of 428 Ghost Squadron of the R. A. F.

V

Vade mecum

Go with me

I came across an old phrase-book in a secondhand bookshop recently, entitled "The Traveller's Vade Mecum in Germany". Anthony Burgess once confided in *The Observer* that "when I was an undergraduate, this tome [T.S.Eliot's *Selected Essays*]… was a *vade mecum*".

Vade Mecum is the name of a Plucker document viewer for the pocket PC.

The phrase might also be loosely translated as "come with me". There can be little doubt that Ernest Bramah had *vade mecum* in mind when he referred in *The Moon of Much Gladness* to "The Official Executioner's Come-with-Me and Complete Torturer's Fireside Companion".

Vae victis

—Livy, *Historia*, V, xlviii. 9

Woe to the vanquished

In 390 B.C. Brennus was the leader of an army of Gauls which captured all of Rome except the Capitoline Hill. He accepted an offer of gold as ransom for the city, but as the gold was being weighed the Romans dared to cast doubt on the accuracy of the scales, whereupon Brennus threw his sword on to the weights. His "*Væ victis!*" reminded the Romans that they were really in no position to question his honesty.

Vae Victis is the motto of the Senhouse family, and is the title of a French war-games magazine.

A (much) later variant is *Vae Vectis*—"Woe to the Isle of Wight".

Vale

Farewell

*Cf. "**ave atque vale**" supra.*

Vanitas vanitatum, et omnia vanitas
—Ecclesiastes, i. 1
Vanity of vanities, all is vanity
"O my jolly companions, I have drunk many a bout with you, and always found *vanitas vanitatum* written on the bottom of the pot."
W. M. Thackeray, *The Adventures of Philip*.

In 1872 the Conservative government under Disraeli was passing numerous public health and sanitary laws. Disraeli himself is reported as claiming that the Vulgate had misquoted the author of Ecclesiastes, who had in fact said "*Sanitas sanitatum, et omnia sanitas*". "Gentlemen, it is impossible to overrate the importance of ... the health of the people."

(The original meaning of *sanitas* was "physical health", but it could also mean "mental health" or sanity.)

Variae lectiones
Various readings
Before the advent of the printed book, all books in circulation necessarily had been written by hand. In the course of copying from the original or from an earlier copy, omissions or misspellings were almost inevitable. Existing copies of any such book may well show significant variation in certain passages, and these variations are referred to as *variæ lectiones*. A book which mentions these different readings is known as a "variorum" edition.

Varium et mutabile semper femina
—Virgil, *Aeneid*, iv. 569
A fickle and changeful thing is woman ever
Kenneth Grahame in his *Dream Days* has a chapter entitled *Mutabile Semper*. The Italians have "La donna è mobile".

The words *Varium et mutabile semper femina* were spoken to Aeneas by Mercury in a dream, while he was in Carthage dallying with Dido. The main import of the message was that Jupiter expected Aeneas to be on his way *instanter*, and that he must leave Dido, who professed to love him dearly. She however, being a woman, might nevertheless turn somewhat nasty if she suspected he was deserting her, and would try to block his passage with her ships, so he had better get a move on, which he did. Poor Dido was most upset by his departure and finding that Aeneas on fleeing the nest had unaccountably left his sword lying on the bed, she threw herself upon it *à la* Juliet and thus did herself in.

In Scott's *Guy Mannering*, Dominie Sampsan is not impressed with the devious nature of Miss Bertram's thinking. He "left her presence altogether crestfallen, and as he shut the door, could not help muttering the '*varium et mutabile*' of Virgil".

Cf. "***pone seram...***", "***rara avis...***" and "***splendide mendax***" *supra.*

Veni, vidi, vici

I came, I saw, I conquered

Julius Caesar, writing to Amantius, thus announces his victory over Pharnaces at Zela in Pontus, in 47 B.C.

Lawrence Durrell in *Sauve Qui Peut*, "What-ho on the Rialto", describes a French lady ambassador who wrought havoc with men's hearts in the Vulgarian diplomatic community, "enmeshing them with her veni vidi vici," and whose tactics included "tapping you on the lips with her closed fan," an idiosyncracy which won all hearts.

Tawdry Hepburn, the San Francisco indie-rock loungecore group, uses "veni vidi vici" as a refrain in "Sink", a song about mythic female dominance borrowed from the rock group Apocalipstick. (*Credite posteri!*)

In October 2005 *The Guardian*, advertising a T.V. series on ancient Rome, used an inscription which read: "*Veni, vidi, volo domum redire*"—"I came, I saw, I want to go home".

Vidi Vici is the motto of 191 Squadron of the R.A.F., whilst *Veni, vidi, Visa* ("I came, I saw, I went shopping") is the motto of Sally Poplin.

Vide "Introduction", the passages devoted to pronunciation.

Venite, exultemus Domino

O come, let us rejoice in the Lord

These are the first words of Psalm 95, although the earlier Latin spelling is *exsultemus*, and the Authorized Version begins "O let us sing unto the Lord". The psalm is used as a canticle at Mattins.

Verbatim

Word for word

> "Having mastered the art of writing in shorthand, I was able to take down Sir Cuthbert's speech *verbatim*."
>
> P. J. Dorricot, *The Nursery Slopes.*

If the person writing was a good speller, he would be able to reproduce the speech *verbatim et litteratim*, that is, not only word for word but letter for letter also.

In *Tom Jones*, Henry Fielding offers to present to the reader the text of a letter *verbatim et litteratim*, his reason for doing so becoming apparent immediately: "Sir, I shud sartenly haf kaled you a cordin too mi promiss..."

Other words which refer to the manner in which something happens or presents itself, and ending in -*im* are *passim* and *seriatim* (*qq.v.*).

Verbum sapienti sat est

A word to the wise is enough

Usually abbreviated to *verbum sap.* or even *verb. sap.* *VerbSap* is the name of an online literary magazine publishing concise prose.

> "*Verb. Sap.* Take the hint from me, old boy. Drop the monocle.... Be a boozer. It's much more fun."
>
> Aldous Huxley, "The Monocle."

Versus (v.)

Against

Literally "towards". Any contest between two opponents can be described as A *versus* B. A famous legal contest, the case of Bardell *versus* Pickwick, is described in *Pickwick Papers*, (although in fact the case was announced in the book simply as "Bardell and Pickwick"). No elaboration is needed of such a phrase as "Wolves v. Aston Villa". *Versus* is sometimes abbreviated to "vs".

An alternative way of indicating a contest is to use *contra* (*q.v.*). In Waugh's *Brideshead Revisited*, chapter 4 of Book 2 is headed: "*Sebastian contra mundum*"—"Sebastian against the world". This has strong echoes of "*Athanasius Contra Mundum*", an expression reflecting the fact that Athanasius, Bishop of Alexandria, (c 293-373), was exiled and restored as Bishop on at least five separate occasions. It seems likely that Waugh adapted this phrase for his own purposes.

Veto

I forbid

The use of "the veto" dates at least from Roman times, but the term became familiar when the veto was used as a weapon in the Cold War. Except in procedural matters, each of the five permanent members of the United Nations Security Council—Britain, China, France, Russia, and the United States—can use its veto to block any proposal supported by the other members of the Council. It was most frequently used by Russia to frustrate the aims of the United States and *vice versa*.

Via

By way of

This word may be used in a physical sense, as when a signpost points to "Lamorna via Castallack", or in a non-physical sense, as when British Telecom states: "You may use your BT Chargecard to dial via 144 from here".

Via Dolorosa

The Way of Sorrows

This led Christ from "Olivet to Calvary", from his arrest on the Mount of Olives, also called Gethsemane, to his crucifixion on the hill called Calvary or Golgotha. The "Stations of the Cross" mark stages on this journey, beginning at the judgement chamber and finishing in the tomb in which Christ's body was laid. When the "Stations" are performed in public, it is customary to sing stanzas from the hymn "Stabat Mater" (*q.v.*) whilst walking from one Station to the next.

> "Now the traveller [in Ypres] along that Via Dolorosa, the Menin Road, begins scrunching into smaller fragments with his boots, bits of the glorious old stained glass of the Cathedral lying broken among its stones."
>
> Report in *The Guardian*, March 1919.

In *Mapp and Lucia*, E. E. Benson portrays Major Benjy as making "the passage of his Via Dolorosa to glean the objects he had dropped" when retrieving his belongings, which included his false teeth, thrown out from Elisabeth Mapp's house.

Via Dolorosa is the name of a Eutropia Universe society, and also the name of a monologue about the Middle East written and performed by David Hare.

Vice

In place of

"Vice" is the ablative case of a noun whose nominative is not used. It appears frequently as a prefix—"vice-captain", "Vice-Chancellor", "vice-chairman", "viceroy",—and less frequently independently.

> "The new man—*vice* Jollifant—certainly sounds a shrimp."
>
> J. B. Priestley, *The Good Companions*.

> "In fact Mr Pendennis was installed as confidant *vice* J. J., absent on leave."
>
> W. M. Thackeray, *The Newcombes*.

Vice versa

And the other way around

F. Anstey wrote a (minor?) classic book called *Vice Versa* in which the *persona* of a boy migrated into the body of his father and, well, *vice versa*. The book was made into a film in 1988 with screenplay by Dick Clements and Ian la Frenais.

Not to be confused with *viva voce* (*q.v.*).

Victoria concordia crescit

Victory grows from harmony

This is the hopeful motto of Arsenal Football Club.

Victor ludorum

The victor of games

Had I come into this world as a horse, I might well have been running tomorrow in the "Petros Victor Ludorum Hurdles" at Haydock Park.

The title *Victor Ludorum* was traditionally given in many public and grammar schools to the outstanding athlete each year. It is still awarded in Hayle Community College in Cornwall to the best boy athlete, while the title "*Victrix Ludorum*" goes to the best girl athlete.

An alternative title is *Dux Ludorum*—"Leader of Games", *q.v. supra*.

Vide

See

An invitation to look at something, widely used in the present *opus*.

Videlicet (*viz*)

Namely

This is a contraction of the phrase *videre licet*—"one can see" or "it is permitted to see". The "z" represents a symbol (ȝ) which resembled a cursive "z" and which was a common mark of contraction in mediaeval documents and inscriptions. Because "*viȝ*", later "*viz*", is a contraction and not an abbreviation, it does not take a full-stop.

> "He knows that it is only possible for him to generate pleasure by the one means, *videlicet*, by screwing."
>
> Philip Larkin, "Round Another Point".

"… a book is what's written,… and I would read a brilliant ugly book without hesitation (*viz* the latest Margaret Atwood, who'd be worth reading if she were printed on baby wipes)."

Column in *The Guardian*.

("*Viz*" is rather unexpected here, suggesting that the "latest Margaret Atwood" is the only "brilliant ugly book" in existence—as a test, try substituting "namely" for "*viz*". It is arguable that here "e.g." would have been a more appropriate linkage.)

Videnda
Things to be seen
Not itself seen very frequently, but it is the motto of the Joint School of Photographic Interpretation of the R.A.F.

Video meliora proboque; deteriora sequor
—Ovid, *Metamorphoses*, vii. 20
I see and approve the better (path), but follow the worse
Jason, leader of the Argonauts, had asked Æetes, king of Colchis, for the Golden Fleece, but the king had set him a number of near impossible tasks to be completed first. Æetes' daughter, Medea, who had fallen helplessly in love with Jason, was determined to use her magic powers to help him (the "*deteriora*") in opposition to her father's wishes (the "*meliora*").
(*Cf.* "***splendide mendax***" *supra.*)

> "Five words sum up every biography. *Video meliora proboque; deteriora sequor.* Like all other human beings, I know what I ought to do, but continue to do what I know I oughtn't to do."
>
> Aldous Huxley, *Eyeless in Gaza*.

> "… he taught me to see and approve better things. 'Tis my own fault, *deteriora sequi.*"
>
> W. M. Thackeray, *Henry Esmond*. ("Sequi" is "to follow".)

Meliora sequamur—"May we follow the better path", is the motto both of Brighton Boys' Grammar School and of Blackpool Boys' Grammar School, and of the Borough of Eastbourne.

Vidi tantum
—Ovid, *Tristia*, IV, x. 51

I caught a glimpse

The full line is *Virgilium vidi tantum*—"I just caught a glimpse of Virgil".

Robert Burns and Sir Walter Scott met only once, in 1786, in Adam Ferguson's house, in the Sciennes district of Edinburgh. Scott wrote: "As for Burns, I may truly say, *Virgilium vidi tantum*." Lockhard, *Life of Burns* (1828).

> "As for the famous Doctor Swift, I can say of him, '*Vidi tantum*'."
>
> W. M. Thackeray, *Henry Esmond*.

Vim
Force, elbow grease

This is probably the accusative case of *vis*, the Latin for "force", used as the object of the verb in "Use some blooming *vim*".

"Vis" itself was used in the name "Hōvis", where the little line over the "o" had always puzzled me. The story goes that Hōvis is a contraction of "Hominum vis", "the strength of men", where hō is an accepted abbreviation of "hominum".

Vincit omnia industria
Hard work conquers everything

This is the motto of Bury Football Club.

Virginibus puerisque canto
—Horace, *Odes*, III, i. 4

To maidens and young men I sing

Horace is defining his target audience, after having disclaimed any interest in the common herd, the *profanum vulgus* of *Odi profanum vulgus* (*q.v. supra*).

Robert Louis Stephenson wrote a book entitled *Virginibus Puerisque*, which included among other matters a number of essays on the problems of young adulthood, addressed to young men and maidens.

Julian Barnes, in *Talking It Over*, observes that he had only had to dangle his forged reference from the Hamlet Academy before Mr Tim to be "unleashed before the cosmopolitan *virginibus puerisque* couchant before their desks."

Virginibus puerisque is the title of a poem by Alan Seeger, who was killed in action in France in 1916 while serving in the Foreign Legion. He was the uncle of the folk singer Pete Seeger.

Virgo intacta
A virgin

Catullus uses this phrase for "A maiden untouched" in his *Ode* 62, line 45. Presumably the opposite is *virgo tacta*, "a maiden touched" but on this point Catullus is not forthcoming. It appears that many Roman girls were given in marriage when they were no more than twelve years old, the Roman *paterfamilias* neatly solving thereby the problem of the wayward teenage daughter creating havoc in his home. It also appears that to the Romans *virgo* was any young girl, married or unmarried, intact or otherwise.

"The Virgo Intacta" are a Jazz-Punk band originally from Leigh-on-Sea, Essex.

Vis inertiae
The power of inertia, of inactivity

Vis Inertiæ, or power of inactivity, is defined by Newton to be a power inherent in all matter, by which it resists any attempt to change its state, either of rest or motion.

> "I have thought of a pulley to raise me gradually [out of bed]; but that would give me pain, as it would counteract my internal inclination. I would have something that can dissipate the *vis inertiæ*, and give elasticity to the muscles."
>
> James Boswell. *The Life of Samuel Johnson, LL.D.*

> "Athelstane,… unwilling to obey, yet undetermined how to resist, opposed only the *vis inertiæ* to the will of John, and without stirring or making any motion whatever of obedience, opened his large grey eyes and stared at the Prince…"
>
> Sir Walter Scott, *Ivanhoe.*

Vis medicatrix naturae
The healing power of Nature

Vis medicatrix naturae is the name of a firm supplying natural medicines, formed in Portland, Oregon, by two naturopathic physicians.

> "Whether I owe my recovery to the Carp, to the Return of Spring, or to the *Vis medicatrix Naturæ*, I am not yet able to determine."
>
> Aldous Huxley, *After Many a Summer.*

"'I am a great believer in nature's remedies, *vis medicatrix naturæ,*' explained Uncle Walter, sneezing a little as he mixed himself a hot whisky and lemon."

P. J. Dorricot, Beyond the Nursery Slopes.

Vis unita fortior
United force is more powerful
This is the motto of Stoke City Football Club.

Vitae summa brevis spem nos vetat incohare longam
—Horace, *Odes*, I, iv. 15
Life's short span forbids us to entertain far-reaching hopes
This sombre thought inspired one of Ernest Dowson's best-known poems, which was engraved on his tombstone:

> "They are not long, the weeping and the laughter,
>   Love and desire and hate:
> I think they have no portion in us after
>   We pass the gate.
> "They are not long, the days of wine and roses:
>   Out of a misty dream
> Our path emerges for a while, then closes
>   Within a dream."

This line is preceded in the Ode by the lines beginning *Pallida mors…* (*q.v. supra*).

Vitai Lampada
The lamp of life
Vide **"Quasi cursores…"** *supra.*

Vivamus, mea Lesbia, atque amemus
—Catullus, Carmina v
Let us live, Lesbia, and let us love

"I don't know. The past is abolished. *Vivamus, mea Lesbia.* If I weren't so horribly depressed, I'd embrace you."

Aldous Huxley, Antic Hay.

Carl Orff in *Catulli Carmina* set several of Catullus' poems to music, including this one and *Odi et Amo* (*q.v.*).

LIVING LATIN

Samuel Taylor Coleridge wrote a vibrant translation of Catullus' poem, "My Lesbia, let us live and love…"

*Vide "**soles occidere et redire possunt**" supra.*

Viva voce
An oral examination (with living voice)

The phrase may also be used to imply reading aloud, and also refers to evidence given in person in court, as opposed to evidence given *via* an affidavit.

> "A brilliant idea occurred to Jeremy. Why shouldn't he offer to translate the book for her—*viva voce* and sentence by sentence, like an interpreter at a Council Meeting of the League of Nations?"
> Aldous Huxley, *After Many a Summer.*

Viva Voce is the name of a Sheffield-based chamber choir, and also of an Indie rock group formed in Muscle Shoals, Alabama.

Not to be confused with *vice versa* (*q.v.*). "A cuckoo is a bird which lays other birds' eggs in its own nest and *viva voce.*" Schoolboy howler.

Vivat
May he/she live

At coronations of British monarchs, the Queen's (or King's) Scholars of Westminster School have the privilege of shouting "Vivat" when the sovereign enters Westminster Abbey.

Vivat Rex—"[Long] Live the King"—is the motto of the McCorkell and McCorquodale families.

Vivit post funera virtus
Virtue lives on after death

Vivit post funera virtus appears on a 1673 memorial in St. Martin's Church, Exeter, to the memory of Winifred Butler, daughter of Sir Richard Prideaux. It is the motto of the Earls of Shannon and of the City of Nottingham, and could formerly be read on the buttons of employees of the Nottingham Corporation Tramways.

242

Vixi puellis nuper idoneus
Et militavi non sine gloria

—Horace, *Odes*, III, xxvi. 1

In those days I lived equipped for ladies' love—And fought not without glory.

Horace is resigning himself to the fact that with advancing years his capacity for close encounters of the amorous kind is sadly diminishing.

In Patrick O'Brian's *The Surgeon's Mate*, Sir Joseph Blaine admits that he had become most painfully aware of "a certain want of vigour… as though I too should sing *vixi puellis nuper idoneus*…"

In *The Oxford Book of English Verse*, the heading "*Vixi puellis nuper idoneus*" is given to Sir Thomas Wyatt's poem, "They flee from me that sometime did me seek".

> "I say to myself *Vixi puellis nuper idoneus*, and I repeat this over and over for five minutes for the beauty of the word *idoneus*. Yet, considering the gulf of time and culture, and my ignorance of Latin, and the fact that no one even knows how Latin was pronounced, is it possible that the effect I am enjoying is the effect Horace was trying for?"
>
> George Orwell, "New Words".

Henry Reed prefaces his "Lessons of the War" poems with a variant on these lines: "Vixi *duellis* nuper idoneus Et militavi non sine gloria", fit for *war*, rather than for women. The poem "Unarmed Combat" echoes the altered lines:

> "It may be said that we tackled wherever we could,
> That battle-fit we lived, and though defeated,
> Not without glory fought."

Viz

Videlicet, namely
  *Vide "**videlicet**" supra.*

Volente deo

God willing
  The phrase is used by Virgil in *Æneid* I, 303. *Vide "**Deo volente**" supra.*

Vox et praeterea nihil
—Ovid, *Metamorphoses*, iii. 397
A voice and nothing more

The phrase is also used by Lactantius (III, fab.V) and refers to a nightingale, which when plucked ready for the pot proves to be "all voice and nothing else". Plutarch included the phrase in his *Laconic Apophthegms*.

In Aldous Huxley's *Chrome Yellow*, Mr Scogan bemoans the fact that whereas in a sane world he would be a great man, "in this curious establishment,… , to all intents and purposes I don't exist . I am just *Vox et praeterea nihil.*"

> "…the fellow is not worth her—a poor groatsworth of a man, *vox et praeterea nihil* (though a very fine *vox*)…"
> Patrick O'Brian, *The Mauritius Command.*

Vox et praeterea nihil is the name of an album by the Ambient group "Controlled Dissonance".

Vox humana
The human voice

The name given to a stop on an organ which has a wailing quality. It is mentioned in John Betjeman's poem "In Westminster Abbey".

> "Let me take this other glove off
> As the *vox humana* swells,
> And the beauteous fields of Eden
> Bask beneath the Abbey bells…"

> "This picture palace had an organ that was nothing but one gigantic, relentless, quavering *vox humana* stop, and listening to it was like being forcibly fed by treacle."
> J. B. Priestley, *The Good Companions.*

Vox humana is the title of a 1984 album by the rock band Daniel Amos.

Vox Populi, vox Dei
—Archbishop W. Reynolds
The voice of the People is the voice of God

Reynolds is quoting Alcuin who used the expression in A.D. 800 but in a very negative context: "We would not listen to those who say '*Vox Populi, vox Dei*', for the voice of the people is near akin to madness."

"'– Because we are the only persons qualified to judge whether a priest suits us or not, since we have had to bear with him for nearly twenty years.'

'*Vox populi vox Dei,*' sighed the old bishop."

Giovanni Guareschi, *The Little World of Don Camillo.*

Vox Populi when abbreviated to "*Vox Pop*" refers to an extract from an interview with a member of the general public (the *plebs*).

F. Anstey wrote a book called *Voces Populi*—"Voices of the People", or "Scenes from English Life", and Longfellow wrote a poem under the title *Vox Populi.*

Vox ultima crucis
The final voice of the cross

In *The Oxford Book of English Verse* the heading *Vox ultima crucis* is given to John Lydgate's poem "Tarye no lenger; toward thyn heritage / Hast on thy weye…", a poem set to music as an anthem by Sir William H. Harris.

Appendix I

This section examines some of the quotations from the main body of the book whose translation may not to the innocent eye be easy to follow. Word order in Latin, and especially in Latin poetry, was flexible: in poetry fitting words to the required metrical patterns of long and short syllables often resulted in related words being widely separated. The order of words in the quotations and translations below has been adjusted so that as far as possible the two correspond.

Abeunt studia in mores
Studia / abeunt / in / mores
Studies / pass / into / character

Amantium irae amoris integratio est
Irae / amantium / est / integratio / amoris
The quarrels / of lovers / is / the renewal / of love

Bis peccare in bello non licet
In bello / non licet / peccare / bis
In war / it is not allowed / to blunder / twice

Bonosque soles effugere et abire sentit, qui nobis pereunt et imputantur
Sentit / bonos / soles / effugere / et abire / qui pereunt / et imputantur / nobis
He feels / the good / days / to fly by / and to vanish / which perish / and are reckoned / to us

Caelum non animum mutant qui trans mare currunt
Mutant / caelum / non / animum / qui / currunt / trans / mare
They change / (their) sky / not / (their) soul / who / flee / across / the sea

Carpe diem quam minimum credula postero
Carpe / diem / credula / quam minimum / postero
Reap the harvest of / the day / trust / as little as possible / in the morrow

Cras amet qui nunquam amavit, Quique amavit cras amet
Amet / cras / qui / nunquam / amavit, / Quique / amavit / amet / cras
Let him love / tomorrow / who / never / loved, / whoever / loved (before) / let him love / tomorrow

LIVING LATIN

Cupido dominandi cunctis affectibus flagrantior
Cupido / dominandi / flagrantior / cunctis / affectibus
The desire / to dominate / (is) stronger / than all other / (human) feelings

Donat habere viro decus et tutamen in armis
Donat / viro / habere / decus / et / tutamen / in armis
(Aeneas) gave / to the man / to have / an ornament / and / a safeguard
  / in battle

Eheu fugaces, Postume, Postume, labuntur anni
Eheu, / Postume, Postume, / fugaces / anni / labuntur
Alas, / O Posthumus, Posthumus, / the fleeting / years / are slipping by

Facilis descensus Averni;
  Noctes atque dies patet atri janua Ditis:
  Sed revocare gradum superasque evadere ad auras,
  Hoc opus, hic labor est.
Descensus / Averni / facilis
  Noctes / atque / dies / patet / janua / atri / Ditis
  Sed / revocare / gradum / -que / evadere / ad / superas / auras
  Hoc / opus, / hic / est / labor
The descent / to Avernus / (is) easy /
  Night(s) / and / day(s) / stand wide / the portals / of black / Dis /
  But / to retrace / (your) step / and / emerge / to / the upper / light
  This / (is) toil, / this / is / labour

Homo sum: humani nil a me alienum puto
Sum / homo: / puto / nil / humani / alienum / a me
I am / a man: / I count / nothing / human / alien / to me

Maxima debetur puero reverentia
Maxima / reverentia / debetur / puero
The utmost / reverence / is due / to a child
Medio de fonte leporum
  Surgit amari aliquid quod in ipsis floribus angat
Medio / de fonte / leporum /
  surgit / aliquid / amari / quod / angat / in floribus / ipsis
From the depths / of this fountain / of delights / wells up / something /
  bitter / which / chokes (them) / in the flowers / themselves

LIVING LATIN

Mutato nomine de te fabula narratur
Nomine / mutato / fabula / narratur / de / te
The name / being changed / the story / is told / about / you

Multis ille bonis flebilis occidit, nulli flebilior quam tibi, Vergili,
Ille / occidit / flebilis / multis / bonis / nulli / flebilior / quam / tibi /
    Vergili
He / died / mourned / by many / good men / none / more grief-stricken
    / than / you / Virgil

Ne pueros coram populo Medea trucidet,
    Aut humana palam coquat exta nefarius Atreus.
Ne / Medea / trucidet / pueros / coram / populo
    Aut / nefarius Atreus / coquat / humana / exta / palam
Let not / Medea / slaughter / (her) boys / before / the people
    Nor / wicked Atreus / cook / human / entrails / openly

Ne sit ancillæ tibi amor pudori
Ne sit / pudori / tibi / amor / ancillæ
Let there not be / shame / to you / (for) the love / of a servant girl

Nullus domus tales umquam contexit amores,
    Nullus amor talis coniuxit foedere amantes
Nullus / domus / umquam / contexit / tales / amores
    Nullus / talis / amor / coniuxit / amantes / foedere
No / house / ever / contained / such / lovers
    No / such / love / joined / lovers / with a bond

Odi et amo: quare id faciam, fortasse requiris
    Nescio, sed fieri sentio et excrucior.
Odi / et amo / quare / faciam / id /fortasse / requiris
    Nescio / sed / sentio / fieri / et excrucior
I hate / and I love / why / do I do / this / perhaps / you ask
    I don't know / but / I feel (it) / to be / so / and I suffer

O mihi praeteritos referat si Iuppiter annos
O / si / Iuppiter / referat / mihi / annos / praeteritos
O / if / Jupiter / would restore / to me / the years / (that are) fled

LIVING LATIN

Quis desiderio sit pudor aut modus tam cari capitis

Quis / pudor / aut / modus / sit / desiderio / tam / cari / capitis

What / shame / or / limit / should there be / in grief / (of) such / a dear / head

Raro antecedentem scelestum/ deseruit pede Poena claudo

Raro / Poena / deseruit / scelestum / claudo / pede / antecedentem

Rarely / retribution / has forgotten / the wicked man, / (though) with halting / foot / long after the crime

Soles occidere et redire possunt:
  Nobis cum semel occidit brevis lux
  Nox est perpetua una dormienda.

Soles / possunt / occidere / et redire; /
  nobis / cum / semel / brevis / lux / occidit /
  est / una / perpetua / nox / dormienda

Suns / may / set (die) / and rise again;
  / for us / when / once / the brief / light / dies /
  it is / one / eternal / night / to be slept

Timeo Danaos et dona ferentes

Timeo / Danaos / et / ferentes / dona

I fear / the Greeks/ even / bearing / gifts

Tityre, tu patulae recubans sub tegmine fagi

Tityre / tu / recubans / sub / tegmine / patulae / fagi[1]

O Tityrus / thou / reclining / under / the shade / of a spreading / beech tree

Video meliora proboque; deteriora sequor

Video / meliora / -que[2] / probo; / sequor / deteriora

I see/ the better/ and / I approve;/ I follow/ the worse

Vitae summa brevis spem nos vetat incohare longam

Brevis / summa / vitae / vetat / nos / incohare / longam / spem

The short / span / of life / forbids / us / to entertain / lengthy / hope

---

1 *Fagus* (second declension) is masculine in form but, being a tree, is feminine in gender, which accounts for the feminine genitive *patulae*.

2 Various words mean "and" in Latin in addition to "et": the word "-que" attached to another word also means "and".

Vixi puellis nuper idoneus
 Et militavi non sine gloria
Nuper / vixi / idoneus / puellis /
 et / militavi / non / sine / gloria
Formerly / I lived / fit / for girls /
 and / I fought / not / without / glory.

Appendix II
From *The Bankolidaid*, Lib.1 By F. Sidgwick

Charmer virumque I sing, Jack plumigeramque Arabellam.
Costermonger erat Jack Jones, asinumque agitabat;
In Covent Garden holus, sprouts vendidit asparagumque.
Vendidit in Circo to the toffs Arabella the donah,
Qua Piccadilly propinquat to Shaftesbury Avenue, flores.

Jam Whitmonday adest; ex Newington Causeway the costers
Erumpunt multi celebrare their annual beano;
Quisque suum billycock habuere et donah ferentes,
Impositique rotis, popularia carmina singing,
Happy with ale omnes—exceptis excipiendis.
Gloomily drives Jack Jones, inconsolabilis heros;
No companion habet, solus sine virgine coster.
Per Boro', per Fleet Street, per Strand, sic itur ad "Empire";
Illinc Coventry Street peragunt in a merry procession,
Qua Piccadilly propinquat to Shaftesbury Avenue, tandem
Gloomily Jack vehitur. Sed amet qui never amavit!
En! subito fugiunt dark thoughts; Arabella videtur.
Quum subit ullius pulcherrima bloomin' imago,
Corde juvat Jack Jones; exclamat loudly "What oh, there!"
Maiden ait "Deus, ecce deus!" floresque relinquit.
Post asinum sedet illa; petunt Welsh Harp prope Hendon.

O fons Brent Reservoir! recubans sub tegmine brolli,
Brachia complexus (yum, yum!) Jack kissed Arabella;
"Garn" ait illa rubens, et "Garn" reboatur ab Echo;
Propositique tenax Jack "Swelp me lummy, I loves yer."
Hinc illae lacrimae: "Jest one!" et "Saucy, give over."
Tempora jam mutantur, et hats; caligine cinctus
Oscula Jones iterat. mokoque immitit habenas.
Concertina manu sixteen discrimina vocum
Obliquitur; cantant (ne saevi, magne policeman)
Noctem in Old Kent Road. Sic transit gloria Monday.

This macaronic poem is full of references to the classic authors which the
reader is invited to identify from the main body of this work.

Appendix III
Motor Bus—A. D. Godley

What is this that roareth thus?
Can it be a Motor Bus?
Yes, the smell and hideous hum
Indicat Motorem Bum.
Implet in the Corn and High
Terror me Motoris Bi:
Bo Motori clamitabo
Ne Motore caedar a Bo –
Dative be or ablative
So thou only let us live:
Whither shall thy victims flee?
Spare us, spare us, Motor Be!
Thus I sang; and still anigh
Came in hordes Motores Bi,
Et complebat omne forum
Copia Motorum Borum.
How shall wretches live like us
Cincti Bis Motoribus?
Domine, defende nos
Contra hos Motores Bos!

A. D. Godley presents us here with a more or less complete declination in Latin of *Motor Bus*. Gathered together and put in some kind of order, the elements appear as:

	Singular	Plural	
Nominative	Motor Bus	Motores Bi	Subject of sentence
Vocative	Motor Be	(Motores Bi)	"O motor bus(es)!"
Accusative	Motorem Bum	Motores Bos	Object of sentence
Genitive	Motoris Bi	Motorum Borum	"of motor bus(es)"
Dative	Motori Bo	Motoribus Bis	"to, for motor bus(es)"
Ablative	Motore Bo	Motoribus Bis	"by, with, from mb(es)"

The accusative is also used after a preposition like "contra". The last four lines *anglice* read: "How shall wretches live like us surrounded by motor buses? O Lord, defend us against these motor buses".

Appendix IV

Some frequently met word or phrases are part of longer quotations, and so do not have their own entries. A number of these are listed below.

Ad hominem
To the man
Vide "argumentum ad hominem".

Amari aliquid
Something bitter
Vide "Medio de fonte leporum".

Amor vincit omnia
Love conquers all
Vide "Omnia vincit amor".

Anguis in Herba
A snake in the grass
Vide "Latet anguis in herba".

Anno urbis conditæ (AUC)
From the year of the building of the city (Rome)
Vide "Ab urbe condita".

A vinculo matrimonii
From the marriage bond
Vide "In vinculis".

Bello flagrante
During hostilities
Cf. "In flagrante delicto".

Caeteris paribus
Other things being equal
Vide "ceteris paribus".

Coelum non animum mutant
They change their skies but not their souls
Vide "Caelum non animum".

Dea in Machina
A goddess in the machine
Vide "Deus ex Machina".

Decus et tutamen
A beauteous safeguard
Vide "Donat habere … ".

Delineavit (del)
Drew, engraved
Cf. fecit, pinxit, sculpsit.

Desipere in loco
Vide "Dulce est desipere in loco".

De te fabula narratur
Vide "Mutato nomine de te fabula narratur".

Dictum sapienti sat est
A word is enough for a wise man
Cf. "Verbum sapienti…".

Dies mirabilis
Day of wonders
Vide "Annus mirabilis".

Dulce decus
A sweet honour, a trustworthy friend
Vide "O et præsidium et dulce decus meum".

Errare est humanum
To err is human
Vide "Humanum est errare".

Fieri curavit
Caused to be done
Cf. "Fecit" and "Poni curavit".

Hoc volo, sic iubeo
This I wish, thus I command
Vide "Sic volo, sic iubeo".

Horribile dictu
Horrible to relate
Cf. "mirabile dictu".

Iacta alea est
The die is cast
Vide "Alea est iacta".

In esse
In existence, actually
Vide "A posse ad esse" and "posse".

In perpetuum
For ever, in perpetuity
Vide "Ave atque vale".

In posse
Potentially
Vide "posse".

Jacta est alea
The die is cast
Vide "Alea iacta est".

Jus primae noctis
The right of the first night
Vide "Ius primae noctis".

Labuntur et imputantur
(The hours) slip by and are reckoned (to our account)
Cf. "Pereunt et imputantur".

Magnum in parvo
Much in a small space
Cf. "Multum in parvo".

Mens sana in corpore sano
A sound mind in a sound body
Vide "Orandum est …".

Mobile perpetuum
Perpetual motion
Vide "Perpetuum mobile".

Monumentum aere perennius
A monument more lasting than bronze
Vide "Exegi monumentum aere perennius".

Mortis in articulo
At the point of death
Vide "In articulo mortis".

Orare est laborare, laborare est orare
Prayer is work, work is prayer
Vide "Laborare est orare".

Quis custodiet ipsos custodes?
Who shall guard the guards themselves?
Vide "Pone seram,…".

Ruat coelum, fiat justitia
Though the heavens fall, let justice be done
Vide "Fiat justitia,…".

Sic itur ad astra
Such is the way to the stars
Vide "Macte nova virtute".

Suaviter in modo
Gently in manner
Vide "Fortiter in re".

Suggestio falsi
A implication of falsehood
Vide s.v. "suppressio veri".

Vitai Lampada
The lamp of life
Vide "Quasi cursores…".

Vale
Farewell
Cf. "Ave atque vale".

Some Mottoes
Football Club Mottoes
Some clubs share a Latin motto with their home town

Arte et labore
By skill and hard graft
Blackburn Rovers

Audere est facere
He who dares, wins
Tottenham Hotspur

Consilio et animis
By wisdom and courage
Sheffield Wednesday
(A motto they share with Eton RDC, and
the families of Maitland-Titterton and
Ramsay-Steel-Maitland)

Nil satis nisi optimum
Nothing but the best is good enough
Everton

Pro rege et lege
For the king and the law
Leeds United

Supera moras
Overcome delays
(Take your finger out?)
Bolton Wanderers

Superbia in proelio
Pride in battle
Manchester City

Victoria concordia crescit
Victory grows from harmony
(again, pull together)
Arsenal

Vincit omnia industria
Hard work conquers everything
Bury

Vis unita fortior
United force is more powerful
(*ergo* pull together)
Stoke City

The Lord Mayor's Show

Many of the City of London Livery Companies have or had Latin mottoes, inter alia*:*

Amicitiam trahit amor
Love draws friendship
Gold and Silver Wyre Drawers Company

Amore sitis uniti
Be united in love
Plate Workers and Wire Workers Company

Corde recto elati omnes
All are uplifted by a righteous heart
Makers of Playing Cards Company

Decus et tutamen in armis
A handsome protection in war
Feltmakers' Company

Ecce agnus Dei qui tollit peccata mundi
Behold the Lamb of God who takes away the sins of the world
Tallow Chandlers' Company

Hinc spes effulget
Hope shines out of here
Innholders' Company

Justitia et pax
Justice and peace
Plumbers' Company

Lucem tuam da nobis Deus
O God give us your light
Glaziers' Company

Omnia subjectisti sub pedibus oves et boves
You have put everything under his feet, including sheep and cattle
Butchers' Company

Producat terra
The earth produces
Tobacco Pipe Makers and Tobacco Blenders' Company

Recipient foeminae sustentaculo nobis
Women receive support from us
Pattenmakers' Company

Verbum Domini manet in aeternum
The word of the Lord endures for ever
Stationers and Newspaper Makers' Company

A Clutch of School Mottoes
Just a few not found in the main body of the book

Beati Mundo Corde
Blest are the pure in heart
Ardingly School

Coelesti Luce Crescat
It grows with celestial light
Cheltenham Ladies' College

Detur Gloria Soli Deo
May the glory be given solely to God
Dulwich College

Discendo Duces
By learning you will lead
Newcastle upon Tyne Grammar
School

Dominus Mihi Adjutor
The Lord is my helper
Douai School, Woolhampton

Dominus Sapientam Dat
The Lord gives wisdom
Royal School for Daughters of
Officers of the Army

Et Nova Et Vetera
Both old and new
Bryanston School

Finis Coronat Opus
The end crowns the work
Croham Hurst School, Croydon

Luce Magistra
With light as mistress
Queen Ethelburga's School,
Harrogate

Omne Vince Perseverando
Overcome all things by persevering
Caterham School

Ora, Labora, Lude
Pray, work and play
Abbey Girls' School, Malvern

Salus Et Felicitas
Health and happiness
Royal Academy of Dancing

Metallum Ponderosum A

Modern pop groups seem for some reason to have taken in a big way to using Latin for titles, both for the group itself and for its compositions. E.g:

Status quo

The group Status Quo have now more or less monopolized the phrase, as a glance at Google will show.

Procul Harum

This band boasts what looks at first sight a Latin title, but after exhaustive research, it turns out, perhaps disappointingly, that the name simply belonged to someone's cat.

Compos Mentis

Compos Mentis is the name of a Melodic Death/Rock Metal band ("Symphonic Rock from Hell") in Denmark, and also of an Australian Funk band,

Domus Mundi

The Austrian symphonic black metal band Hollenthon chose Latin for the titles of the tracks of their album Domus Mundi ("Home of the World"). These include:

a) *Hinc Illae Lacrimae*—
b) *Non Omnis Moriar*
c) *Pallida Mors*
d) *Ultima Ratio Regum*
e) *Lex Talionis*
f) *Vita nova*—"New life", perhaps "my music will put new life into you"?
g) *Magni nominis umbra*
h) Lastly and less transparently comes *Malis Avibus* which probably means "For naughty birds", but whether the birds were avian or just groupies is a matter for conjecture.

Metallum Ponderosum B

Memento Mori
Nowadays the medium of conveying doubts about intimations of immortality is often music. The band Anathema had a song called *Memento Mori* in "Pentecost III", as did The Streets (i.e. Mike Skinner) in their 2006 album "The Hardest Way to Make an Easy Living".

Elixir vitae
In 2003 the rock band *Low Flying Owls* made its national album debut on Stinky Records with *Elixir Vitae*.

In Hoc Signo Vinces
This saying was adopted by the band Deadsy as its band manifesto.

Carpe Diem
The title of a song in Metallica's Re-load Album is "Carpe Diem Baby", and the lyric concludes: "Come squeeze and suck the day, come carpe diem baby."

De Profundis
The Industrial band Professional Murder Music in 2005 released a record called *De Profundis* on Wormhole Records.

Veni vidi vici
Tawdry Hepburn , the San Francisco indie-rock loungecore group, uses *veni vidi vici* as a refrain in "Sink", a song about mythic female dominance borrowed from the rock group Apocalipstick.

Thin Red Heroes

Regiments of the British Army have long boasted mottoes reflecting their courage and the glorious achievements.

Decus et tutamen
An honour and a protection
West Essex Yeomanry

Domine Dirige Nos
O Lord, show us the way
Royal London Militia

Invicta
Unconquered
Kent Volunteer Fencibles

Justitia turris nostra
Justice is our tower
The Hackney Territorials

Nemo me impune lacessit
No one gets away with mucking me about
Black Watch

Primus in urbe
First in the City
London Rifle Brigade

Pro aris et focis
For our altars and hearths
Fife Light Horse

Quis separabit
Who shall separate?
The Sligo Rifles

Quo fata vocant
Whither the fates call
Northumberland Fusiliers

Semper Fidelis
Always faithful
East Devon Militia

Tenax et audax
Tenacious and audacious
25th County of London (Cyclist) Battalion

Vestigia nulla retrorsum
No steps backwards
5th (Princess Charlotte of Wales) Dragoon Guards

Heart of Oak

Many ships of the Royal Navy have or have had Latin mottoes and why not?

Cave
Beware
HMS Sesame

Cavendo tutus
Safe by keeping good watch
HMS Cavendish

Ex tenebris lux
(Not much) light out of the darkness
HMS Glow-worm

Fortiter in re
Boldly in action
HMS Sussex

Mors janua vitae
Death is the gateway to (the after?) life
HMS Valhalla

Nil desperandum
No reason to despair
HMS Dauntless

Omnibus tempestatibus
In all weathers
HMS Stormcloud

Pro justitia pro rege
For justice and for the king
HMS Southampton

Sis ut leones
Be as the lions are
HMS Sea Lion

Timeant Danaeios
Let them fear Danae's men
HMS Danae

Ventis secundis
With following winds
HMS Hood

Vento favente
With a favourable wind
HMS Boreas

Lux

Lux, unlike Life, is more than just a Soap. Here are some more mottoes.

Fiat Lux
Let's have some light
Moorfields Eye Hospital

E Tenebris Lux
From the dark places, light
National Coal Board

Lux ex Tenebris
Light from the dark places
Wigan & District Mining and Tech.
Coll.

Lux in Tenebris
Light in the dark places
Services Kinema Corporation

Lux et Veritas
Light and Truth
Yale College, U.S.A.

Lux, Salubritas et Felicitas
Light, Health and Happiness
Clacton-on-Sea, Essex

Lex Mea Lux
The Law is my Light
Lord Birkett (of legal renown)

Post nubes lux
After clouds, light
College of Aeronautics

Sic virescit lux
Thus light flourishes
Sheffield and Rotherham Police
Authority

Lux Perpetua Luceat Eis
May eternal light shine on them
(Up for grabs)

Now descending to the Ablative:

Luce Scientiae Vinces
By the light of Science, you'll conquer
South Wales and Monmouth School
of Mines

Luce Scribimus
We write by light
RAF School of Photography

And one other closely related:

Dominus Illuminatio Mea
The Lord is my Light
University of Oxford

In Excelsis

The squadrons and branches of the air forces, first of the Royal Flying Corps and then of the Royal Air Force, adopted, in extenso *and* ab initio, *Latin mottoes, e.g.:*

Aere Invicti
Invincible with the brass
Central Band of the RAF, Halton

Corpus non animum muto
I change my body not my spirit
57 Squadron

Custodes Urbis
Guardians of the city
903 County of London Balloon Squadron

E Nocentibus Innocentia
From harmful things, harmless things
5131 Bomb Disposal Squad

Experientia Docet
Experience teaches
No. 6 Elementary Flying Training School

Insula Defensor
The island fortress
Malta Sector RAF

Mare Transeo Internum
I travel across the inland sea
Malta Communications and Target Towing Squadron

Non Nisi Veritas
Nothing but the truth
Institute of Pathology and Tropical Medicine RAF

Securitas In Coelo
Safety in the sky
Air Traffic Control Centre, RAF Watnall

Ubique Loquimur
Everywhere we speak
No. 38 Group Tactical Communications Wing

Viribus Audax
Bold in strength
RAF School of Physical Training

Appendix V
Obiter Scripta

These were composed to brighten up a former website of mine called "Living Latin". I hope they may brighten up this *opus*.

Adventures Underground

It was mid-summer in Rome and the weather was sultry, sultry enough to make me want to escape from the sun and seek somewhere cool and shady. A notice caught my eye advertising guided tours of the sewers, and, remembering my tour of the sewers of Paris many years before, I decided to find out if those of Rome were any better or worse. As it happened I was the only customer for the two o'clock tour, but my guide, a Signor Publius V. Maro according to his name-tag, welcomed me courteously and preceded me down the manhole. The descent seemed easy but I suspected that the task of returning to the daylight might be something of a struggle.

I suppose once you have seen one sewer you have seen the lot. However, the sewers turned out to be well lit, certainly not enveloped in the Stygian blackness I had expected. The waterway was wide and a path ran along both sides. Publius V. pointed out several features of interest, and I was admiring a particularly fine mosaic on the far wall of Leda half-heartedly fending off a swan when the sound of a human voice came to my ears. I looked up-stream and saw an elderly man dressed in a rather tatty toga, staggering down the opposite bank of the stream shaking his fist at the ceiling. His words came across the water clearly: "*Ceterum censeo delenda est Carthago.*" He repeated them every few steps and we could hear his voice long after he was out of sight.

"What was he on about?" I asked Publius.

"Oh, that was just Cato the Elder muttering threats against Carthage. In his opinion Carthage must be destroyed."

"What has he got against Carthage?" I asked, trying to remember where (and what or who) Carthage was.

"He has some conspiracy theory—or maybe it was a Carthage girl who threw him over when he was young. Nobody ever took him seriously".

"Oh," I said.

Then we heard footsteps and a small procession came into view. In front was a young, handsome, confident-looking soldier, twirling a short sword and occasionally throwing it up and catching it again, nine times out of ten by the hilt. Following him were a dozen dispirited-looking nondescripts, dragging their feet and murmuring among themselves. Their leader looked over his shoulder, turned and, walking easily backwards, called out, "*Nil desperandum Teucro duce et auspice Teucro*", then turned and walked cheerfully on.

"Who was that?" I asked.

"Oh, that was Teucer. He's just been thrown out of Salamis by his father, and he's off to seek his fortune elsewhere."

"What did he say?" I asked.

"He said not to despair, with Teucer as leader and under Teucer's lucky star."

"I see, a bit like 'Have no fear, Teucer's here'," I suggested.

"Exactly."

The procession wound out of sight, Teucer still twirling his sword and humming a merry tune, his followers trudging along and looking quietly desperate.

I began to wonder who might be next, and as I wondered another figure hove into view, a scholarly-looking bloke who was scribbling on a tablet, occasionally looking heavenwards, or at least roofwards, and then busily scribbling again.

"Who's this?" I asked.

"That's Publilius Syrus. He composes mottoes for Christmas crackers, inspiring sayings. He calls them *sententiae maximae*, highest thoughts, but we just call them 'maxims'. Hi, Sy, what's new?" he called out.

Publilius Syrus stopped, took a sheaf of papers from somewhere in his garments, selected one paper, folded it into a pellet, stretched an elastic band between his thumb and forefinger and fired the pellet across to Publius, just missing the latter's nose. Then he walked on, still scribbling, while Publius picked up the pellet and unfolded it. He handed it to me.

"Read that," he said.

There were just three *sententiae* written on the paper.

"*Beneficium accipere libertatem est vendere*," I read.

"To accept a favour is to sell one's liberty," translated Publius.

"*Bis dat qui cito dat.*"

"He gives twice as much who gives quickly."

"*Necessitas non habet legem.*"

"Necessity knows no law."

"Sterling stuff," I suggested. Publius made no reply.

Suddenly we heard the sound of running footsteps, and there appeared a very prosperous-looking middle-aged man trotting briskly along and breathing hard. He saw us and pointed ahead of him. "*Abiit, excessit, evasit, erupit,*" he shouted and trotted on until he was out of sight.

I said nothing but looked enquiringly at Publius who was smiling somewhat enigmatically.

"Poor old Cicero! I knew this would happen. He's too trusting. He should have clapped Catiline in irons."

"Who's Catiline?"

"Cicero was holding him on a charge of high treason against Rome. Now apparently he's escaped, he's fled, he's eluded the watch, he's broken through the guards. And the only bright thing to be said about it all is that you now know four different ways in Latin of saying he's slung his hook."

"I suppose so," was all I could thing of saying.

A few moments passed with nothing happening except for half a dead mule floating down the stream. On the wall by my right shoulder I noticed in the stone the inscription "Kilroy was here 1944", and above it the faint remains of another inscription of which all that was left or legible said "Qui era Dan". I knew of Kilroy by repute but there are so many Dans in the world...

Then a man appeared carrying in his arms a pile of some eight or nine books, which he seemed to have some difficulty in balancing. "Uh-uh," said Publius.

The man looked across and with some pride in his voice called out "*Exegi monumentum aere perennius.*" As he said this the pile of books swayed forwards and the man had to break into a run to keep up with them, accelerating hard as the books threatened to topple over. He was soon out of sight.

"So who was that?"

"That was Horace, a very light-weight poet. He has a medium-sized brain in an out-size head. 'I have completed a monument more lasting than brass'. Huh. A brass farthing is about all I'd give for all his work put together."

"I've heard of Horace. I remember the name because it was the name of our school porter. You don't think much of him, then?"

"He's strung together a few odes, a handful of letters and satires, and a do-it-yourself book on poetry, and all Rome goes crazy about him. It would be a different matter if he'd written, say, an epic poem in twelve books, on a really important subject, like the Trojan War. But that's your modern reading public for you, hooked on the meretricious and the tawdry." He looked the picture of disdain, and spat. "Ars Poetica? Poetica my *nates*, more like." He spat again into the turgid flood.

Delicacy made me forbear to request a translation of this but I determined to look it up in the dictionary *quam celerrime*—what? Oh, sorry,—as quickly as possible.

We had now reached the exit. As I had feared it was uphill work getting out but we made it and I shook his hand and pressed into it a €10 note.

"Very many thanks, Signor Maro," I said, "A very enjoyable tour. Thank you for interpreting for me."

"My pleasure," he replied. "Come back next time you're in Rome and we'll do a different tour."

"I'll look forward to that. By the way, I hope you don't mind my asking, but what does the V stand for in your name?"

"Virgil", he said.

Military Matters 1

It was a pleasant day in July when I next met Publius V. He was still advertising guided tours of the sewers, but when I greeted him he grabbed me by the arm and insisted on taking me, via the sewers, to an underground bunker used by the Roman military. We sat at the back of the room and no one seemed to notice us. The twenty or thirty young men present had their eyes elsewhere.

On a small dais at the front of the room stood a burly figure in full fighting garb, minus the helmet. He was standing beside a large board covered with a cloth and he was, it seemed, about to give a lecture on military tactics. His body language and the inflections of his speech reminded me of a certain flight sergeant who fifty years earlier had lectured me on matters military, and with the help of these and explanatory mutterings from Publius, I was able to follow the lecture fairly well. It went something like this.

"Now I expect you're wondering what I'm going to talk about. I'm going to talk first of all about being ready." He made a sign and a soldier standing by the board raised the cloth a few inches to reveal the words: **Qui desiderat pacem, praeparet bellum**". Publius translated : "Whoever seeks for peace, let him prepare for war".

"Right, you say, we've got the **Pax Romana** ('The Roman Peace') in place, so why prepare for war?" Well, those of you who've got their eyes open will have noticed above the front door as you came in the words "**Si vis pacem, para bellum**", of which this here is just a lah-di-dah version. A saying attributed to Flavius Vegetius Renatus, but that need not concern you. Rome is always ready for war, you are always ready for war, and that includes polishing your spears every night. Nothing like the sunlight glinting on a forest of spears to put the fear of Jove into the Hun."

The cloth rose a few inches further to read: **Praemonitus, praemunitus** (Forewarned is forearmed).

"Now this is where intelligence comes in, and I don't mean your intelligence, because Juppiter help us all if we had to depend on that, I mean the network of spies, scouts and informers we employ to keep watch on the movements of potential enemies. Our foes are always looking for an excuse to attack Rome (a '**Casus belli**') and we've got to be ready when the attack comes. Always on the alert, '**Semper paratus**'."

Up went the cloth again. "**Bis peccare in bello non licet**—(In war one may not blunder twice). Think about this one. You put a foot wrong in battle and that battle's going to be your last. You'll finish up six foot down under a slab saying '**Flebilis Occidit**' above your name, rank and number. But you stand firm and obey orders and you'll get the chance to fight again another day.

"Now make sure you've got all the equipment you need before the fighting starts. Look at Flaccus here"—the soldier by the board took two steps forward smartly—"he's wearing what some poet fellow referred to as a '**decus et tutamen in armis**' (A beauteous safeguard in battle). It may look to you like a leather corselet his mater has run up for him, but you'll be very glad to be wearing a flak-jacket like this if the Hun gets his sights on you.

"Now why have you joined the army? Perhaps to impress your girl-friend, hoping to be a **miles gloriosus**. No harm in that, always supposing you do something to be *gloriosus* about. But a word of warning. You may have heard the recruiting signifer say, '**Dulce et decorum est pro patria mori**'—(It is sweet and proper to die for one's country)—trying to whip up your patriotism in his own inimitable way. Well, *verb. sap.* which you will know stands for **verbum sapienti sat est** (A word is enough to a wise man)—we expect a fair quota of casualties in battle and those casualties may be you. So some advice."

Up went the cloth again. "**Omne ignotum pro magnifico est** (Everything unknown appears stupendous). Right, you're in Britain, manning Hadrian's wall. Somewhere up in front of you hidden in the mist are the Picts, each one reputed to be seven foot high with five rows of teeth and tiger's blood flowing in his veins. **Faex tauri** (bullshit). Don't you believe it. They're short-arsed creatures with wives and mortgages, just like you, and remember, you've got Rome behind you. Their motto may be **Nemo me impune lacessit** (No one mucks me about) but you're there specifically for the purpose of mucking them about, and you're born to be a winner, every one of you.

"One more word of warning. Keep your eyes open. Anyone here from Greece?" No one there was from Greece. "Right, so I can say without fear of contradiction, slippery customers, these Greeks. They say don't look a gift horse in the mouth. I say, **Timeo Danaos, et dona ferentes** (I fear the Greeks, even when they bring gifts). So if anyone, Greek or otherwise, gives you a horse, you'd better look very carefully into his mouth and into every other available orifice as well. And don't ask me why the Greeks are called Danai—you can ask the centurion tomorrow when he briefs you about the campaign. Right, fall out, *quam celerrime*, and remember what I said about polishing your spears."

Publius and I made our way back to the sunlight, arranging to meet early the next day for the centurion's briefing.

Military Matters 2

"Salvete. I'm Marcus Naso, your new centurion. My job here today is to bring you men up to date with the latest developments on the northern front. It seems that a large contingent of Goths or Visigoths—we aren't quite sure which yet, but our spies are working on it and to be blunt it doesn't much matter—they're all barbarians—are gathering in some strength and making menacing gestures. Anyway, we've been delegated to go and sort them out, and I'm sure we'll make a very good job of it.

"Now remember, a soldier's life is a very noble calling. As one of our greatest poets said, *"Arma virumque cano"*—("I sing of arms and the man," translated Publius, looking, I thought, rather smug)—and I'm sure all Rome will be singing your praises by the end of the week. You too can be heroes along with the great warriors of the past. It can be said of you, *"I, bone, quo virtus tuo te vocat, i pede fausto. Grandia laturus meritorum præmia"*—("Go, good (lad), where thy courage calls thee, go with propitious step, (certain) to carry away the rich rewards of thy merit" supplied Publius) "– and you can stand shoulder to shoulder with Ascanius, to whom Apollo was moved to say, *"Macte nova virtute puer, sic itur ad astra"*—("God speed thy youthful valour, boy, in this way one attains to the stars").

"Now I gather my signifer upset one of you yesterday by mentioning that *Dulce et decorum est pro patria mori*—("It is sweet and proper to die for one's country"), but just remember, *"Mors janua vitae"*—(Death is the gateway to life") though just what kind of *vita* no one yet knows. Anyway, men, I'm sure you'll do your best and keep up the reputation of the Legion. Right, any questions? No? Now, I'm sure you all know the saying, *Dulce est desipere in loco*—(It is pleasant to let one's hair down on proper occasions)—so I've authorized Signifer Stertus to give each of you a sestertius and you can go and *desipere* a bit down at the tavern this evening, but remember *reveille* is an hour before sunrise, so don't overdo it. Dismiss."

The Girls Get Together

It was mid-summer in Rome and the weather was sultry, sultry enough to make me want to escape from the sun and seek somewhere cool and shady. I remembered my tour of the sewers with Publius Virgil Maro and his promise to take me on a different tour when I was next in Rome. I sought him out and found him still offering tours of the sewers.

"Salve!" I said.

"Ciao!" he replied, impassively. "Nice to see you."

I reminded him of his promise when we last saw each other, and without a word he beckoned me to follow him down the manhole. The sewer hadn't changed noticeably since I was last down there. However there was a new mosaic on the far wall showing Semele trying to dodge a shower of gold, having clearly hit the jackpot of some celestial fruit-machine.

"This time," said Publius V., "I shall show you a sight vouchsafed to few," and he led me up a side passage sloping upwards from the main sewer. After some fifty yards the passage levelled out and Publius stopped at a grill in the wall at head height, through which came flooding light.

"Cop an eyeful of this," he said.

I looked through the grill and saw in a well-lit room a throng of women, some young, some old, some beautiful, some with faces which had clearly seen better days. All were more or less neatly attired in the costume of ancient Rome and I decided I was looking either at a modern fancy-dress ball or at a meeting of the Women's Institute of some two millennia back. Snatches of conversation came to me as I stood and gazed in awe at the sight.

"Video meliora proboque, deteriora sequor." The speaker was clearly upset and her hearers showed signs of sympathy and compassion, as they appeared to offer advice and encouragement and handkerchieves. Publius' voice sounded in my left ear.

"That's Medea, her father's Æetes king of Colchis. Jason came along looking for the Golden Fleece but Æetes would only help him if he carried out certain tasks which made the labours of Hercules look like spare-time activities for Brownies. Medea of course fell in love with Jason and now she's torn between supporting her father—that's the *meliora* bit—or helping Jason by means of her not inconsiderable powers of magic to finish the tasks and get the fleece—that's the *deteriora* bit. 'I see and approve the better path, but follow the worse.' She's helped Jason despite her father telling her not to and now she's lying low in Rome for a bit until the storm at home blows over."

One of the other girls had put her arms round Medea and was clearly congratulating her and telling her a tale of encouragement. Several of the others suddenly clapped their hands and a general cry of "Splendide mendax!" went up.

"That's Hypermnestra——" began Publius.

"Who?" I interrupted.

"It's a Greek name—that accounts for the funny spelling. Let's call her Hype. Her father is also a king, Danaus. He's blessed with fifty daughters and his idea of honeymoon high jinks is to have each daughter stick a knife into her husband at some time during their wedding night. Can't think why. Possibly some kind of tax fiddle at the bottom of it all. Anyway, Hype had other ideas. Just before dawn on her wedding night, she thanked her husband for a really nice time, and slipped him a tidy sum of money so that he could bribe the guards and make his way to the frontier. They're now living in Rome and running a bed and breakfast gaff. How to interpret 'Splendide mendax'? 'Splendidly false'? 'Nobly untruthful'? You choose. Anyway, as you can see, the other women are right behind both of them."

The group moved on, still engrossed in mutual congratulations, and another group took their place. Suddenly one pointed, and they all looked in the direction in which she was pointing, and so did I. The words "Simplex munditiis" floated across to me ears.

I saw a very pretty girl approaching, a dazzling blond in contrast to the Mediterranean complexion of most of the other women, dressed minimally in a short tunic which covered about half her body though not necessarily the essential half. The contrast to the other women's costume was marked. No frills or furbelows on this one, in fact not much of anything below, either, as far as one could see. She came up happily enough and joined the group, who all seemed pleased to see her.

"That's Pyrrha, one of Horace's former fancies," said Publius.

"Fiancées?" I suggested.

"Fancies. She's very much into the pretty youth market. Horace was much too old for her, really. Not her type."

"What were they saying about her?"

"'Simplex munditiis?' 'Dressed elegantly but simply.' No frills or furbelows."

"That's what I thought."

"Well, just take a look at that face and figure. And that hair. I think you'll agree with me that the last thing that one needs to attract the fellows is clothes."

Pyrrha moved on, and the group dispersed, but not before I had heard several of them agree: "Semper eadem". I looked at Publius.

"'Always the same'. Never changes. Doesn't need to. The old formulae are the best."

Two girls came along in close embrace. One was clearly distressed, and the other was offering words of comfort. "Amantium irae amoris integratio est." The unhappy one looked up and nodded, attempting a smile, then sank into her grief again. They both moved on.

"'Lovers' quarrels are the renewal of love'. Another of Terence's platitudes. 'We'll make it up tomorrow and be even more lovey-dovey than before'. I reckon more loving couples have fallen out arguing about that one than for any other reason. The more I see of Terence's tripe in the amphitheatre, the more I'm in favour of stage censorship."

I didn't see that I was called on to argue about this, especially as more action was imminent within walls. Two older women were talking in low tones, and I had to strain my ears to catch what they were saying. I heard: "De gustibus non est disputandum" and "caecus amor est" before they passed out of earshot.

"Flacilla's daughter has fallen in love with an oyster merchant from Naples. Her father refuses to have him in the house because he smells of fish. All Flacilla's friend could say was: 'There's no arguing about taste' and 'Love is blind', to which Flacilla would no doubt be saying, had we been able to hear her, 'And devoid of all sense of smell as well'."

Next came along two girls in close embrace. One was clearly distressed, but was chattering so rapidly that I could only catch a few words of what she was saying. I did hear "Quia amore langueo" before the two passed on, her friend patting her on her shoulder in sympathy.

"Showing off," said Publius. "'Because I am languishing for love'—she's got her hooks in some poor fellow but he's presumably putting up a bit of a fight."

"Why do you say she's showing off?" I asked.

"She's been reading the Hebrew Bible," he explained. "Lifted that one out of the Song of Solomon. When they start doing that, I think it's time to leave."

We left the lovely visions of Roman womanhood and made our way back to the light of day, passing another mosaic showing Europa having trouble with a bull.

"Next time you're in Rome we'll do a different tour again," said Publius.

"I'll look forward to that," I said. "Vale."

"Ciao," he said.

Postscript

As we mentioned in the Introduction to this book, wherever we go in our journey through the intricate paths of the English language, we cannot escape the influence of Latin. Latin has long been a linguistic meadow from which innovative writers throughout the centuries have culled the blossoms they needed to put their burgeoning thoughts into words, and the identification of these writers and the chronology of their inventions and borrowings is a fascinating study.

We meet Latin more directly in the scientific names which have been given to living creatures, a subject which requires a book (or books) to itself. Each creature has a generic name, identifying its *genus*, followed by a specific or special name, identifying its *species*. Some names are classical Latin. *Bufo* was Latin for "a toad" and the scientific name for a common toad is *Bufo bufo*, a rare case of the two names being identical. (Another case is the wren, *Troglodytes troglodytes*.) The natterjack toad, *Bufo calamita*, is also a toad of the *bufo* genus, but of a different species. Its name might be thought to suggest some connection with ill-luck, but *calamita* was the name given by the Romans to a small green frog who lived among reeds (*calami*). (*Calamus* was also the name given to a pen made from a reed—*cf. lapsus calami* in the main body of this book *s.v lapsus linguae*.) A sparrow in Latin was *passer*, and the house sparrow is *Passer domesticus*, while the Spanish sparrow is *Passer hispaniolensis*.

(Confusingly, the *Puffinus puffinus* is not the puffin, but the Manx shearwater. The puffin is *Fratercula arctica*. "*Fraterculus*" is Latin for "little brother", but the ending *−a* is a feminine ending, and so technically the puffin is the "little feminine brother of the Arctic regions".)

Naturally the Romans had names for those plants and creatures with which they were familiar. In Latin *rana* was "frog" and *ranunculus* was "little frog", but the latter name was also given to the crowfoot plant, so the water crowfoot is *Ranunculus aquitilis* and the ivy-leaved crowfoot is *Ranunculus hederaceus*. The crowfoot was of the same genus as the buttercup, and so the common meadow buttercup is *Ranunculus acris* ("the acrid little frog") while *Ranunculus repens* is the creeping buttercup.

Much can be gleaned from the specific name about the habit or qualities of the plant or animal. *Pratensis* indicates that a plant's habitat is meadows, while *officinalis* indicates that it has medical uses. *Repens* and *reptans* both mark its habit of regenerating itself by "creeping" and putting down fresh roots at intervals. From the verb *reptare* comes the word *reptilia* which the Authorized Version translates correctly and all-inclusively in Genesis i. 24 as "creeping things". Modern versions of the Bible choose to translate *reptilia* as "reptiles", thereby rather unkindly excluding ants, millipedes, butterflies, spiders, scorpions *et alia* from the creation myth.

These ancient names were not enough to go around when Linnæus and others began their great task of assigning scientific names. The use of much imagination was clearly called for. Many plants have Greek generic names with Latin specific names, so *Cephalanthera rubra* is the red helleborine, a red (*rubra*) flower whose anther (*anthera*) looks very like a head (*kephale*). Others have Greek names or Greek forms of names for both genus and species: for example the corky-fruited water dropwort is *Œnanthe pimpinelloides*, the "wine-flower" with a resemblance to the pimpernel or burnet. This is indeed a field with rich etymological pickings.

While we are on the subject of Greek, it is worth looking at two of the very few Greek words or phrases which have been adopted by English speakers. The words "phenomenon" and "criterion" are singular in Greek and should so be in English. Their plurals are "phenomena" and "criteria" respectively and thus it is incorrect to speak, as a small number of people do, of "a phenomena" or "a criteria".

Again, the phrase "hoi polloi" seems now to drop easily from the English-speaker's lips. In Greek "hoi" is "the" and "polloi" is "people", and "hoi polloi" (οἱ πολλοί) are "the (common) people". It is unnecessary to speak of "*the* hoi polloi", which is "the the people". We are slowly being educated in Japanese to the extent that we talk of "Mount Fuji" or of simply "Fujiyama" rather than of "Mount Fujiyama", so the correct use of "hoi polloi" should not present too much of a challenge.

Finis

www.ingramcontent.com/pod-product-compliance
Lightning Source LLC
Chambersburg PA
CBHW032037080426
42733CB00006B/106